Routledge Revivals

Principles of Economic Sociology

First published in 1939, *Principles of Economic Sociology* has a two-fold object: first, to develop an economic theory of primitive life, secondly, to show the social principles behind the making of economic decisions, whether among primitive or advanced peoples. Economic theory was first developed with regard to Western exchange economics. Since then, it has been explored among the activities of totalitarian states. Here the process is carried a step further, by tracing economic theory in the lives of primitive peoples. It shows how the Bantu of Africa make economic choices, dispose of their resources, and apply capital to the meeting of future needs, always in a manner dictated by their own culture, yet fundamentally on principles similar to those of advanced peoples.

The importance of groups in the making of economic decisions is stressed. Economics is enriched by a study of the structure of groups, since this plays a fundamental part in the forming of decisions. The author hopes that his work will encourage economists to use a knowledge of primitive peoples to test their theories and help to coordinate the two major branches of social science, economics and sociology. This is an important historical reference work for scholars of African economics, economic sociology, and economic history.

Principles of Economic Sociology

The Economics of Primitive Life as Illustrated from the Bantu Peoples of South and East Africa

D. M. Goodfellow

Routledge
Taylor & Francis Group

First published in 1939
by George Routledge & Sons

This edition first published in 2024 by Routledge
4 Park Square, Milton Park, Abingdon, Oxon, OX14 4RN

and by Routledge
605 Third Avenue, New York, NY 10017

Routledge is an imprint of the Taylor & Francis Group, an informa business

© D. M. Goodfellow, 1939

Publisher's Note
The publisher has gone to great lengths to ensure the quality of this reprint but points out that some imperfections in the original copies may be apparent.

Disclaimer
The publisher has made every effort to trace copyright holders and welcomes correspondence from those they have been unable to contact.

A Library of Congress record exists under LCCN: 40001992

ISBN: 978-1-032-94583-5 (hbk)
ISBN: 978-1-003-57155-1 (ebk)
ISBN: 978-1-032-94584-2 (pbk)

Book DOI 10.4324/9781003571551

PRINCIPLES
OF ECONOMIC SOCIOLOGY

The Economics of Primitive Life as
Illustrated from the Bantu Peoples
of South and East Africa

By

D. M. GOODFELLOW

B.Sc. (Econ.), Ph.D., London

*Late Lecturer in Economics in the
University of Cape Town*

LONDON
GEORGE ROUTLEDGE & SONS LTD.
BROADWAY HOUSE: 68-74 CARTER LANE, E.C.

First published   .   .   1939

Printed in Great Britain by T. and A. CONSTABLE LTD.
at the University Press, Edinburgh

To

K. A. KENNEDY

CONTENTS

Fitting economic formulae to the primitive. The practical importance of this. There can only be one body of
economic theory. No gulf between the civilized and the
primitive. The social anthropologist and the economist
compare notes. Economics does not assume a Western
exchange system. Some misconceptions. The absence of
Western economic forms. Form and function in economics. The indirect satisfaction of wants. The economic
application of resources. Its reality among the Bantu.
The alleged carefree nature of the savage. Social mechanisms for economic disposal. The so-called dominance of
custom. Choice at the margin of subsistence. Control
by groups and by the individual. Values a cultural product. Economic disposal is part of any cultural scheme.
The *minimum sensible*. Self-interest.

Co-ordinating economics and sociology. The uniformities of human culture. The basis of fact in the social
world. Processes in social knowledge. The social world
not truly external. Arriving at the constructs. Testing
the constructs.

What is social fact? The existence or event. Active
observation by the sociologist. The assumed facts of
science. The hypothetical human needs. Their logical
standing. Specialism and these needs. The fact of
relationship. Relationships our main subject-matter. Describing the relationships of facts. Law in social science.
Law as description. Frequency of associations. The
invariable properties of social facts.

PRINCIPLES OF ECONOMIC SOCIOLOGY

CONTENTS

PRINCIPLES OF ECONOMIC SOCIOLOGY

Decision as to how much labour to be applied to agriculture made by group as economic unit. Personal preferences must be taken to coincide. Organization of wants further ensures this. Reciprocal relation between productive activities and organized wants.

Economic ownership in land. Relationship between its economic and other social aspects. Best mixing of land and labour a fundamental problem to the Bantu. No real superfluity of land. Actual sale among one tribe. But limited among all. The real cost of cultivable land. Competition for suitable fields. Deciding what area to break in. Much foresight needed. Economic leadership of headman. Consequences of inefficient choice. Land frequently changes hands, though not by sale. Difficulty of distinguishing amount of resources expended upon land. But indications given. Heavy labour cost of obtaining fields. Lack of money must not prevent our seeing a real price of land.

How the agents of production are mixed in accordance with the valuations placed upon them by members of the groups. We cannot say that a fund of capital is released to be turned into productive equipment. Therefore no choice as to how this is to be used. Also no entrepreneurial function in this sense. Surplus of consumption goods, but used to maintain only the human frame. Bantu society is virtually non-progressive. However, always some slight choice in application of productive resources. Difference in degree, rather than in kind, from Western communities, but very significant.

No burning question as to what new capital goods shall be created. Function of money does not extend to this evaluation. But does extend to goods of lower order. Lack of money correlated with lack of lengthy economic processes. *Minimum sensible* very effective in consumption goods. Practically no interest as a distributive share. Consumption interest does exist. Entrepreneurial interest better assumed to be non-existent. Headman as entrepreneur, but not with control of resources of highest order. His importance as economic manager.

CONTENTS

Two important differences in degree between Bantu and Western society. More fundamental fact of economic attribution does exist. Agencies of production various and substitutable. Variations in returns. Problem of sharing work and its proceeds. Realization of contribution of factors. Formation of market "prices", essential to attribution, does extend to units of labour. Extreme value of Bantu labour in production. Difficult to disentangle rewards to labour. Proceeds go to group. Organizations of consumption then secures sharing out. But not on basis of shares to individuals. Valuing the labour of a group. The marginal valuation. Economic use of labour fully secured without strict sharing of proceeds to individual labourers.

Economic aspects of ownership. To what extent the economist can take ownership for granted. The essentials of group ownership. Full play for individual preferences. Ownership of consumption goods. Mistake to say that this must always be individual. No purely individual needs, and no purely individual ownership. Social relations of consumption. Ownership of productive goods. Similar to that in Western communities. How the consumers set the pace of production.

Conveyed ownership. Placing factors of production in hands of headman. Definite valuations upon these factors. The reward of economic management. Difficult to think of Bantu manager dissatisfied with his reward. Difficult for him to withhold his services. Why we must question individual ownership of consumption goods. Bantu social unit considered as a market. Extent of freedom of choice. Valuations must and do change.

Customary disposal of resources, far from being non-economic, implements economic management. Society as an economic mechanism. Illusion of fixed disposal. Number of parties sharing in each exchange. Large enough to secure effective substitution. Even rules of kinship contribute to, rather than hamper this. Most efficient entrepreneur is secured. Optimum size of unit approached. Conclusion.

xi

PRINCIPLES OF ECONOMIC SOCIOLOGY

PART II

CONTENTS

xiii

PRINCIPLES OF ECONOMIC SOCIOLOGY

xiv

CONTENTS

PRINCIPLES OF ECONOMIC SOCIOLOGY

CONTENTS

PRINCIPLES OF ECONOMIC SOCIOLOGY

PART III

INTRODUCTION

WITHOUT subscribing to any racial theories, we shall agree that there are great cultural differences between various sections of mankind. Nothing is more urgent than to achieve a clear comprehension of these differences, for only thus can we arrive at fundamental similarities. The principles of economics have been developed on the basis of Western life. Nothing is more important than to show whether they extend their validity to the more primitive cultures. This affords a testing-ground for economic theory which its exponents will doubtless welcome. It also should help in the enormous problem of making efficient contacts between ourselves and more primitive people in many distant parts of the world.

This book attempts something more. Co-operation between the various social sciences appears, to the author, to be a matter of extreme urgency. The day is past when this need can be met by each specialist doing a little light browsing in the works of his colleagues. It is very possible that progress is now to be made less through each specialist pursuing his own line of study, than by a consolidation and adjustment of work already done. Works on economics are full of problems upon which progress cannot be made until real working contact is established between economists and sociologists. Sociological studies require at every point, not merely advice from economists, though even this would always be useful, but active co-operation in every detail of the work.

Otherwise, we may see the spectacle of groups of students independently studying the same subject-matter—man in society—yet developing each his own terminology to such an extent that he can scarcely communicate scientifically with those who ought to be his fellow workers.

At the present stage of social science, the author is well

aware, it is difficult to enunciate economic principles in a way acceptable or even intelligible to many expert sociologists, social anthropologists and social psychologists. It is equally difficult to bring the principles and discoveries of these latter specialists into effective relationship with economic theory. It is scarcely to be hoped that this book will, in itself, establish such a relationship. But a beginning must be made.

The vital and penetrating interest shown by Professor Malinowski in his analysis of the economic life of a primitive people virtually made possible the writing of this book. His sustained and unstinting help have made possible its completion.

He, as no other scholar, has made it clear that human life can be studied only by giving equal, and equally expert, attention to every aspect of that life. It is the author's hope that he has been of some service in the elucidation of the economic aspect. Only thus can a real acknowledgment be made to the work of a great teacher and inspirer.

PART I

A

CHAPTER I

THE APPLICABILITY OF ECONOMIC THEORY TO SO-CALLED
PRIMITIVE COMMUNITIES

IT has long been recognized that the formulations of economic theory have in them a certain universality. Many are the references in standard works which may legitimately be taken to show that the writers believe themselves to be handling "Laws of Human Nature", or facts so fundamental that, explored though they might be upon the basis of Western communities, their value would be found to hold in any community whatever.

Yet extremely little exploration has been made in the fitting of economic formulae to those types of society which are taken to differ so fundamentally from our own as to merit the term "primitive". This at once indicates a line of sociological study which not only may be fruitfully undertaken, but which, in the interests alike of economics and of other branches of social study, must sooner or later be faced. Does the method of modern economic theory apply equally to the Trobriander and to the Londoner? to the peasant of Eastern Europe and to the Chinese aristocrat? The question is far indeed from being an idle one. The very form in which we have put it reveals the chaos in which we should find ourselves should a negative answer be returned or even should any doubt remain in our minds. The aim of this book is to show that the concepts of economic theory must be taken as having universal validity, and that, were this not so, the result would be not only scientific confusion but practical chaos.

The practical weight of the problem is easily indicated. Our economic relationships now embrace in the most vital way peoples of very divergent cultures; trade is conducted and employment carried out between the most primitive of

3

human creatures, such as the natives of the Andaman Islands or the Aborigines of Australia, and the most highly organized of London and New York firms. We have no doubt whatever that these Western businesses conduct their activities according to the dicta of modern economics, for these dicta were arrived at very largely by studying such businesses. But, should it happen that the assumptions of economic theory fail to fit the other term of the equation, that they give no guidance to the future conduct of the Andaman or the Aborigine, then the scope and usefulness of economic theory become so restricted that, in order to give guidance in the affairs of the modern world, the economist has before him no less a task than that of devising a "new economics" which would apply to the primitive people. The inevitable further task of establishing some correlation between the two "systems" of economics would then be so vast that we choose not to attempt to consider it.

Actually, once it is baldly stated, the proposition that there should be more than one body of economic theory is absurd. If modern economic analysis, with its instrumental concepts, cannot cope equally with the Aborigine and with the Londoner, not only economic theory but the whole of the social sciences may be considerably discredited. For the phenomena of social science are nothing if not universal. The groups, the behaviour, the fundamental social relationships such as those of kinsmen and neighbours, are qualitatively the same the world over. Wherever we look at Mankind we see motives of accumulation, of competitive display, of obligations towards kinsfolk, of religious organization and political activity; these, and such, make up the body of fact with which social science must deal. The fundamental differences between "civilized" and "savage", so dear to nineteenth-century sociologists, have now been so effectively exploded that we need not here waste space upon them. Quantitative differences between cultures most certainly exist; the people of one will have mechanical machinery while those of another may lack even the wheel; in one case literacy will be so common that almost everyone reads a morning newspaper, while in another case even the

4

wise men of the people may have nothing corresponding to written characters. But if we turn our attention to these quantitative differences we shall find at the very outset that we are robbed of our hard-and-fast line between the savage and the civilized. Within one complex modern community such as the United States of America we must find many grades of culture; we shall find many people using machines but very few capable of originating them; we shall find people who can merely spell out the headlines of newspapers in their own language, and others who can write creatively. Turning to Europe, we find that under the term "European culture" we include such divergent peoples as the truly Western product of the great European capitals and the simplest of peasants who, at any rate until very recent years, must have been classed as much nearer, in cultural affinity, to the African tribesman, the subject of this volume, than to the highly sophisticated member of the great urban communities.

When it is asked, indeed, whether modern economic theory can be taken as applying to primitive life, we can only answer that if it does not apply to the whole of humanity then it is meaningless. For there is no gulf between the civilized and the primitive; one cultural level shades imperceptibly into another, and more than one level is frequently found within a single community. If economic theory does not apply to all levels, then it must be so difficult to say where its usefulness ends that we might be driven to assert that it has no usefulness at all.

Yet when, as inevitably happens, the social anthropologist and the economist begin to compare notes, a tendency shows signs of arising whereby the former may claim that economics, which he describes as "Western exchange economics", cannot quite apply to his primitive peoples, while the latter, although he regards his system as consisting of logical deductions from universal truths, finds himself in doubt as to whether these may correspond sufficiently to actual fact among peoples who are termed primitive. The problem, we believe, arises almost entirely from the difficulty of co-ordinating social studies. Economist and social anthropologist have one thing in common, the source of their strength and of their weakness; they are specialists. Each has carried his study to a high stage of validity and effectiveness; the very degree of their success makes it difficult for one to know what the other is doing. Hence the especial need for a study in co-ordination. The social anthropologist has the keenest need and desire to understand the economic aspect of the cultures upon which he works; the economist is no less desirous of testing and applying his equipment in every conceivable social setting. But, on the first approaches which they may make to each other, it is only too likely that they will be found to use terms in slightly different ways and to be unfamiliar with the exact nature of each other's working concepts.

The fundamental propositions of economics have probably not been in the mind of the anthropologist when he was making his enquiries; hence he is in the position of having to take these propositions, which, admittedly, were formulated with Western exchange communities in mind, and to test them out against the facts which he gathered in "the field". It is not surprising that this task has not so far been undertaken in a systematic way; nor is it surprising that, as appears to the present writer, the few efforts so far made do not show every sign of following the most fruitful lines. Yet we have conceded too much in saying that modern economic theory has been formulated with Western exchange systems in mind. It has been shown that Robinson Crusoe has something more than a strictly methodological significance; that an individual in his position would indeed feel the pressure of needs upon resources, would in fact make choices between the applications of his various resources, would encounter varying returns and would have to choose between present and future and between work and leisure. Wicksteed, on the other hand, has shown how the greater part of the apparatus of economic theory may be evolved without going outside a single household. This being so, it would be surprising if modern economic theory failed to apply to the peoples known as primitive.

We shall find that any difficulty which may arise in seeing that the savage disposes of his resources along ordinary economic lines, will arise through misconceptions very similar in character to those which, for a time, prevented the realization that people of low cultures conduct their affairs according to definite principles of law. It is not necessary here to recall how the savage was believed to have nothing corresponding to civil law, to be a blind slave of custom and, in general, not to be amenable to the legal principles which had been formulated in Western communities. It has now been shown very clearly that although the savage may not have formulated legal systems, yet he is in no way lacking in means of defining and enforcing obligations; in fact, that early legal theorists were misled by the absence of written codes and of formal courts. The "automatic obedience to custom", once the reality of savage law had been established, was seen to be a simple error; the savage obeys his customs, not automatically, but just as other people do; because there are sanctions which secure his obedience and because the whole of his training gives him the values which make him a good member of his own society. Legal principles were found to apply just as clearly in South Seas communities as in our own. It has been necessary to refer to the great step forward embodied in this realization because an analogous step must be taken with regard to economic theory.

It is almost superfluous to point out that the *forms* taken by the agencies of production in Western economics are almost undiscoverable in those of savage communities. Rent, wages, interest and profit assumed great importance in nineteenth-century economic discussions because they could, to some extent, be distinguished as separate shares given to separate bodies of people. In a primitive community we do not expect to find them in clearly distinguishable forms, although we shall find their distinct beginnings in Bantu societies. Likewise, special organizations to carry out cultivation or manufacture need not be expected among the Bantu; the functions are always actively carried out, but often by organizations, of which the family or household is the most important, which exist to carry out almost all necessary functions, including the religious, the legal, the political,

7

and the educational, and which conduct manufacture and agriculture alongside of these other activities. Anything resembling a modern mercantile firm is, among the Bantu, conspicuous by its absence. Yet distribution is conducted and the elements of sale by specialists are by no means lacking. To attempt to apply the categories of production, exchange, distribution, and of rent, wages, interest and profit, to Bantu society would be to choose the most difficult of all approaches. Yet we must remember that these categories are not inapplicable among the people whom we study. It is often possible, as will be seen in forthcoming pages, to distinguish shares of product given to people on account of their labour, or their organizing power, for the use of their land or cattle, or even as a surplus corresponding to profit, accruing to them through the uncertainties of the situation. Yet we mention this point now mainly for three reasons: first, because the difficulty of discovering the *forms* of modern economic life may well lead to a mistaken belief that the *functions* of that life are not to be discoverable among our less advanced people; second, because these forms are not without their relevance for primitive communities; third, and most important, because modern economic theory has supplied us with a technique which transcends these forms and has the great merit of being applicable to the economic aspect of life, simply as an aspect, and independently of the forms prevalent in any given culture.

First among the principles which we must use in studying the economic aspect of Bantu life is that of the indirect satisfaction of wants, with which is closely associated the fact of division of labour. It is as true of African society as of any other that the people do not work each to satisfy his or her own needs. The division of labour is elementary, being largely dominated by such natural or social facts as differences in age, sex, or rank. Yet, no matter how elementary the division may be, it is a fact that we see people manufacturing goods and rendering services because they expect these to be valued sufficiently highly by other members of the community. In a Bantu household the women are able to concentrate on

8

certain services and the men upon others. A woman produces more grain than she and her children will wish to consume; the way in which the surplus is used to feed her husband and his unmarried brothers is dependent upon these men valuing the women's produce in some ascertainable way, and, in return, performing their own services, which in their turn are evaluated by the women. Even if this evaluation were conducted without any conscious effort, it would still establish an effective relationship. But, as we shall see, the people appear to be very conscious of the importance of the reciprocity, as is best seen when one party believes the other to fail in his or her duties, when scarcity or plenty changes the value of either set of services, or when people are contemplating a marriage and carefully compute the value of the services which the prospective partner is likely to render. When grain is plentiful in a community, the value of an extra wife may noticeably diminish, while in time of scarcity, when baskets of grain take on a very high value in relation to other commodities, the women will be justly valued as standing between the household and starvation.

If this indirect principle, controlling the investment of working power in accordance with the estimated value of the product, can be seen, as we hold it can, even in the relationship between the women and the men of a household, then it may be seen even more clearly in situations depending upon a wider sphere of exchange. More specific exchange takes place also within a given household, as when one person may specialize in tending cattle and will certainly be rewarded accordingly. It is clear that the principle of the indirect rendering of services is as real in Bantu society as in Western. Each person, or group, carries out productive activities upon the basis of an estimate of the demand of other persons for the product; this demand thereby originates the activity and values the units of product according to the urgency of the needs which they satisfy and the possibility of securing equal satisfaction by the use of substitutes, which, in their turn, will be produced upon such a demand coming into evidence.

It is in this way that we begin to see the concept of wants

as controlling the means of their satisfaction. The legal principle operates alongside of this principle of economic indirectness, and is indispensable to it. There must be effective sanctions for the carrying out of obligations; it is the economic principle which lies at the root of the obligations. The fact that this division of labour is quantitatively very much less than in a Western community in no way lessens its importance. The principle is just as valuable to the more primitive community as to the more complex, and we cannot begin to appreciate the universal applicability of economic method until we grasp this fact.

The principle of economic indirectness is, in turn, but part of the wider one of the economic application of resources. The question is whether the savage can be said so to dispose of his resources as to feel that no unit would have given greater satisfaction if put to a different use. This concept is at the basis of modern economic method. As we shall see later, it is to be taken simply as a methodological assumption, and not as a statement having content. Can we assume that the savage so disposes of his total resources as to obtain the maximum satisfaction? Our reply is an unhesitating affirmative, in the sense, and in the sense only, in which we should reply in the affirmative if asked whether the assumption is useful in Western communities. There can be no doubt that the Bantu enjoys a flow of resources which he must apply to the satisfaction of a series of needs. He has labour power and land, then cattle, grain, and other disposable commodities, continuously coming to hand; he has the needs for nutrition, for warmth, for government, for religious experience and for many similar things which we are yet to examine more closely. It should be evident that the diversion of an undue proportion of his goods to the satisfaction of any one need will leave the others unsatisfied, and a feeling of frustration in the man. It must have been easy for him (in the old days) to devote so much time to house-building or removing, when the time was needed for the fields, that the family would be left short of food. It must have been easy to kill valuable animals for sacrifice to such an extent that the household was left short of flesh and milk at another season. It will be seen throughout this book that economic choice is constantly exercised by the individual both in disposing of resources for consumption and in the disposal of resources for further production. An individual who disposes unsuccessfully of his supplies will enjoy less satisfactions than his neighbours; a household which ineffectively applies its resources to the creation of further commodities will likewise see its members less well supplied with consumable produce than are their neighbours. The assumption of the economic disposal of resources appears to work. Yet it is just here that doubts have arisen.

These doubts may be comprehensively stated under some four headings. There is first the question as to whether the alleged carefree nature of the savage may rule out effective economical disposal of his resources. Little time need be wasted on this proposition, although it is well to note it, for, mistaken though it is in itself, it suggests one or two genuine points. The fiction of the lazy savage has by now been thoroughly exploded; some of the most lowly peoples have been found to be industrious gardeners and tireless craftsmen. Yet proof of these activities is no proof of a keen desire to dispose carefully of units of resources. With the savage as with ourselves, a point must arrive at which his main satisfaction will be derived from not worrying too much about the way in which he may consume his worldly wealth. An Englishman sooner or later reaches the point at which he decides that, in order to expend his income so as to get the maximum of satisfaction from the last sixpence, he would have to give to the matter much more than sixpennyworth of care and attention. It may be suggested that peoples of different cultures are willing to go to different degrees of trouble in the careful planning of their expenditure. This is a matter upon which we can have only personal impressions. It is probable, however, that some peoples, of whom the Latins of South America are reputedly an example, may put much less stress upon the economic disposal of their resources than do certain other peoples, generally supposed to reside in more Northern climes. It is also certain, among individuals, that some, even within a group of acquaintances, are much more economically minded than others. Yet we should never suppose from this that the assumptions of economic theory apply to some individuals and not to others, or that they break down when applied to the South American whose main occupation appears, at least to the superficial observer, to be to lie in the sun.

The uneconomically minded person, so-called, is simply a person who puts a relatively high value upon his time and attention; he does not squander these upon attention to details. If part of his resources are expended in ways other than they would have been had he devoted more attention to the matter, the fact still remains that his whole resources, including his powers of attention, have been disposed of in the ways which give him his greatest satisfaction. He may have paid a good deal for his carefreeness, but this in no way breaks down the basic assumptions of economic theory. The possibility always remains that he will change his habits, and we cannot suppose that such a change would suddenly bring him within the scope of economic principles. Thus, even if the Trobrianders or the Bantu happened to be very careless in their domestic economies, this fact would not invalidate our contention that the main body of economic theory applies to them just as much as to ourselves.

Yet all our evidence points to the fact that even these widely divergent peoples are relatively careful in spending their resources. There is overwhelming evidence that they dislike waste; a Bantu family has very efficient means of making its resources go as far as possible. Social mechanisms show this, in that the head of the household has ultimate control of the great majority of food stores. The housewives cannot draw upon these without his knowledge or permission. The need for economic disposal along careful lines is often paramount, for the penalty for neglect may be starvation. A herd of cattle, likewise, is certainly not squandered by any Bantu owner; all evidence points to the fact that he most carefully weighs the alternative uses to which his animals might be put; some will be used for a sacrifice, some for a wedding portion, some to relieve a necessitous relative, some as gifts (*i.e.* taxes) to the chief. It is no mere form of words to say that cattle are highly valued among the Bantu; this statement points to one of the central facts of their lives, and its meaning lies in their *behaviour*, which carries out an extremely careful disposal of these objects of wealth, so that *the central assumption* of economic theory is readily applicable.

A more important objection to the application of modern economic assumptions to peoples such as the Bantu is that their lives are so dominated by custom that they cannot be said to exercise free economic choice. The present writer has not yet seen this objection clearly stated in print, but he does find a tendency to say that, of course, free choice, as known in Western communities, does not exist among savages. It is held of some of the poorer tribes that they are so near the margin of subsistence that they cannot exercise economic choice, while it appears to be a tacit assumption of many writers about primitive peoples that an entity called custom controls their lives in such a way that they dispose of their resources with but little willed choice.

With regard to both of these points, we should say that we are already thoroughly familiar with them in discussions of Western economic life. Very large numbers of Western and European people spend their lives very near what may be called subsistence level. Peasants and unskilled labourers have normally just enough resources to meet what appear to be elementary physical needs. Yet we never say that economic theory does not apply to these people, and in this we are right, for, no matter how scant the resources may be, they still must be disposed of along economic lines. We might even go further and say that the fewer the resources, the more need there is for the housewife to expend them carefully, thus adding to the total family income of real satisfactions through the increased exertion on her part. It is doubtful even whether the fact that Western wages are paid in the form of money gives to the European labourer any freedom to waste his resources which is denied to the Bantu, whose income is in the form of readily usable products. Just as the European labourer's income may be expended in "worthless" ways, so the Bantu who is near the starvation level may well consume all his resources at a feast which will bring him no return, or exchange them for trinkets. Even the savage who is normally near starvation has freedom of choice to "waste" those resources which he has, and a correspondingly greater need to apply them with due care.

But by no means all Bantu tribes are, or were in the past, on what is called the "margin of subsistence". Yet it appears to have been assumed that they, in common with other primitive peoples, have been so dominated by custom that free economic choice has not been to them the reality which it is to us. The supposition has been that "custom" may make primitive peoples behave in ways unlike those which we know in the Western world. It might appear that the savage has held expensive feasts because these were customary; has kept large herds of cattle because custom so dictated; has given part of his crops away against his own interest, because it was customary to do so; has allowed his chief to plunder him, again because it was the custom.

Any such statements or suppositions are entirely meaningless. Custom is merely another name for behaviour, and these statements merely state that such-and-such behaviour is carried out; they solve no problems. All that social scientists can do is to observe the ways in which human beings behave. When any piece of behaviour is repeatedly observed, it is described and given a name, so that it may be observed and discussed upon future occasions. A custom is therefore a unit of behaviour, isolated for purposes of observation. When customs are carried out in very well marked ways by considerable groups of people, on specific occasions, they become those organized activities which have sometimes been called Institutions. Thus to say that savage behaviour is customary, or even dominated by custom, is to be guilty of tautology. To say that he pays taxes to his chief because of "custom", is merely to say that he pays them. We shall see throughout this work that organized custom remains a most useful concept in describing Bantu behaviour so as to appre-

14

ciate its economic aspect, but we must never suppose that a piece of conduct is disposed of as soon as we have called it a "custom".

We shall find that resources are indeed disposed of according to the dictates of social values and rules of behaviour, describable in terms of custom. In this way we hope to obtain a full appreciation of the economic aspect of Bantu life. It will be found that this, instead of invalidating the assumption of the economic disposal of resources, gives us the terms on which this disposal takes place.

Two threads are clearly visible: on the one hand, society lays down the main lines along which resources must be disposed of; on the other hand, the individual or the group is left free to achieve the social ends by his own planning. We may say that this gives us economic disposal in two different senses. In one, the society or the culture lays down the broad rules for the economic disposal, and in the other, the individual or his group manages his own resources in conformity with social rule. But these together only give a total management of resources along strictly economic lines. Any economic management must be with a view to realizing values already in the minds of the people. These values are themselves a cultural product, and are inculcated into each individual almost from the first hours of life. A man grows up to value certain social forms and activities, be they the ceremonies at the crises of life or the more continuous conventions of daily existence. One of the main lessons of his life is to dispose of his resources so as to realize these valued things to the highest degree possible. Thus in behaving in the customary ways, he exhibits no conduct presenting any new difficulties to the assumptions of modern economists. It would be quite as true to say that the people of America or Europe are so dominated by custom that they cannot dispose economically of their resources. Exploring the point with a primitive people in mind, we are brought to realize that we are dealing with a sociological principle of universal import. All over the world, people are not free to dispose of their resources, as it were, de novo. Everywhere the main lines of expenditure are laid down; the aim of the individual's choice is to realize the maximum satisfaction along these lines.

The principle of economic disposal is an essential part, or aspect, of any cultural scheme. One of the basic facts to be observed in any culture, however primitive, is that it has mechanisms whereby the individual is taught not to waste; to acquire values in consonance with those of his fellow-beings, and to manage his affairs according to those values. Even if the savage, therefore, could be said to be "dominated by custom", this, far from meaning that he did not dispose economically of his resources, might mean just the opposite; for custom may best be regarded as the mechanism through which this essential aim is achieved. Customary behaviour is simply the entity of which we are now studying the economic aspect.

A further way in which it is sometimes argued that the savage so behaves as to render economic assumptions less illuminating when applied to him, is that in which he may be said to fail to perceive small units of commodities, or to have a large *minimum sensible*. It may be said that time means little to him, therefore that if it is customary for him to devote a certain number of days to a piece of work or to a ceremony, he will do so without further calculation. The same may be said of the units in terms of which he thinks; if it is customary for him to make a gift of a certain number of baskets of grain on a certain occasion, then that he will do so. Against any such argument we can but invoke all the factual evidence of the best modern anthropology. It has been shown again and again that the savage can be careful to the last basket of grain and that he can bargain to the last goat-skin. Further, that if the goat-skin is too valuable, some extra small service will be expected in return to make the bargain even. Perhaps the most effective demonstration of the futility of such an argument is afforded by the introduction of currency by Europeans. When this occurs, the people will be found to balance their accounts and their bargains down to the smallest coin available.

It remains only, in this connection, to answer the argument that savages may not behave in ways consistent with their self-interest. The Trobriand Islanders have been quoted as giving away a large part of their produce to their wives' brothers instead of keeping it for themselves. This behaviour, so far from exemplifying disinterested, non-economic action, merely indicates an extension of kinship ties. It is quite on a par with a European father giving a large part of his income to his own wife or children. To introduce such considerations and to try to prove from them that savage behaviour may be of so peculiar a nature that it actually reverses ordinary economic assumptions is regarded by the present writer as fantastic.

CHAPTER II

SECTION I

The Beginnings of Co-ordination

THIS book being an attempt to co-ordinate the two studies of economics and of sociology, it is of the greatest importance that we should at this stage make a statement of what we accept as the fundamentals of social study. Excellent though it be that working scientists should pursue their activities without too frequently exploring the ultimate bases of their work, the time does come when such explorations are advisable, and in such a work as this, utilizing the concepts and comparing the results of two major branches of the social sciences, it seems that some attention to fundamentals is required.

We have already seen that we assume certain uniformities to exist wherever human culture is to be traced. These uniformities, like all the uniformities of science, are constructions of our own minds. We interpret our sense data so as to arrive at such entities as human needs; these same needs translated into active wants; human groups, not fortuitous or meaningless, but directly correlated with fundamental needs; and, by no means least, units of behaviour which we call customs, organized activities, or simply institutions, by means of which we are able to trace similarities in the behaviour of man no matter what his geographical situation or his cultural level.

It is thus that we arrive at our basis of fact in the social world. We cannot too often repeat that such facts are our own constructions, and that the uniform relations which we find among them are *a fortiori* results of our own mental application and existences in our own minds. We have no knowledge of the social world save that based upon the reports of our senses. And since the social world, possibly even more than the physical world, has in it such a complexity of content that we can proceed only by selecting those features which seem to us to have significance, we see at once that we do not attempt to explain the whole of man's social life. Out of what our senses report to us we select those impressions which indicate significant facts, and the essence of these facts is that we should be able to classify and compare them, to establish their more important and less variable relations; in short, to treat them scientifically.

In seeking knowledge of the social world our main processes must closely resemble those by which our knowledge of the physical world has so far been obtained. The social, the physical, and no doubt the mental phenomena of nature make up what may be called the external world. There must be differences, whether of detail or of importance is a matter of opinion, between the methods employed for research into these three divisions of nature. But the fundamental method must be the same. The basic instrument is scientific thought, that type of mental operation which defies description, but which has about it the well-known qualities of hardness, of willingness to examine evidence, of imaginative powers sufficient to invent hypotheses and critical powers strong enough to destroy these hypotheses if it is right to do so.

The main difference in method required to cope with these three parts of the universe arises from the fact that only one of them, the physical, is truly external to the scientist. The social world, the world of human needs, persons and groups, relationships and activities, is not truly external to any enquirer. He is himself a person with needs and activities and with a complex of relationships extending outward from himself to his fellow-men. Hence no sociology can escape being partly introspective. Even when we look at a group of African natives, we are almost sure to interpret their behaviour and the meanings of things to them partly in terms of our own behaviour and of our personal values. An anthropologist, for example, who in his personal life is deeply religious is not likely to report the same things of a primitive people as would another anthropologist whose main passion is for economic theory. The personal equation in such matters is not something to be lightly passed over; it goes to the root of our problem of knowledge. Both anthropologists, since we take them to be examining the same African tribe, will have precisely the same field of sense data. But how much further will the agreement go? Upon the answer to this question depends the possibility of valid and universally acceptable knowledge about the social world.

We may say at once that if these two scientists are so truly scientific that, as it were, they can depersonalize themselves, then they will be able to arrive at constructions of social fact in complete agreement with each other. We do not, however, regard it as either possible or desirable that sociological enquirers should jettison all those personal interests which give richness to a personality; a man who is really keen on religion is likely to discover facts and relationships which the other may miss, while a specialist in economics is almost certain to get a view of the primitive society which is not achieved by those lacking his special interest. Even apart from such differences in personal keenness, the fact remains that each of the major aspects of life today must be studied by specialists, and that any anthropologist is likely to be a specialist in little more than one aspect. Thus the experts in religion and in economics, respectively, are taken to be applying the instrument of scientific thought to the same group of African people. Both have the identical field of sense impressions. The next step, we suggest, is the construction, out of this sense data, of the ordinary objects of the external world. Even at this early stage the worlds of the two men may begin to diverge. Each will see the natives; no difference will arise here. But a difference will appear as soon as the scientists pass from the stage of merely perceiving the bodies of the natives to that of conceiving them as personalities, prone to certain types of behaviour. Each anthropologist constructs the personalities of the natives in terms of his own interpretation, determined by his interests and prior knowledge. Each sees them as dark-skinned, as having hair of a certain texture, and so on. But the expert in religion sees them further as beings who have certain views of their ancestors, who possibly dream of those ancestors, who may regard a snake as a personification of an ancestor, and who are actuated by religious motives and feel themselves to be part of a community bound by the same religious views. Such, in the round, is the African constructed by the religious expert by the well-known process of interpreting his sense data so as to give himself the objects necessary for his scientific work.

The economist, proceeding from precisely the same sense data, arrives at precisely the same concept of the natives as dark brown bodies, but then he proceeds to visualize them as people who dispose of their time and their energy in certain proportions so as to achieve certain results with the least expenditure of each; he thinks of them as linked with each other on the basis of such ties as the rendering of indirect services, and so on. The economist's native is in one sense the same person as the native of the religious expert, but in another sense they are quite unlike each other. Reports upon religious sacrifices and ceremonies may describe these in terms of social and religious needs; or in terms of the economic resources consumed. The two scientists in a sense see different things. When they both watch an African behaving in a certain way, one may know that he is carrying out a religious observance, while the other may think that he is spitting upon the ground from a mere physical impulse. Yet the significant point is, that the two scientists, in interpreting such a simple unit of behaviour as that of an African spitting upon the ground, will not really disagree. One will be able to interpret the action, or custom, much more fully than the other. To him, the religious expert, the action is a more significant construct than to the other. Yet when this has been explained to the economist he, in his turn, will read new meaning into the action and for him it will become a significant piece of data which may well have its economic aspect. He may find that the custom of spitting is carried out before or after a meal as a way of thanking the ancestors who have helped to provide the meal. It takes its place in the economist's category of sacrifices, the symbolic giving of something back to the higher powers in return for favours received. Thus should the economist find on further investigation that the custom is carried out after some meals but not after others, he may work on the assumption, that is, proceed to test the assumption, that the meal for which this thanks is given is more valued than the meal which is merely eaten, and this may enable him to describe more completely the relative exchange values of commodities to the natives.

The basic possibility of valid knowledge of the social world is thus established by the fact of agreement between the constructs of different scientists. These constructs are not the same at the outset; the custom which is observed may be full of meaning to one anthropologist even though he actually sees only a few traces of it; to him it is a scientific fact, classifiable and with relations to other facts. To the other scientist it is not yet a scientific fact. It may be so meaningless to him that in the course of years of diligent enquiry it might never appear in his note-books. It is when contact is established between the two specialists that the custom becomes a scientific fact to both, a "thing" with unchanging properties, constructed from sense data.

Should disagreement appear at this point it will be the clearest sign that the method of one or both has been defective. This supplies the testing which is an essential part of scientific method. Should the economist have reason to question the significant existence of the sacrificial spit, then further enquiry by both is called for. The point here emerges that the social world is a real unit. The further proof of this is that if one specialist, say the one in religion, pursued his studies to a sufficient length he would arrive at as complete a knowledge of the society as the human mind may ever achieve. In order to describe fully the religious processes he would be obliged to branch into all other aspects. Sacrifices could not be fully described without describing their economic inter-relations. Nor could the religious aspect be fully appreciated without a full discovery of its political, educational and other aspects. The only reason why we write in terms of each of these aspects being dealt with by a specialist is that this brings out the fundamental need for a scientific superimposing of the constructs formed by each. This superimposing, when successful, gives us the assurance that objects of utility to science have been constructed from out of the field of primary sense data.

Section II

The Grammar of Social Science

It is customary to say that the ultimate appeal of science must be to fact, and it is further said that science is a method of exploring facts. When facts have been clearly related to each other, it is said that laws arise. Since we are here writing of social science, and not of particular social sciences, that is to say, of the body of method by means of which the social world may be explored, it is necessary for us to define the type of fact of which the social world is composed. What is a social fact? We shall find it useful, though in no sense conclusive, to think in terms of facts of two kinds.

First, there is the existence or event. A Bantu village exists; it is an event occurring in time and space; in this same category are social groups, such as a household, or a local community. Such facts correspond to the primary constructs of the scientists whose work we have just been discussing. They are singled out from the great mass of sense data. They are so singled out because human thought must begin with comprehensible objects. These correspond roughly to the objects of common sense, such as chairs and tables, of our everyday world. It must not be thought, however, that it has always been easy to distinguish them, to confer upon them a reality in people's minds. A chair to an Englishman is a number of visible surfaces which he can at once interpret, from his present perceptions and his past experiences, as a chair. A raw African, seeing precisely the same surfaces for the first time, may scarcely manage to disentangle them from the rest of his field of sense data, and he will certainly not at once recognize the object as the article of furniture which it is to us. He will begin to "recognize" the chair when he has seen

23

people using it and, perhaps better still, when he has been told to bring it and has tried sitting on it himself.

In just the same way it has not always been straight sailing for anthropologists to recognize the primary objects in human societies. Seeing some thousands of natives living in a given district does not at once make apparent such objects as religious societies, age grades, groups who co-operate in agriculture, clans, or even such apparently simple entities as families. All of these facts or events have to be carefully constructed; the sense data relevant to them have to be selected and organized. The great mass of irrelevant sense data, telling of unique events and of accidental occurrences, must be jettisoned. Always, a great mass of experience must be ignored before the relevant features are brought into existence in the scientist's mind.

To show how little elementary simplicity there may be about these sociological primary objects, it is only necessary to indicate the problem of the clan. A type of human group was observed in certain primitive societies; it was labelled the clan; thenceforward enquirers began to discover clans in other parts of the primitive world. Here were elementary existences, objects, or events, which seemed simple enough. It was only when further enquiry was made that it was found that these clans, even if something did exist to correspond to the name, performed so few functions in common, and had so little effective reality, that it became necessary to regard the term merely as denoting a hypothetical existence, something which was worth looking for, but which it was dangerous to begin by supposing to be a plain object of common sense.

An additional significance is thus given to the mental processes by means of which we saw our two experts pursuing their work of describing the culture of a primitive community. We saw that each investigated his own aspect, and that valid knowledge could be taken to have been achieved when the constructs of each coincided. We now see that the first result of these processes is to bring into existence the primary facts of social science, and so to equip the scientists with their first material for investigation. Chief among these primary social facts are the objects of material culture, the linguistic equipment of the people, and the basic social groupings. Should it still be necessary to contend that it is no automatic or easy task to bring these primary facts into existence in the minds of the investigators, it is only necessary to glance at the simplest class of them, the material equipment. At first it may seem easy to define the existence of a digging-stick, an altar, or a dwelling-house. Actually, as every anthropologist knows, this may be a difficult task. A piece of wood can be recognized as a digging-stick, not from the first sense impressions of that piece of wood, which may tell us nothing, but only from seeing it in use and carefully noting the usages, supernatural beliefs, technical knowledge and economic value which pertain to it and which give it its existence as a digging-stick, distinguishing it from other bits of wood which are apparently just the same. To perceive a religious altar, again, requires active interpretation of sense data. A tree and a broken jar, perhaps a few grains of corn which the chickens are eating, can be interpreted only by the specialist, as an altar at which a sacrifice has just been performed. Only then does it become a definite construct, a fact of the type which has permanence and invariable attributes, and thus is the raw material of scientific investigation.

Let us note, in passing, that facts are discovered by no mere passive receptivity on the part of the scientist. Always, he is part of the reality which he is disentangling. Only by active observation, by moving about in the life which is his subject, does he achieve knowledge. Rigid experiment is not his, but the method of observation based upon active participation, which is of the essence of the experimental method, is his essential instrument.

Having established the primary objects or elementary facts of the social world, we must ask whether it has been found necessary to assume the existence of other facts, namely, those whose existence cannot be derived from sense data, but which may be hypothetically assumed to exist in order to enable the scientists' minds to discover other and more definite facts.

These hypothetical entities might correspond roughly to

25

facts of physical science such as the atom and electron. Whether or not these can be isolated and made into objects of sense, they are indispensable to physical science because they help to clarify certain relations in the thought of the scientists.

It is enough to mention that there is no hard-and-fast line between these and the primary objects of sense. Already we have seen an instance, the clan, which hovers between the two spheres. In some societies clans have been observed as existing events or facts; in others, the clan is best regarded as a hypothetical entity, as something which may exist, and to which in any case it is quite useful to attribute certain functions, at least until these can be more definitely related to other social groups. Thus if food taboos are found to be important, complicating religious and economic adaptation, it is necessary for us to discover for which social groups they are realities; by whom they are enforced and practised. Our first indication may be that they are attached to a widespread group of people who have certain other things in common, and who are said to make up a clan. It is then quite practicable to discuss their food practices with men whom we classify as members of that clan. Some practical progress may result. Later, however, we may discover that the taboos are highly valued by different groupings of people, possibly by age grades, possibly by extended families. When we know this, we proceed to investigate among these other groups, and the clan may recede into the background so far as food taboos are concerned. But it has its utility until we can relate the taboos to more definite groups. The concept of a food taboo in itself is simply such a hypothetical fact. We are learning quickly that food preferences and avoidances among savages are as complex and "unreasonable" as among ourselves. It is by no means easy to say that a certain kind of meat is definitely avoided by a well-defined group of people. Individual preferences will break the rule, and so will occasions of need. But science cannot deal merely with an immense number of individual cases. It must single out classes of sufficient significance and simplicity. Thus it becomes not only convenient but essential to assume that there are some uniformities in peoples' practice, so that a food taboo becomes an hypothesis, which we assume to be a fact. It is a piece of shorthand, simplifying for us a mass of complicated data. It has thus the basic character of a scientific law, stating invariable relationships between objects. It is the kind of scientific, or hypothetical, fact just as necessary to the description of the social world as to the external world of physical science.

Having now furnished ourselves with instances of the simpler facts, constructed from sense data, and of facts which are largely hypothetical, it is advisable to introduce another of our indispensable instruments, giving us a more completely hypothetical kind of fact. Our business throughout is to describe human behaviour. This is an impossible task unless we allow ourselves to think in terms of certain uniform drives. It must be made very clear that these exist only in our own minds; but, being equipped with them, we can proceed to relate human behaviour to them, thus achieving some uniformity and basis for prediction in what would otherwise be an unmentionable chaos. The uniform threads to be seen running through human conduct are taken to be those corresponding to certain main human needs. Their scientific utility is derived from the remarkable circumstance that each need corresponds exactly to one of the aspects of human culture which it is practicable to study. The main needs have been classified by Malinowski as those for political organization; for a legal system; for education, whereby the young are trained into the values of the community; the need for some artistic expression; the need for knowledge, and its application; the need for some contact with the supernatural, that is to say, for magic and religion; and, what concerns us chiefly in this book, the need for the economic application of resources.

That these needs are but hypothetical entities or facts, needs no stressing but must not be forgotten. They can never be isolated and made the objects of sense perception. Nor must we make the mistake of supposing that they are entities which can be known by their effects. We can have knowledge only of these effects, that is to say, of the actual society. Logically, the hypothetical needs would be found to have the same standing as the "wants" of economics, for it can always be said that people act to satisfy their wants or needs, and if we are pressed to tell how we know of these, we can but reply that we know because of the ways in which the people have acted. *The argument is circular, but assumptions whose logical standing in relation to the outer world may be insignificant are yet indispensable to the thought processes of scientists.* By having these assumptions of uniformities in his mind, he has yet another instrument whose purpose is to abstract simplicity from the outer confusion.

On the basis of these assumptions, scientists become specialists, in economics, education, or whatever it may be. Each specialist pursues the aspect which is isolated for him by his assumptions. The complex social world, already reduced to facts of the main types which we have indicated, is explored, on the basis of these further, hypothetical, facts, along the lines of the vital aspects.

One result of this is that further facts are established. The social world is reduced still further to manageable items. These, being studied from their various aspects, are studied thoroughly, and further interrelations established between them, giving us larger facts taking on more of the nature of natural laws which describe the invariable associations found in human society and thus provide any basis we may have for the making of probability judgments about the future.

The purely hypothetical human needs therefore enjoy a high scientific standing because of their complete coincidence with the aspects from which it is found possible to study human society. The object of this book is to see what new facts and relationships between facts can be arrived at by exploiting thoroughly one aspect, the economic.

The final type of fact which we shall distinguish is that of relationship, not between other facts of science, but between human beings, human groups, and between them and their material and linguistic equipment. This may be taken as the highest type of fact, of a definite sort, amenable to sense impressions, in the study of human society.

In a way, these relationships are the fundamental objects of our study. Regarded as facts, they are in a class apart from the first constructs from sense data, from the facts which are scientific assumptions, and from those which are more completely hypothetical, such as the main human needs. For the relationships are functional correlations between these other types of fact. Having equipped ourselves with the first three sets, making up for ourselves a social world composed of units amenable to scientific manipulation, the next step is to describe the relationships between these units. Thus, property is one of these relationships, kinship is another.

In examining a case of the property relationship, we first clarify to ourselves the facts which are the terminals of the relationship, that is to say, for example, the person or group on the one hand; the valued objects, whether material or abstract, such as legal rights, on the other; and then we proceed to describe the relationship as fully as possible. This can be done only by noting fully all the facts, of any type, further brought into relationship with the two main facts, the person and his property. Our observations must be active, and quite possibly we ourselves may enter into the relationships in order to clear points up. Should we wish to know whether the relationship between a person and his property is such that he may dispose of it without consulting any other persons, one way of discovering this would be to offer to buy it ourselves, though it must be stressed that, while the attainment of knowledge depends upon the active participation of the observer, this participation is also, in all instances, a disturbing influence. We shall, therefore, concentrate upon observing all possible instances of the actual use of such property by such owners; we shall enquire closely as to any conceivable ways in which other persons may be involved, knowing that the man may quietly consult some of his relatives before carrying out a sale. By observations of this type we may succeed in achieving a description, useful as a working guide, of the property relationships, in each given case. The man may or may not be able or inclined to sell his property at all; he may or may not have such complete control over it as to be able to sell it should he wish to do so. If this control is not sufficient, this would be an indication to us that the person's ownership is not absolute but that other persons, possibly his relatives or his chief, share in the ownership.

The descriptions thus arrived at, of the relationships between facts, are perhaps the main objective of the social sciences. It is for this reason that we refer to them as a higher type of fact, meaning by that, facts which were the sole reason for our going to the trouble of constructing the earlier types. When we have achieved them, we shall have achieved the description of useful parts of human society and behaviour.

The fact of relationship is discoverable between all of the other facts, giving a web of relationships coterminous with human culture. Relationships exist, and must be described, between individuals and between groups, giving larger units of social grouping; between groups and their organized activities, as when a certain assembly of kinsmen and neighbours carry out agricultural production; between men and women and their material equipment, such as implements and houses; between groups of men on the one hand, and such methodological facts as clans and totems; between all other facts, and such hypothetical assumptions as human needs.

It is in describing such relationships that we arrive at the facts which must guide the administrator, the missionary, the "social engineer". The fact that men have duties and obligations towards their kinsfolk, that this fact involves the transfer of property, the assembling of these kinsfolk for such purposes as ceremonies controlling agriculture and satisfying the needs for religious expression, is a fact which at once gives possibilities of influence and control. No colonist, however unscientific in his outlook, is likely to overlook the rudimentary facts of the kinship situation. He knows that, in certain circumstances, he may succeed in employing a young man by approaching that young man's father. But he is not in the least likely to formulate the further significances of kinship among the natives.

The social scientist makes this more complete description. He is able to approach, not to completeness, but to a useful rounded whole, by making full use of the whole range of facts composing his equipment. He will expect to find the kinship relationship connected, in its turn, with material goods, so will try to discover the ways in which the manipulation of these is affected by the facts of kin; he will observe isolated facts of behaviour, such as food observances, and, in the hope of relating them, will resort to the assumption of some organization behind them which he may choose to call a clan. He will keep in mind the whole range of hypothetical human needs, and so may discover in what ways kinsfolk are related in order to satisfy these needs.

The result will be a description of facts with relationships, many of which will appear to be invariable at least as far as experience goes, as that a father invariably provides for his wife and children or other closely related kinsfolk, or that closely related kinsmen cultivate fields together or assemble for religious expression. The description of these relationships, especially when they are invariable or of known frequency, gives us the beginnings of social law. The present writer does not regard it as very fruitful to discuss the nature of law in the social sciences. It appears to be sufficient, at this stage, to regard a law as a statement of invariable relationships, so that the type of fact discussed in this paragraph is indeed the beginning of social law.

It will be seen that social law of this type is definitely not a statement of the ways in which a society may change, or pass from one evolutionary stage to another. It is a piece of description of the ways in which the various facts, making up a human society, are related to each other; it is a description of the actual functioning of the society. To the extent that the relations described are invariable or of known frequency, and exist between sufficiently well-defined and unchanging social facts, social law is discovered. This brings out the great importance of establishing clearly the range of facts with which we deal; which make up the social world of the scientist. It is for this reason that we have attempted carefully to enumerate the main types of facts, and to establish the epistemological validity of each, based as it may be either upon the coinciding sense impressions of observers, each a specialist in his own field, but with similar training in method; or upon the fact that we are entitled to work with hypothetical assumptions and entities of purely methodological import, always remembering, however, that the sole use of such entities is to enable us to discover relationships between facts which are capable, in their turn, of being checked by the sense observations of scientists. The first step to the attainment of law in the social sciences is the construction of the entities of the social world. Social law will then state constant associations between these entities, and we shall be in the position of having that definite knowledge of the social world which is the essential basis for probability calculations about the future, and hence for social control.

Section III

Making the Assumptions

Our next step is to clarify the point that every social fact has properties which, by the definition of "fact", are invariable, and that a scientist who is a specialist will examine facts from the aspect of these properties. Given the fact of a small community of African people, the specialist in education, for example, may examine this community from the point of view of the learning processes which are likely to be going on within it. He may find whether an apprentice to the native medical profession is receiving instruction from established medicine men; whether young craftsmen are learning the tricks of their trade; in what ways the children of the group are becoming aware of the behaviour which they must learn if the group is to persist. Through the specialist examining this aspect of the group life, additional value is given to almost all facts. He may find, for example, that a religious observance is never carried out without some opportunity being given for younger people to learn both the practical details and the spiritual value of the observances. Thus the description of religious ritual is enriched by a description of its educational aspect. It becomes, indeed, not merely a religious fact, but a fact with, in all probability, every one of the main aspects.

Its political significance may even overshadow its religious meaning. As will be seen later in this book, it may perform valuable economic functions; the legal, artistic and even scientific aspects are not likely to be lacking. Thus what at first appeared to be, and was quite rightly described as, a religious ritual, becomes, following scientific activity, a fact with a much more varied significance.

A similar process can be observed in the description of almost any social fact. The sittings of a law court are, for everyday speech, a legal fact; for scientific discourse their significance for other than legal matters may be immense. The court may be the main source of the political authority of a chief; it may be the occasion for a considerable transfer of wealth. For purposes of convenience we must continue to refer to the religious ceremony as religious, to the court as legal; but as scientists we must keep in mind that each of these is a social fact having, in all probability, the complete range of aspects, and to be explained in terms only of the satisfaction of all the human needs with which these aspects coincide. The circumstances of all specialists examining each social fact, every one from his own aspect, and of the facts satisfying the needs of all, is the primary guarantee that these facts have scientific validity.

The only safe assumption upon which the economist may work is that all facts, of whatever type, must have their economic aspect explored before they can be completely described. Complete description, naturally, results from exploration of all aspects. At first sight it may appear that only certain facts will repay, or require, investigation from the economic point of view. It will be obvious that such facts as implements, houses, agricultural activities and payment of taxes to a chief will have important economic aspects. The temptation is to regard the economic exploration of a community as complete when these and similar items have been dealt with. Economics in Western communities has achieved its results largely by using such facts as its data. But in primitive communities it will be seen that such a selection of economic facts, or economic institutions, as they are sometimes called, will not

C   33

be the economist's best contribution to a complete sociology. For one thing, as we have just seen, they are by no means solely economic; their other aspects have enormous significance. For another thing, many other facts, not corresponding to those which we think of as economic in Western communities, have in primitive societies very important relationships with the disposal of resources. A religious object such as a ceremonial hoe may attain to great value and, should extreme need ever arise, it may exchange for considerable quantities of other commodities. Even a comparatively small food taboo will affect the relative values of foods, and thus influence agriculture. Religion among the Bantu has strongly economic aspects, sacrilizing the desire for plenty and the need for efficient economic management, controlling the consumption of flesh in the peoples' diet through the practice of sacrifice, and in other ways. Malinowski has laid the foundation of economic study along these lines by showing the great control over economic resources exercised through the fact of the kinship relationship and through such practices as ceremonial feasts and tribal ceremonies.

In exploring a primitive community from the economic aspect, we have first to construct a set of scientific objects or facts somewhat different from those employed by economists in Western communities. The fundamental facts of the social world are the same the World over. Everywhere, there is material equipment, language, and social grouping. Everywhere the same assumptions such as fundamental human needs may be expected to play their part, as also will those assumed facts, such as the existence of the "average man", corresponding to the assumed existence of clan and totem, which we have discussed. But it is obvious that many of the most significant facts in the world of the Western economist are almost peculiar to that world, or assume in it a significance not to be found in savage cultures. Joint-stock enterprise with limited liability, is, we need scarcely say, not in the social world of the savage; rent, as a payment for the use of land, is seldom discernible as a social fact in primitive communities, not because savages are in any way incapable of making and taking payments for the use of land, but because, as it happens, land is in nearly all cases either very plentiful in relation to the need for it, or is so tied up with groupings such as the family that it never comes into a market. The management of concerns by men who do not own them, or who own only a very small part of them, is also virtually indistinguishable in primitive communities, so that it is not one of the facts of the social world which we shall use in dealing with those communities. Large-scale marketing and transport are likewise not facts which will provide the economist with data when he works out the principles of his science on the basis of primitive peoples.

In Western economics it is decidedly useful, and has been indispensable in the growth of the science, to talk of entities such as rent, interest, wages, and profit. Sometimes these payments to agents are distinguishable in a concrete way, but, we should say, much more frequently they are simply assumed facts whose epistemological value lies not so much in our being able to see them, as in their being useful in enabling us to give full descriptions of how the proceeds of manufacturing or other productive activity are shared out. Even the contents of a weekly pay envelope may by no means correspond exactly to wages in a scientific sense. They are payment for labour, but their amount is likely to be affected by economic uncertainty in such a way that the sum which common sense designates as wages really includes payment not only for labour but also for risk-bearing. Thus the epistemological standing of wages is similar to that of the clan or the totem in the foregoing discussion. Wages are a methodological fact, and this applies also to the other classical shares of the agents of production.

It is of great importance for us to make this clear, since there is a decided tendency to approach the economics of primitive communities with the observation that the main facts of economics, that is, of Western economic life, are lacking in them and consequently to assume that the principles of economic theory may fail to apply. The truth is that these principles will be shown to be even stronger than before, after it has been demonstrated that they are just as workable in primitive communities, with their different sets of social facts.

35

The facts of sense data against which economic theory will be tested in primitive communities are such facts as the family, the religious group and activity, agriculture, activities of mainly educational import such as initiations, the activities marking the crises of life, such as birth, marriage and death. These are all facts susceptible of being constructed from sense data. All of them are present, in one form or another, in Western communities, but, not there having the same significance, have not to the same extent been included in the data of economists. Further, facts which appear to be the same may in reality be different, should they perform a different set of functions. Thus, the family among the Bantu corresponds to the Western family in some of its essential functions, but has others to which the Western family will not lay a general claim, more particularly in that it is a much more comprehensive economic unit among the Bantu. In these ways it will be seen that the objects constructed from sense data are not the same in the two cultures.

It is only necessary to mention that the further purely hypothetical entities of production, consumption, distribution and exchange have already, for all practical purposes, taken back places in the world of the modern economist, to see that economic theory has in recent years so simplified and improved its technique that it can be adapted, with much less of a wrench, to the study of primitive communities, than would have been possible a quarter of a century ago.

All of the specialists working upon the nature of human society study the same subject matter. They take from the raw material of sense data such objects or facts as seems significant. It is a guarantee of the significance of these facts that they are regarded as useful by all of the scientists, whose views, so long as the studies progress smoothly, will coincide. Thus the facts of all types, which will be useful to the economist, will be significant to the educationalist, the jurist, and the other experts. The objects of primary sense data, such as material equipment and groups of people; the assumed objects of science, such as clan, totem, and the "average man" of statistics; the hypothetical assumptions such as those of human needs;

and finally, the facts of relationships between these other facts, giving us the statements of invariable relationships which are in effect social laws; all of these make up the social world to be studied.

SECTION IV

Economic Choice and Economic Value

Two points of extreme importance are now to be introduced. First there is the point that, in addition to the assumed needs with which we have so far been dealing, there are needs of another and more primary order. These are the physical needs, such as nourishment, procreation, sex, the maintenance of a correct temperature and the supply of an air composition suitable to human survival. Purely for purposes of method, we regard these as facts of the first order, that is to say, as facts capable of being constructed from sense data. The five senses, together with our past experience, enable us to appreciate the fact that the human body requires a certain intake of food and of the other primary necessities. It is perhaps best to regard these as minimal necessities; they are at the root of human existence; but, as Malinowski has shown, it is useful to work on the assumption that it is one of the characteristics of man that he does not satisfy these elementary requirements in any direct way. In his efforts to get food, man first of all evolves a system of productive activities and obtains his food only through the instrumentality of this system. Similarly with regard to procreation; this is not carried out by man, as by the other animals, in any direct way, but only through the instrumentality of elaborate family systems. It is *via* these indirect means of satisfaction that there arise the more elaborate needs such as those for economic disposal of resources and for religious and educational and legal behaviour. The fundamental facts of the social world are best explained to our minds by assuming that human behaviour, with its component systems of activity, is actuated by these social needs. The primary needs themselves, however, have often a most direct bearing upon social activity, and the need for religious expres-

37

sion will be obliged to flow into channels which also give the stomachs of the people sufficient food. These primary needs are therefore always to be kept in mind as among the facts of the social world, entering into all other relationships.

The other great social fact which we have not as yet stressed, but which obviously underlies all others, is that of human behaviour. On the one hand, it is a fact capable of construction from sense data; on the other hand, it has a standing of its own as being an aspect of all other facts. It is in this way that the study of psychology is given its unique place in social science, as studying that behaviour from the point of view of the individual human mechanisms involved. From our present point of view, human behaviour is studied in the form of those relationships which we saw to be our most important type of fact. The relationships of kinship, for example, are, from another point of view, organized units of human behaviour. These are very fruitfully to be studied from the various main aspects. Again, the relationships between people and groups at a time of marriage give a standard type of behaviour capable of being studied as a unit. Thus the units of human behaviour, whether those small units often described as customs, such as the custom of two brothers sharing responsibilities to their younger kinsmen, or the larger units, sometimes called institutions, in which people assemble to carry out sacrifices, to hold courts of law, or to serve the political authority, constitute the most important relationships between the facts of the social world, and thus are the main units of social study, to be fully described through expert approach from all profitable aspects, of which the economic one is that which concerns us most directly in this book. Having seen that the economic is one of the aspects from which it is necessary to study the facts of the social world, we now turn to the specific methodology of this science.

The history of economic method has afforded clear proof that induction, by itself, is a method of discovery only, affording very little evidence of significant relationships between stable facts. It gives no proof that these relationships or facts are anything more than unique. While the essential method of science is to achieve a complete description of facts, the history of economics has shown the importance of stating what is meant by facts in such a connection. Were economists to confine themselves to the facts of sense data, they would be confronted with such a multifarious mass of material as would baffle any human minds which tried to describe stable relationships within it. Economists have thus, very rightly, from the beginning utilized assumed existences which, while they cannot be seen or heard, act as shorthand symbols, bringing unruly numbers of facts under comprehensible headings. Economic method has then described these simpler, hypothetical facts, showing their significant relationships to each other, so that economic science has been able to provide that valid knowledge of the social world which can stand the final test of giving probability judgments about the future.

In exploring these scientific facts, economics is still using inducive method; all that it has done is to assume the existence of uniformities in social nature, to treat these uniformities as facts, and to explore relationships among them. But the existence of such scientific facts gives scope for a further step in method which is by no means exclusive to the higher realms of science; which is, indeed, employed by the least scientific of ordinary men in the daily walks of life. Men are everywhere able to say that if such and such a thing exists, then such another thing must exist alongside of it, or follow after it, or have preceded it. Examples of this are numerous and obvious. If the most primitive man sees the outside of a hut, he will feel certain that it has an inside; if he sees an animal fall on being hit by an arrow, he will feel certain that the arrow has been fired. Such conclusions are so elementary that we refer to them as logical necessities. We do not think it necessary here to enquire into the basis for belief in such logical necessities. It is enough that they are part of the mental equipment of the simplest of human beings, and have doubtless achieved this fundamental position in the course of human development because, barring freak accidents, they have been found to work. Their further validity, however, is shown by the fact that modern science has not only developed these

39

logical relationships into the formal reasoning of mathematics, but even accepts them as rendering scientific proof.

It is with this method of logical deduction that modern economics manipulates its simplified objects of science. It argues that, these objects being as it defines them to be, certain consequences must follow and certain relations exist between them. The thorough exploration of hypothetical facts by means of this logical method has proved a most potent way of discovering significant relationships in the social world.

What are the hypothetical facts, or objects of science, with which economics has filled its world? or, in other words, what are the simpler existences, assumed to represent the over-complex social world of sense data, to which economics applies the method of logical necessity? First, there is the fact of the existence of economic resources. All kinds of material objects, human energy, and even units of time itself, are assumed to be describable under this heading, so as to become a fact amenable to scientific manipulation. The width of this fact may be seen at a glance when we indicate that it embraces everything in the physical world which has significance for human conduct or, in one word, value. Units of resources which are not available in absolute plenty, come under this heading; these are said to have economic value when brought into contact with active human wants.

This leads us to our second scientific fact. We have referred repeatedly to the hypothetical needs of human culture and to the less hypothetical needs of the human organism. We now must see that there comes a stage at which these needs, acting as drives in human behaviour, crystallize into much more direct imperatives. When they come to bear actively upon economic resources they are said to be economic wants. Their characteristic, then, is that they can be satisfied, ultimately, only by destroying portions of economic resources. Further, by the time they have changed into economic wants, they have become linked, not only with the general units of behaviour which we have already described, but with specific types of behaviour of which choice, and manipulation of available resources so as to satisfy wants to the utmost possible, are the examples. Thus, economic wants become the second great scientific fact in the social world of the economist.

The third assumed scientific fact is that which we have just now indicated, the specific type of behaviour, running through all other behaviour, known as the economic. This implies that, whatever else men do, there must in their behaviour be some element, very large or infinitely small, of realization that their wants can be satisfied only in part, and that to achieve any satisfaction they must balance these wants against available resources, as well as against each other.

It is difficult indeed to think of any behaviour of Bantu peoples which does not involve this specific activity of economic choice. Whether they hunt, sacrifice, entertain, or teach their children, they appear to be exceedingly aware of the economic aspect of their behaviour. This specific type of behaviour, indeed, runs *pari passu* with all others and hence is best regarded as one aspect of all behaviour. Yet the choice is, in itself, an activity, so that it has been legitimately incorporated into the social world of the economist as a scientific fact or event. It is, however, only an assumed, hypothetical fact, a piece of mental shorthand on the same footing as the facts of resources which are always limited in relation to needs (which must be only an assumed, scientific fact, because the needs themselves are a hypothetical fact), and the fact of economic wants, which arises when the human needs are brought into direct contact with the economic resources. In this way we see the basic equipment of methodological fact created for its own purposes by economic science. The prime justification for the creation of such facts lies in the limitations of the human mind, which, without them, could never hope to introduce order into the infinite complexity of the social world. It is one of the fundamental tenets of modern science that, so valuable are such hypothetical facts or assumptions, very imperfect ones are better than none. Many are the examples in physical and other science of crude assumptions having led to valid knowledge.

A further fact, or relationship, emerging from the manipulation of these three facts, is that of economic value. When

41

limited resources are applied to the satisfaction of wants by men exercising the activity of economic choice, relationships appear between units of the economic resources. Thus, one unit will be said to be worth two of another. This corresponds to what is termed price in Western communities. Anything which has economic value, that is to say, which is scarce in relation to wants and consequently has power to determine human conduct, is capable of having that value expressed in terms of price, and of having its power to yield satisfactions measured by the degree of the price. This is not to say that all objects of economic value do in fact find their expression in price. It is well known that many of the most valued things are never so expressed. Yet even those things whose prices are never figured are valued just as certainly as those which are. However, for practical purposes, it is best to think of economic resources, which are either actually or potentially in the circle of exchange, as having between themselves that type of relationship known as value.

Here we again encounter one of the formal differences between the civilized and the primitive worlds which may lead people into believing that there are functional differences, which may prevent the application of economic method. In primitive communities there is little or no real money; hence the fact of price, as we know it in our own societies, is not there to be discovered. It is tempting to argue from this that its reality does not exist among savages and, should even a trace of such a belief exist in the mind of any sociologist, it would indeed be impossible to make a fruitful application of economic method. There is no doubt whatever in the mind of the present writer that the strict comparison of values, the function of price, does exist in any community, however primitive. He believes this, first of all on *a priori* grounds; savages can most safely and fruitfully be assumed to have economic wants, limited resources, and to have choice in the disposal of these resources, just as we ourselves can be assumed to have these things. Hence it would be strange indeed if units of resources did not have their respective values known in the way which gives the reality of price. On the other hand, as a matter of sense experience, savages do exchange and substitute units of resources. They are never liable to substitute a valuable cow in the provision of a meal, for which a few handfuls of maize would suffice. When a woman supplies another with a basketful of one kind of food, the return will be made either in kind or in the form of something else which is valued. If the return is made in the same kind of grain, the quantity does not need to be the same as that first given, for it may have become either more or less valuable in the meantime. Should the return be made in the form of other things, it is clear that there must be the relationship of equivalence of value. There can be no doubt but that economic value is just as real a fact in a primitive village as in London, although the relationships are carried in the minds of the people and are not conveniently expressed by the concrete medium of money. In this way we claim economic value as a universal fact of the social world, to be assumed by economists wherever they apply their method.

These hypothetical facts which are the primary equipment of the economist were not brought into existence in any easy way. The history of the science tells how they were introduced, or created, at various stages when previous assumptions did not appear to be giving the best of results. Like all such scientific hypotheses, they were the result of acts of imagination by scientists who were struggling to reduce to order the multifarious data of life. Yet they were acts of disciplined imagination; that is to say, they seemed to embrace realities, susceptible to interpretation from immediate sense data. Thus, the fact of resources, capable of meeting human wants, being always limited in relation to these wants, had to appear to agree with facts of experience. It might not do so completely, but, the more it did so, the more would deductions from it tally with sense perceptions at a later stage. It might be that all of its sociological implications had not been fully explored. Were these to be explored from other aspects, by other specialists, with results that clashed with those of the economist, the hypothetical fact of the limitation of resources in relation to wants would be gravely shaken. We shall therefore, at this stage, make a short examination of this assumed fact, pressing its sociological implications some distance into fields other than the economic.

Were the fact of the limitation of resources in relation to needs to be found inapplicable in some societies, such as those known as "primitive", its usefulness, again, would be challenged. If it failed in one part of the world it might fail in another. We may still read in competent anthropological accounts, of peoples who have "plenty of everything"; who, it is implied, do not feel the pressure of needs upon resources. Were this to be so, the whole usefulness of economic theory in non-Western society would be challenged. Since the main purpose of this book is to maintain this usefulness, we shall delve into the assumption.

The fact of resources being always limited in relation to human wants is, while being one of our assumed facts of science, also a statement of an invariable relationship, thus being one of the highest class of facts, approaching the status of a law of human culture. Although it is an assumed fact, it has a direct basis in sense experience. Economists have found it useful as describing a very large set of phenomena discoverable wherever the entities of human resources and of human wants were considered together. There appears to be no logical necessity for resources always to fall short of satisfying wants. As a matter of common sense, it would be quite easy to imagine a people whose resources were plenty, whose wants were few. It has long been the practice of romantic writers to imagine that such peoples do exist. It is only as the methods of social anthropology are applied to one level of culture after another that we find the romantic illusion being shattered. Purely as a matter of accumulated evidence, it appears that in the South Seas, among the Indians of America, throughout Africa, and certainly in Western civilization, there exists this fundamental relationship whereby, no matter how circumstances change, resources are still limited in relation to needs.

The existence of this fact is not in any way shaken through our failure to find any logical necessity for it. Yet we do not, at this stage, confess to this failure. Logical necessity, so far

44

as we can know, consists simply in invariable associations of properties. If it is found to be the fact, in an immense range of cases, that human resources are limited; and if it is further discovered in a very large range of cases that human beings are constantly striving to satisfy wants as well as they possibly can, and are even producing what are called new wants; then a kind of logical necessity is set up for the relationship which we are discussing. It must follow from the relationship of the other facts. Such a logical necessity at once indicates that we must have this assumed fact, of the limitation of resources in relation to wants, in our minds when we come to explore any people, no matter how primitive. The scientific standing of the fact is sufficient to require us to do so.

Thus we have a further reason for approaching primitive cultures, not on the assumption that a new or special economics will have to be evolved in order to describe them, but on the assumption that the methodological equipment of existing economic theory will give us the most fruitful approach, at least in the first instance, until facts were discovered which it may fail to place in scientific order. Such facts would appear when, and only when, a people were found who were in the happy position of being able to satisfy every want to the point of repletion, without effort, and then to develop no new wants. Such people would have no need to economize. The rest of the method of modern economics would certainly not apply to them. Indeed, we should be in no necessity of producing a new economic system to cope with such a people, for their lives would have no economic aspect. We should be just as ready to discover a people whose culture had no legal aspect, no religious aspect, or any other of the aspects whose existence we take to be of the essence of human culture. Once we grant that culture must have these main aspects, we grant that any people on the face of the globe must economize their resources in order to satisfy their wants so far as possible and, given this premise, it is extremely difficult to see how the whole of the logical apparatus of modern economics can fail to apply.

To look further into the relationship between wants and resources, we must see at once that this is a relationship between two quantities which, we know from experience, may be extremely variable. Wants may change almost in one generation from those of the scale of the humblest peasant to those of wealthy European people. When a peasant becomes wealthy he and his family probably have no difficulty whatever in expanding their wants until they have to be just as economical in the management of their new income as in that of their previous resources. Conversely, and fortunately, we know that wants can be curtailed in times of depression or with other changing circumstances. On the other hand, resources can fluctuate, sometimes in an alarming manner. Given this variability of the two primary facts, how are we to assume that there is an invariable relationship between them? The appeal, in the first place, is, as we have indicated, to the facts of experience; even a millionaire has to dispose of his resources in an economic manner, knowing well that should he fail to do so he or his descendants may not continue to be millionaires. At the other extreme, the poorest savage, on the very rock bottom of existence, has to economize all the more carefully on that account. Should he fail, for example, to make provision for the simple forms of capital required in his culture, he does not need to be told that he will starve.

Some possible exceptions to the pressure of needs on resources may be indicated. In the first place, it is sometimes said that a people's needs are expanding more than their resources. An example to hand is that of Bantu who, in contact with European influences, develop needs for new clothing, for sewing machines, for such new food items as tea and sugar, and who, to all appearances, develop these needs before they are able to satisfy them. The result may be that these people obtain such goods on credit from European traders, and an awkward situation may result. Yet it is obvious that these Bantu will not obtain such credit unless the traders, who are experienced people, are reasonably sure that their resources will in the near future expand in such a way that the accounts will be settled. Thus the additional wants stimulate the people to new ways of adding to their resources; at first, they actually intensify the relationship of which we are writing. Should the resources not successfully be increased, the credits will soon be stopped and the new wants abandoned. The pressure of wants upon resources receives only an additional illustration from such a case.

On the other hand, it may be said that sometimes resources increase so quickly as to outstrip wants, to satisfy all of these, and to leave a proportion of the resources unused. This is entirely possible, and cases of it have been observed. Yet it is most obviously a phenomenon of short duration. Munition workers during the European war provide an example very much to the point. These people suddenly found that their real incomes had increased substantially and unexpectedly. Yet it was very clear that in a short time they had developed wants corresponding roughly to those of a middle-class standard of life, and, when their incomes fell once more, the position was reversed, for they had to undergo the uncomfortable process of curtailing their wants, and social friction gave concrete evidence of this. Thus we can admit only that there may be a slight time lag when resources take the initiative in moving upwards. These apparent exceptions test the general rule and increase its validity.

Thus human wants, according to this important assumption, not only may but *must* expand and contract in such a way that they always press upon resources, even though these resources themselves are not without fluctuations. In what way can we give a fuller account of human wants, showing their relations to other aspects of life, so as to indicate that, these relations being as they are, wants indeed have this quality of variability? The relationships which we can describe are roughly as follows; people, given the choice, will prefer the greater to the lesser; having the desire to satisfy their wants (which follows from the definition of wants), they will satisfy each and all as well as possible; they will encounter practical limitations in the satisfaction of wants. These simple propositions may be tested out, in respect of peoples at any level of culture, in any of the main spheres of their lives. These correspond to the facts, constructs from sense data and assumed facts, which we have discussed. Thus with

47

regard to the material equipment of life, and thinking in terms of the Bantu, we see that even the simplest implements and dwellings are subject to these propositions.

The people will always choose a better supply of hoes or dwellings in preference to an inferior supply, whether in quantity or in quality. They will satisfy their wants for implements and dwellings to the best of their ability, taking into account the other things which they must sacrifice in order to do so. They will also encounter very definite limitations in their power to supply themselves with the implements and dwellings which they desire. Social opinion will make them keenly aware of this. It is indeed a fact that the simplest material possessions of Bantu peoples are shot through by this social consciousness of their success or failure of satisfying their wants in relation to them.

Coming to social groups, we find overwhelming evidence of the same propositions with regard to the character of human wants. A group shows just the same attitude to its possessions as do individuals. Further, we find that individuals have desires to achieve or to maintain membership of certain groups. Admission to an age grade or to a council of elders may depend upon ability to pay the fees, while the general power to remain in the highest social circles among the Bantu depends very largely upon ability to entertain, to contribute to certain tribal expenses and, in general, has all the characteristics of other human wants.

Coming to the important hypothetical needs, we find that every one of them ultimately takes expression in the form of a set of wants. It is in this way that the needs are converted into wants, the wants being much more near to the character of sense data than are the hypothetical needs, which are indispensable in describing the fuller implications of the wants. In the matter of religion, for example, we find throughout its practical expression a series of wants which must be satisfied, and which definitely press upon resources. In Bantu religion the sacrifice takes a prominent place. It nearly, though not always, involves the expenditure of resources, such as the killing of an animal. The physiological needs of the people are not for a moment forgotten; every bit of the carcase is put to a practical use. Yet much of its value comes from its power to satisfy religious needs. Should their resources in cattle increase, the wants which these cattle have the power to satisfy will be found to expand in such a way that every animal still appears to be wanted. For example, they will be able to sacrifice on occasions when it had previously been impossible, and for other reasons will continue to value the herds. It is even possible that a religious desire for the cattle may come to interfere with more practical, or physical needs. It is enough at this stage to show that these people had a very keen desire, from the religious point of view, to have as many cattle as possible, in that their wants for these cattle were never completely satisfied.

It is unnecessary to show that the other hypothetical needs are all at one point or another expressed as economic wants. Legal and political activities, in particular, make demands upon resources no less than do the religious activities. They all centre upon the same body of resources; cattle, for example, entering at every stage into legal and political activities. Everywhere the same elementary propositions about the nature of wants can be shown to operate. The wants, taken as a whole, certainly appear to press upon resources, even though wants taken separately might have their urgency reduced. In this way we see that to describe the functioning of actual wants, constituting economic demand, it is necessary for us to resort to each of the great hypothetical needs, and also to the needs for material equipment and for human grouping as well as to the needs for physiological satisfactions. Only by describing the relationships between the results of all these needs can we arrive at such comprehensive descriptions of human behaviour as will constitute social law. But, and this is our immediate point, we shall fail in our efforts unless we make use of such concepts, supplied by economic science, as those of human resources, human wants, and that invariable relationship between them whereby the one always presses upon the other.

CHAPTER III

THE THEORY OF PRIMITIVE ECONOMICS

THE substance of Bantu life, examined from its economic aspect, is treated in other chapters of this book. Our object is now, briefly, to state the essentials of economic theory as they seem to have most significance for a primitive culture. It is obvious that many of the more advanced theories of modern economics cannot be tested against the background of Bantu life; curves of indifference, measurements of the elasticity of substitution, and other parts of up-to-date equipment must be admitted at the outset to be applicable only where the measuring rod of money is present. It is possible that in the future some economists will obtain such an insight into the culture of some primitive people as to be able to use the most refined economic concepts, but we are not yet at that stage. On the other hand, we are well able to apply the basic concepts of economic theory to the people who are our subject matter.

We have already made it clear that we start from the assumptions of limited resources, of wants pressing upon these resources, and of the people having the power to dispose of the resources in ways calculated to satisfy the wants as far as possible. The management of limited resources, of an economic nature, as carried out by the Bantu peoples, is thus the heart of our subject matter. We must study the ways in which the time, the human energy, and the materials provided by Nature are disposed of so as to provide the people with those complex satisfactions which may be said to begin with bodily warmth and to extend to such satisfactions as that of communicating with supernatural powers.

We shall see that the evaluation of units of resources is the dominating factor in the use to which they are put, and that this evaluation arises from needs, translated into economic demands. It will be evident further that the value attached to units of resources will vary as the wants, which they can satisfy, are increased or diminished. It will be seen that a social evaluation, equivalent to price, emerges from the individual valuations, since, should one person value units of a certain commodity more highly than does his neighbour, an exchange will very probably take place. It will also be seen that units of personal service are valued, and shares in the ultimate product given, on the basis of this valuation.

It is necessary at the outset to state that we are describing the disposal of resources by individuals, who invariably act as members of several groups, in order to render satisfactions to themselves, both as individuals and as members of these groups. No distracting influence has been more persistently dragged into discussions of primitive economics than that of the supposition that the savage is more "communistic" than is the member of a Western community. It has, indeed, been realized that Western economics are on a family, rather than an individualistic, basis. It is doubtful whether an individual ever, even in the most personal matters, makes an economic choice simply *qua* individual. Even in providing himself with proper nourishment he certainly has to consider certain implications of his action from the point of view of his social group. Should he eat too much, his children may not have enough. Should he eat unwholesome food, his family may suffer from the resulting loss of his health. Should he eat food that is socially taboo, his earning power is very likely to suffer. The most individual economic decision, therefore, has strong social aspects. Actually, in making his economic decisions, the individual nearly always acts not merely for himself but on behalf of some group with which he is vitally connected. Food is not bought for one man but for a family. This is even more true of the Bantu than of European peoples, for the individual who eats in restaurants has scarcely a significant counterpart in an African village. Further, the Bantu head of a household, in determining which services are to be produced, must always act in response to the felt and expressed wants of the members

51

of his household. Not only so, but the production of these services will depend upon the willingness of members of the household to contribute their share of work. Whether we think in terms of the Bantu household, the individual house of each wife, or the extended household which co-operates in a given district, we see that production is carried out and satisfaction enjoyed in behaviour which is always social, that is to say, analysable into the behaviour of people as members of groups.

In studying the economic, as in studying any other aspect of society, we do well to recognize the dual principle that all valuations and actions are those of individuals, but that these individuals invariably lead their whole lives within, not one group such as a suppositious clan, but a whole series of groups of different kinds. There are the kinship groups, the neighbourhood groups, the occupational groups such as work parties, and, at the top of the scale, the great political group known as the tribe.

Two courses appear to be open to us; we may, if we choose, regard economic theory as dealing with the choices of individuals, so that, when we describe the economics of social groups, we shall have to posit a different branch of study, Public Economics: and we agree with de Marco that this would be a concrete science as opposed to the more abstract science of pure economics, accepting de Marco's methodological corollary "that Public Finance cannot use logical abstraction to the same extent as does general economics". Or, on the other hand, it is open to us to work on the assumption that the whole method of economic theory is equally applicable to individuals and to groups. It will be gathered from foregoing remarks that the present writer prefers the second method, or, to put the matter more definitely, that he regards all economic decisions as the outcome of group life though expressed, necessarily, either by some individual or by some executive authority which stands to the group as the father does to a Bantu household.

It is significant that de Marco felt the need of assuming the existence of two kinds of wants, collective and individual. Collective wants, he gives as those which arise from the very fact of social life, with that of defence against external enemies as the type. "Individual needs, on the other hand, are those which arise and remain within the life of a man who is isolated, or who believes himself to be isolated." Hunger and thirst are the type of such needs. De Marco is careful to point out that all wants are in the last analysis felt by the individual, this applying just as much to his "collective" wants as to the others. Yet a dangerous assumption seems here to be made; by any sociological definition, there can be no such thing as a man who is isolated or who even believes himself to be in this condition. We can build up a body of sociological description only by working on the basis that man is an organism which invariably has relationships with other men and is conscious of these relationships. Not only so, but that both his relationships and his awareness of them enter into the satisfaction of his most personal needs, such as those for nutrition and warmth. Malinowski has shown that even the nost individual wants and actions have their social aspect, that even the digestive processes of an individual by no means concerns him alone. It must follow that his economic decisions also are essentially social.

De Marco's assumption of collective wants also requires further examination. He describes them as those which arise not from the mere addition of the wants of all the individual members of a group but from the needs of the group itself as expressed through its executive, some individuals possibly not feeling the wants, or not so intensely as others, as soldiers not all wanting the hats which are part of their uniform, or some members of a community placing a much smaller evaluation upon, say, military defence than is expressed by the total expenditure of the group upon that item. While ready to admit that the concept of collective wants may have more utility than that of individual wants, we doubt whether it should be accepted in this form into sociological discussion. From the very nature, or definition, of a soldier, he must "want" his uniform. His wants, like those of all of us, are conditioned by the group to which he belongs.

By the mere fact of his being a soldier, also, his wants are culturally determined and translated into economic demand. It is scarcely necessary to point out that his so-called individual wants are similarly controlled. He must be taken to want such quantities and types of food as soldiers in fact receive. Since he has no way of expressing any individual wants in such matters, we do not appear to be justified in assuming such wants to exist.

With regard to the member of a group who is taken to disagree with the valuation placed by the group executive upon such a matter as defence, we should again say that we have no means of knowing how this individual does evaluate defence. Our only evidence of the strength of an economic demand is that the economic subject actually *makes* that demand in the course of his or its economic management. Since the individual under consideration has no means of expressing his own personal evaluation of the defence of the group, or of that perfectly unascertainable proportion of it which may be taken as defending him, that evaluation is unknowable to us. It might be higher or lower than the evaluation expressed by the executive, but, in the first place, we should be very much mistaken to accept as guidance any mere personal opinions expressed by the individuals, for how often have we not heard persons expressing their opinion of the extravagance of the State in such matters as defence and social services, when, had that person really had to deal with the matter out of his own resources, he might well have spent more upon such services than he was called upon to do by the State. In the second place, it is now obvious that the individual does not and cannot make such evaluations; as a member of a given group or culture he has needs determined by the setting and expressible only through the executive of his group.

We would agree with de Marco when he says that Public Economics (or Finance), ". . . . seeks, in its investigations, to approach as near as possible to reality, and therefore makes an effort to study real phenomena . . .". In order to do this, the economist has to consult the sociologist, whose work it is in connection with such a problem to describe the concrete relationships involved, subsuming them under such shorthand symbols as may describe wide ranges of facts with sufficient definiteness to be scientifically valid. In this case, the symbol, or concept, which may throw light upon the matter is that of social reciprocity, that is, the set of relationships giving coherence to any existing society through the fact of a constant give and take between the members. Malinowski has shown in what a vital sense this obtains among the primitive peoples whom he has explored, and all the evidence in the other chapters of this book fully bears out his conclusions. A group or society does not hang together from any mystical impulse to unity. History is full of the dissolutions of societies and of groups—more frequently, of course, of groups. They continue to exist because, in general, each person feels that in return for what he gives to other people he receives a corresponding service.

This feeling is, like all feelings of satisfactions or dissatisfactions, purely subjective. Our only objective evidence of its existence and strength is the behaviour of the person. He may feel so strongly that he is not getting fair reciprocity that he may cease to be a member of a group, should the group be of a voluntary nature; that he may refrain from introducing new members, including his own children, into the group; and that he may express his dissatisfaction in a definite manner by withholding his co-operation in the group life. Thus any group, whatever its nature, may begin to show signs of incomplete efficiency. It may go out of existence or it may change its policies.

Only by such concrete symptoms can we know that individuals are actively disagreeing with the collective wants of their group. Nor should we forget that in talking of collective wants, in de Marco's sense, we are assuming some power to make comparisons between the subjective satisfactions of individuals. Whether we have any valid means of deciding that a service supplied, in response to a collective want, gives so much satisfaction to one citizen and more or less to another, is discussed later, but the sociologist does not expect anything like complete harmony within a group. In the formation

55

of collective wants it is certain that some individuals will tend to feel dissatisfied, and it is just here that we find that any society or group has mechanisms to overcome such dissatisfactions. Such are feelings of loyalty, mottoes and ideals, customary behaviour and the law of the group. These all work mainly on the basis that satisfaction is a subjective thing, that a man is satisfied to the extent that he feels satisfied. Consequently, these ideals and customs operate upon peoples' feelings. A man in a modern community, who might otherwise have expressed dissatisfaction at the expenditure of his society upon defence, is influenced by the ideals, ethics and customs of his group and as a result does not feel the dissatisfaction. The actual law of his group may act in an even stronger way; since he knows that he may come into conflict with the law should his feeling of dissatisfaction become too strong, he, consciously or unconsciously, controls or changes the feeling. He does not express it, and a feeling which is not expressed tends not to exist.

We must conclude that no useful purpose is to be served by hypothecating two such types of wants as the individual and the collective. We must assume all wants to be collective, adopting de Marco's use of that term, though, as we have seen, by no means all his implications. In particular, we deny the possibility, which he assumes, of the general divergence between the evaluations of individuals and those of the executive of their group—of the soldier not wanting his head-gear. We arrive at the point that all wants are collective and collectively expressed. The active economic subject can be defined only as that group or executive which has the power of economic disposal over resources. This may be any type of group, or association of groups, operating through any type of executive, including an individual such as a head of a family who must *feel the pulls of the units within his group.*

It becomes necessary to abandon any hypothetical distinction between an individual and a public or group economy. The systems of modern economics have been worked out mainly on the assumption of an individual economy. They could have been worked out equally well, and without sub-

56

stantial difference to the result, had they used the assumption of groups, rather than individuals, as the active economic subject. The case is paralleled by the work of Joan Robinson, who has shown that, although economic theory has been developed on the hypothesis of competition, it could have been worked out equally well on the contrary hypothesis of monopoly. In other chapters of this book we have examined the operations of individuals and of groups as economic subjects in Bantu society. Throughout these chapters we see resources being managed by the household, by the house of the wife, by the sub-clan, by the groups which assemble for specific purposes such as initiation and religious sacrifice, as well as by the political group.

In the smallest of these, the house of each wife, we see economic management carried out by the adjustment of the valuations of its members. The man and the wife may well have different views as to the rate at which the stores of food should be consumed, or as to whether one kind of grain is to be valued more highly, as it becomes more scarce, so that other grains should be substituted, at some rate, for it. Differences of opinion are to be found as to whether a cow is to be kept for milk or to be disposed of in order to get the working powers of an additional wife. Should these differences become too acute, the family may break up; divorce may result. So long as this *impasse* is not reached, this family operates as an economic subject.

Traditionally, it would have been accepted that the husband was the economic subject. This was perfectly justifiable as a simplifying assumption. But realism demands that we pass, in the traditional way of scientific method, from this assumption to a more complex one which embraces more reality. The valuations which control the economic management are just as much those of the wife as of the husband; nor do they stop there, for we may see that at a very early age children begin to exercise economic judgement which they can doubtless express by their willingness to do certain types of work, as well as by their preference to consume certain types of commodities. It will further be seen that the house of the wife is generally but

57

a unit of a larger household. The husband is likely to be the head of this household as well and, under him, it is usual for it to co-operate in the most vital forms of economic management. This larger household therefore becomes a most important economic subject, whose final, expressed evaluations are the resultant of the evaluations of the houses of the wives within it and of their individual members. In describing the economic management prevalent in Bantu culture it will not be found impossible to think in terms of the individual as the subject, but in the view of the present writer it is very much more profitable to think in terms of the interaction of individual preferences finding ultimate expression in the behaviour of groups which thereby become, by definition, the active economic subjects.

We are led to disagree with de Marco at his contention that Public Economics cannot use logical abstraction to the same extent as can General Economics. All of the logical propositions of economic method have equal applicability whether they work upon the assumption of the individual, or of the group, as the economic subject. The active groups can be seen disposing of their resources just as does the hypothetical individual. The only difference is that we work on a wider basis, approaching reality more closely, and seeing that economic choice is expressed, not directly by an individual ". . . who is isolated or who believes himself to be isolated ", but indirectly through cultural means. We agree, in part, that this is giving concreteness to the science, and it is the duty of sociology to do this. But we do not see that a real opposition is introduced. By taking account of the social facts offered by sociology, economics approaches nearer to the concrete simply by widening its hypotheses. The full use of its logical method is still possible and indeed more necessary than ever.

CHAPTER IV

OWNERSHIP AND THE ECONOMIC SUBJECT

Section I

Ownership and Disposal

HAVING seen that social groups of various kinds may profitably be regarded as the effective economic subject in Bantu society, as in any other society, we proceed to show in what ways these groups exercise that power to use economic goods which is known as ownership. Having done this, we shall show some of the processes by which active wants are formulated within the economic subjects.

Like all peoples, the Bantu have effective distinctions between various types of economic goods. It is as true of the Bantu as of any other people that Nature supplies them with extremely few goods ready for immediate use. A few wild berries, resorted to in time of famine, represent perhaps the whole of this category. We must visualize the Bantu, through that social organization which is the primary instrument in their economic management, as proceeding to apply their personal powers to certain materials provided by Nature so as to fashion them into commodities, that is to say, into goods capable of technical manipulation under the guidance of economic management. It is thus that the material of the primary environment comes to be changed into that secondary environment essential to human culture, and of which the main characteristics are that instead of being an undifferentiated mass of resources, it is a collection of goods susceptible to ownership and to consequent economic management. Further, that these goods are limited in relation to effective human wants so that, at any level of culture, they are certain to be the subject of defined ownership, since without this their economic management would be impossible.

The extent to which the Bantu or any other people convert the primary environment into a secondary environment of manageable goods is conditioned by such a non-economic factor as the state of the people's knowledge, and by another factor, more relevant to economics, namely, the felt pressure of their aggregate wants. These two factors determine the extent to which the natural resources remain latent or are turned into manageable commodities. The felt wants, however, are the more ultimate determinant for, should they increase, it is highly probable that the people would succeed in increasing their knowledge and thus their technical capacity to exploit the resources of Nature. The felt wants may be taken as determining the economic choice involved in the expenditure of a greater or smaller amount of labour. Should these wants remain fixed at a certain level, they may be satisfied by the devotion of a certain proportion of the people's time and energy to the manipulation of the raw natural resources. In any given community there appears to be a tendency for the aggregate of human wants to change only within limits, for it is clear that violent fluctuations would tend to disrupt the society. It further appears that this aggregate of felt wants, while it can vary as between individuals, yet has a certain uniformity within any effective social group with economic functions, for, should one individual expand his desires and make a consequent readjustment as between his leisure and his working time, he is seldom able to express this change entirely on his own initiative. It is in such a matter as this that the effectiveness of groups as economic subjects can be seen in Bantu society. Should, for example, a younger brother be much more willing to work than the rest of the household within which he must operate, he will be held back by the rest of the household so that his preference will become only one of the pulls within the economic subject. Thus the conversion of part of the primary environment into disposable goods is carried out by the people, operating through their social organization, this organization being not only a kind of technical instrument for the exploitation of resources but also the group of effective economic subjects which carry out complete economic management.

OWNERSHIP AND THE ECONOMIC SUBJECT

The resources of the primary environment having been converted into economic goods, they take on the character of property. The various ways in which the property relation functions among the Bantu are described in other chapters. It is from this that we see the true nature of the economic subject. Neither sociologically nor economically is ownership a simple matter. The sociological fact of property, enforced by custom or law, is invariably at the root of economic disposal of resources, and indeed has its necessity in this economic disposal. Nothing is more important to the integration of a culture than the economic utilization of its scarce resources, and it will be found everywhere that this is reflected in very clear formulations of the principles of ownership. True economic disposal could not take place unless social mechanisms guaranteed effective ownership. Conversely, the fact that primitive peoples have been shown to possess well-developed systems of property is a further reason for believing them to dispose of their resources according to economic principles.

It is thus that the ownership of all classes of goods is clearly defined in Bantu society, being attached to groups of individuals which thereby are the active economic subjects. Beginning with goods for immediate consumption, we find that even these are complex in their nature. They embrace, among the Bantu, such elements as grain, as the milk and flesh of cattle, as the medicines of doctors, and, coming to personal services, the activities of rain-makers and of chiefs. No two of these sets of consumable resources are owned in precisely the same way, or by the same active economic groups. Some of the differences will be seen to arise from the fact that, though all of them are consumable goods, they are by no means all consumed simply for the satisfaction of immediate cravings.

Grain, of which, incidentally, there are several kinds with different economic implications, is the type of commodity nearest to a simple consumable good. Yet, as will be seen in other chapters, its modes of consumption relate to a considerable number of distinguishable needs, and it is managed accordingly. It is produced under the ultimate management of the man who is head of a household, which may include several families, some of them being the families of his wives, and others the families of his younger brothers and their wives. Under the guidance of the head of the household, whose functions have in them much of those of the entrepreneur, each married woman in the household is peculiarly responsible for the cultivation of fields allotted to her by the headman, and the produce of these fields goes into her personal store-houses. She is responsible for the day-to-day administration of her own grain, but its ultimate control is in the hands of the headman, who, in his turn, is likely to consult closely with the other men of the household. Thus the control even of grain resources, while intensely personal in the sense that all of these people keenly feel their interest in the grain and their share in the power of disposing of it, cannot be said to be individual. This is reflected in the variety of uses to which it may be put, and in the multiplicity of considerations which may affect any one of these uses. As regards any one day's meals, they may be liberally prepared and consumed, or may be eked out by the use of other food resources such as pumpkins or bananas. While the immediate decision in such a matter will be made by the women, the unit which controls the day-to-day expenditure of the primary resources of grain, is no individual, but an active group which integrates the views of a number of individuals, giving especial weight from the short point of view to the woman responsible; over the longer period, to her husband and the headman; and always to the other individuals whose welfare depends upon the effective management of the resources of the whole household.

The weights of the opinions of these several parties is, further, likely to vary with the varying uses to which the grain is put. We have seen the situation as it appears when the grain is used, as clearly as possible, simply as daily sustenance. A slightly different complexion is given to the matter when it may be used for special entertaining. The importance of this is that the prestige of the head of the household will be influenced by the entertainments which he can give to various people of importance. This will increase the range of his contacts, so that he may be favoured by the chief, or himself become a sub-chief, or make much more advantageous marriage connections which may lead to the acquisition of valuable cattle.

Thus, in the matter of using grain for entertaining, it is probable that the weight of responsibility is shifted in the direction of the man himself; his wife, it appears, may provide food as far as possible in accordance with his desires, while the other women of the household will suspend judgment.

The grain, once more, has yet a different aspect when it is regarded as the necessary means to supporting the working power of the group. With these people, the failure to maintain good supplies of grain food until the time of the next cultivation of the fields is likely to result in a distinct diminution of their working power, so that if grain is wastefully employed one year there may be a smaller yield, and actual starvation, in the next year. It is in this way that grain takes on some of the character of capital. It is a produced good, used for further production. We do not mean that any part of the grain store is singled out by the people in this way; we mean that this consideration is always present in their minds and that at certain periods in the year, notably when it seems that the liberal enjoyment of good stores after harvest has depleted resources, and when the next harvest is quite a long way off, it comes to dominate the situation. It is here that control by the man, who is to such a large extent the entrepreneur of the group, as well as its executive authority, becomes dominant. This was expressed in the old days, by some tribes, through the existence of special grain pits so placed, in the middle of cattle kraals, as to be unapproachable by women. Thus, as the apparently simple consumption good, grain, shows its variety of functions, we find its control being vested in different combinations of the people making up the economic group or subject.

In yet another way does grain become a form of capital. At the appropriate time in the season, when much laborious field work has to be done, mainly by the women, it is the practice of nearly all the Bantu peoples to organize work parties at which neighbours assist at the cultivation of each other's fields, thus, certainly not securing a technically efficient cultivation, but effectively lightening the felt burden of the labour. The decision to call together a work party appears to be made in most cases by the women whose fields are to be operated upon. The fields belong to her in a real sense since, under the general guidance of the head of the household, she is responsible for their cultivation; the food from them goes exclusively into her store-houses, and her standing within the community depends upon the success of her efforts. But the calling of a work party is an expensive matter, for it is rewarded by beer, made from the woman's grain, and possibly by meat supplied with the husband's agreement. There is also an immense expenditure of energy by the women of the whole household in converting the grain into beer.

The grain comes from the stores of the woman whose fields are to be worked. Thus the decision to call the party lies chiefly with her. Her neighbours are not likely to begrudge their help in making the beer. This is a supply of latent power reserved for such an occasion. The existence of sufficient grain may be attributable very largely to the husband's foresight, but the decision to use it on this occasion must lie with the woman. Thus, once more, grain takes on the form of capital, securing the production of fresh stores. Being connected specifically with the fields of one woman, the weight of her choice becomes dominant within the economic unit. In these ways we see the economic management, by a group which is the active economic subject, of an important resource which, in some of its aspects, is a consumable good, but in others of its aspects is an extremely important form of capital. We see that the weight of the pulls within the group is varied according to the predominance of one or other of these aspects, which correspond to the wants satisfied by the grain. These wants affect the evaluations of the commodity in the minds of the different persons within the group and thus secure effective economic management. In this way the primary conversion of the latent resources of Nature takes place into the goods required for immediate consumption and those required for further production.

OWNERSHIP AND THE ECONOMIC SUBJECT

Groups and Economic Management

It is indisputable that choice of an economic nature is involved, no matter in which of these ways the grain is used, and that there is further choice, again of a strictly economic nature, as between these main uses. Technically or physically, the grain is one commodity; economically it is not so uniform. Thus *its very economic nature depends upon these choices:* if it is used mainly for consumption it is a consumption good. If it is used in the other ways it takes on the character of a productive good. We have seen how the nature of the economic subject, the collection of people making final decisions, changes with the changing purposes dominating the use of the grain. It is never possible to say that a purely individual want is satisfied, yet every want is registered by individuals and the final decisions taken by certain of these individuals who are in an executive position, but between whom, and the rest of their group, there must be a felt reciprocity if the group is to function well and to achieve a recognized level of well-being. It is unnecessary at this stage to develop further our argument as to the nature of the economic subject. This appears in many examples in other parts of this book. It is enough to remark that the economic choices made by a constantly changing, but always a collective subject, registering the pulls of its individual members, require no reconstruction of the body of economic theory. This functions just as well on the assumption of choices made by groups as on that of an "individual" economy; the fact that decisions are indeed made habitually, in any culture, on behalf of groups, enables us to make an advance from the assumption of an "individual" economy to an assumption which is nearer reality. It will, no doubt, still be extremely convenient for economics, in the course of its work, to hold to the assumption that choices are made by individuals. Yet it is probable that the sphere of the study known as Public Economics, in which the individualist assumption is no longer serviceable, will be enlarged. In

E

Western civilization, just as among the Bantu, economic life is organized on a group basis, for this is the nature of all society.

We have seen the operation of economically effective groups among the Bantu in determining the nature of the grain resources and in deciding the uses to which they shall be put. We have seen that the growing of this grain is one of the first results of the peoples' activities when they are directed toward taking from the general resources of Nature, their primary environment, goods which can be obtained by the application of labour and directive power. These activities lead to the production of the grain, but it is the further activities, those which we have just described in some detail, which lead to the production of satisfactions from the grain.

The production of grain and the productions of satisfactions from it, are two entirely different phenomena. They are not to be confused, nor is either of them to be underrated. Both are essential, and in both the economic principle functions to the full. The extent to which they are interdependent has been shown by the fact that a large part of the satisfaction produced by the proper management of the grain consists in its being made available for the further filling of the store-houses. The undifferentiated character of Bantu culture is shown in this, that there is a not a sharp physical distinction between important production and consumption goods. Further, the complex character of wants is demonstrated when we show that, while grain can be used to satisfy the immediate wants of the belly, it probably satisfies simultaneously a whole group of other wants, such as those connected with social intercourse, but mainly, in this connection, the want for a capital resource which, through supporting the human physique and through obtaining the services of other labourers, will lead to further production of the resource itself.

The production of grain, therefore, and of satisfactions from it, are subsumed under the same economy. To some extent they might be designated under some such terms as production and consumption; but this consumption is so clearly a part of the general economic management that we must decide to abandon it as a separate category, thus following

66

the lead of modern economic theory. This affords one of the many illustrations of the point that, while the method and categories of Ricardian economics would have fitted but clumsily to primitive social systems, those of modern economics have achieved a universality which enables them to cope almost equally with the Bantu and with the European.

While modern changes in Bantu Africa tend to obscure the fact, it is still evident that that much discussed resource, cattle, was, and to a considerable extent still must be, managed on precisely the same lines as is grain. It is significant that cattle, of all Bantu property, may at first sight be said to belong to individuals; namely, to the head of each household. Yet upon further examination we discover that probably the whole of each herd is shared out among the various wives, each of whom has her own animals, is entitled to their milk, has a large say in their being paid away to obtain an additional wife, and has to be consulted before they are disposed of in any way. The cattle are thus managed by groups for the benefit of the various members of the group. The distinction between their technical and their economic management is very marked. The technical management is entirely in the hands of the men; they show a devoted interest in them and, within limits, have a very detailed knowledge not only of their utilitarian but also of their artistic points; the women, on the other hand, are practically forbidden to touch the animals and in many circumstances even to go near them; they do not appear to value them as the men do and may have practically no knowledge of the extensive terminology associated with them. Yet, for a man to dispose of cattle without the consent of the wives to whose houses they are attached, would be unthinkable. They must always be used to satisfy the wants of the group, in this case mainly, though by no means exclusively, the actual house of the wife. Thus, the wife and the needs of her children exercise a very strong pull within the economic subject.

The cattle are also used, like the grain, to satisfy, not single wants but groups of wants. It is very misleading, in general, to think of a want as a simple thing, such as a want for nutriment. While wants are merely data in economics, it is important, especially when widening the application of economic theory, to describe closely the data. Beginning with the assumption that wants are simple, we may proceed to the assumption that even the simplest want may well be complex, as when a simple bowl of porridge is "wanted" not merely to satisfy hunger but also to establish important social relations, probably with strong religious and other aspects. While the evaluation of the good is established by the strength of the want together with the existence of substitute goods, that strength in its turn is determined by the pulls of the various needs which are expressed in the want. Thus, in the case of cattle, their economic management is controlled by their power to satisfy a series of wants. Their simplest use, and that in which they come nearest to producing a consumption commodity, is that in which they give milk as food. The importance of milk in the diet of the people varies enormously among the Bantu tribes. Yet its economic character is much the same among them all. Its main utility, especially when it is scarce and consequently very valuable, is in the nourishment of young children. This may be either directly, or through their mothers. Yet it is correct to argue that even in performing this function the milk is by no means regarded as a mere consumption good. In keeping children alive and making them strong it is acting as a productive good or capital, in the full sense. It is well realized by the people that their main hope of economic security and progress lies in the maintenance or increase of the working power of their communities. The milk given to the children or to their mothers is thus invested for further production and, should a time come when other food resources fail, milk may very actively take on the function of enabling the people, by nourishing them, to cultivate their fields.

But cattle satisfy other complex wants. It is clear, for example, that, at least until recent times, it was the custom among the cattle-owning Bantu to kill numbers of cattle at that period in the year when their flesh was most needed as food, and particularly when the people needed that extra stimulation which could be derived from the consumption of flesh. Here was the decision to turn the cattle into flesh being determined by the want for more human energy, in order to produce more grain. Yet even this want would not be relied upon to bring men to the most important decision of killing the highly valued animals, for we are told that at this period in the year the women required to be furnished with new cloaks of hide, always in the correct fashion, and would egg their husbands on till they got what they demanded. A further most important need which played its part in the expression of the want for meat was that of communication with the ancestors, especially when a member of the group was ill. A sacrifice was necessary in order to conciliate the ancestors and bring about his cure. But, the sacrifice having been made, and the carcase being available, no part of it was ever allowed to waste. The ancestors were allowed to eat only the "spirit" of the beasts. The flesh was eaten by the people and there is every evidence to show that the need of a cattle sacrifice was one of the main occasions upon which people took the decision to part with a living member of the herd and to have its carcase instead. Yet another way in which cattle were used, this time almost entirely as capital, was when numbers of them were given as payment to a person who was believed to have the power to bring rain at the time when it was necessary for the crops. Thus, while it may be increasingly true today that cattle perform few of the real functions of capital, it is clear that, until very recently, they were indispensable, and that their high value resulted from the manifold important uses to which they were put, in all of which the function of capital was clearly evident.

Having examined the economic management of the two most important resources of Bantu peoples, grain and cattle, we have practically seen how their capital was applied to the production of further supplies. We have also seen that the existence of capital, especially at the times when it was most needed, depended clearly upon the regulation of consumption so that the people did not consume everything as quickly as they may sometimes have been tempted to do. A balance of present and future needs was always arrived at. This was obtained partly by deliberate management, as by a husband controlling the wife's inroads upon the grain stores. Yet it is clear that the provision of capital did not entirely depend upon the choices of the subjects, made with this sole end in view. The evaluations determined by the culture of the people also provided a regulating influence, so that the necessary balance between immediate consumption and more distant productive uses was maintained. While grain was saved with a full consciousness that it would be needed to give the people strength at their next sowing, it was also saved with a view to the enjoyable beer drinks which accompany this sowing. In providing for them the people were providing capital. The same applies eminently to the managing of cattle. The culture imposed high values upon such activities as beer drinks and the flesh food which was available at the time of the hard work, and thus indirectly governed the maintenance of the society's capital. The hard fact of the decision to save was always present, but it was implemented indirectly, through the social demands. That this was as true of people living very near to the bare margin of subsistence as of those who were more fortunate, is evident, for all had to maintain their capital if their existence was to continue, and the same mechanisms are seen among all.

The maintenance of capital is thus correctly regarded as a normal feature of Bantu, as of any other, society. We see, and will see even more fully in other chapters, that the economy of the Bantu cannot be said to be characterized by its directness, as opposed to the indirect or round-about production of modern societies. The difference lies in the fact that modern societies have a vastly superior scientific equipment, whereby the capital accumulated in the round-about process can be applied in ways which increase the total powers of man. Although the Bantu lack this scientific knowledge, their culture does recognize the absolute need for the use of resources as capital, and provides very effective ways for its accumulation, which is secured much more by indirect processes of satisfying various wants than by any direct process of saving, though this is not insignificant.

OWNERSHIP AND THE ECONOMIC SUBJECT

The food having performed the functions of capital in maintaining the working power of the people, these powers are applied to the cultivation of the soil. The economic aspects of this technical process are fully explored in other chapters. We may here point out simply that the first, possibly the fundamental economic choice, lies in the amount of labour which the people will devote to the agricultural work. In this, as in all other instances, the decisions are made by the individuals, acting through group executives, in response to their individual valuations, and they are always given effect by the groups which carry out the work. The people work in order to satisfy wants which they know will arise and which are safely anticipated because of the uniformities of the culture. It is in this way that the changing of wants, through giving rise to uncertainties, may diminish incentive to work. Having the various wants in mind, and having also their technical equipment, the people decide as to how much labour they should put into the fields. They have other demands upon their personal energies, demands also corresponding to definite wants, and these compete with the demands of agriculture, thus giving to that labour its real cost. It costs the people what they have to forego in the way of other activities.

CHAPTER V

SECTION I

Consumption Activities

THAT these other activities have clear evaluations placed upon them there can be no doubt, and these evaluations correspond to the functions of the activities in the maintenance of the people's culture. There are times in the year when non-agricultural activities impose a very great strain upon human energy and time. The heavy preparations for initiation ceremonies, the tribal visits to the chief among certain peoples, family visits; these and many other occupations compete with that of agriculture. To a great extent they are timed so that the competition is as slight as possible; yet there is evidence throughout the daily lives of the people that, could they be persuaded to attach less importance to visiting, to funeral feasts, to initiation schools and to the rest of the long lists of organized activities, they would have much more time and energy left to cultivate their fields. Their physical and technical equipment, and hence their food supply, would be improved. It is easy to proceed from this point to argue that these competing activities should be curtailed for the benefit of the people. It is just such an argumentative step as this that the practical man is tempted to take, but which the social scientist has to point out to be totally invalid. The data of economics are technical equipment and resources on the one hand, and wants on the other. These organized activities are the means of organizing the people's wants, just as definitely as their agricultural system organizes their physical productivity. Just as the organization of agriculture must be described because it is strongly advisable that the economist should be thoroughly familiar with that term of his data, so it is equally desirable that the organization which formulates and expresses wants should be understood, so that we may estimate more clearly the true nature of the choices open to the people in the application of their resources. It is for this reason that we have, in other chapters, examined such activities as birth and pregnancy customs, initiation schools, and marriage, on precisely the same footing as the organization of agriculture and of handicrafts.

It is just as logical and useful to neglect one as to neglect the other, yet it was the practice of classical economics to give such wealth of attention to the technique of manufacture and agriculture that there was some danger of the technical side swamping the economic, while, on the other hand, wants were, if any specific attention were given to them at all, to be "taken for granted". In strict logical theory both technique and wants may be taken for granted, but when we use this theory as an implement to increase our knowledge of a given human culture, it becomes necessary to describe both the "givens". To do this for a civilized community would require a degree of objectivity which we are only just beginning to obtain through the method of social science. It may be one of the most valuable results to be secured from the study of primitive peoples, that we are able in their case to describe the organization of wants as well as the organization of physical production, so that content may be accurately given to the formulations of economics. Thus, if we were to recommend a Bantu people to abandon some of the organized activities through which they consume their resources, and to devote the time thus saved to increased agricultural production, we might find ourselves in the absurd position of advising them to reduce their wants and to increase their production. We suggest that this is absurd because the values which control production rest in the expressed wants; it is to satisfy these wants that agriculture, such as it is, is carried on. Hence, to reduce the wants might well lead to a reduction, rather than an increase, in the amount of time and energy devoted to the fields. The choices open to the people depend just as much upon the "demand" term of the equation as upon the technique of their agriculture, taking demand here to mean the consumption uses which compete with the productive uses to which the human resources might be put.

SECTION II

Collective Wants

These organized activities through which, in the main, Bantu resources are consumed, indicate the truly collective nature of all important Bantu wants. The amount of resources expended, for example, must be decided by the pulls of all the people contributing to, and concerned in consuming at, these organized activities. An individual, *qua* individual, might not agree with the evaluation placed by his group upon a unit of consumption behaviour, whether a simple family meal or a great religious or political activity; he might think that resources were being overstrained in relation to the value obtained. His opinion will exercise due weight, corresponding to his importance in the community and to the energy with which he expresses his opinion. But, as we have seen, we can, beyond this, only assume that he expends, in practice, that proportion of his resources upon the organized activity which corresponds to his own personal evaluation, for we have no other means of estimating this evaluation.

Thus, when the important decision is made as to how much of the time and energy of a group is to be devoted to agricultural production, we see that the determining force is the personal decision of all the members expressed as a single unit, and that there will be a working correspondence between these personal preferences owing to the fact that all of the individuals share in the organized wants. It is with these wants in mind that the decision as to the amount of time and energy to be devoted to agriculture is taken. They decide this, in the aggregate, just as they decide the amount of time and energy to be devoted to visiting, to ceremonies, and to all the other organized consuming activities. It is the function of sociologists, specialists in fields other than economics, to describe these organized activities from their various aspects, that is to say, from the points of view of the needs which they satisfy. These will certainly show that, although there may be consumption of resources on a very large scale, including time and energy which might be devoted to agriculture, this fulfils definite purposes, as in the case of initiation ceremonies with their educational functions and visits to the chief with their political functions. But, as we have seen, each organized activity will probably contribute to the meeting of almost every one of those fundamental social needs upon the assumption of which we are working, and it is only by studying the activity from all its aspects that we may see its true place in the integration of the community and hence the evaluation of goods, time and energy devoted to it.

Thus the activity of agriculture, which may be taken to compete with other activities, consumptive in nature, is really antithetical to them, providing the means for their satisfaction, while they reciprocate by providing the values which make agriculture worth while, and decide the extent to which the total resources of the people should be invested in it.

Section III

The Economics of Land

In no respect does the economic management of resources by active groups among the Bantu stand out more clearly than in the ownership of the right to cultivate, and to enjoy the produce of, pieces of land. It is only recently that the full sociological implications of land-tenure have been explored. Malinowski, in his epoch-making study of the Trobriand Islanders, has shown the amazing complexity and vitality of these implications. Our much more limited study of the subject, bringing out its economic aspect, must begin with the remark that the correct mixing of land and labour appears to be one of the most difficult choices confronting the economic subject among the Bantu. The alleged superfluity of land among the Bantu in general is not found to bear close examination. As in many other matters, there are great differences in this as between Bantu peoples. In only one people, the Kikuyu, do we know of land, in primitive conditions, being sufficiently scarce to give rise to something like an economic price for it or for the right to use it, and to rights changing hands at this price. On the other hand, among practically all of the peoples regarding whom we have evidence, it is clear that really suitable land is limited. All of the families are not equally lucky in the areas which they can secure, while the physical exhaustion of the soil in many cases leads to migrations which are obviously a drain upon the peoples' resources. A head of a household, expressing the needs of those under him, can well show lesser or greater skill in obtaining really good pieces of soil. Should he be relatively unsuccessful, there is no doubt but that his people, women as well as men, may have to expend a greatly increased amount of labour in making up for the defective quality of the soil. This deficiency may well consist of the fields or gardens being less near to the homestead than they might have been, so that a truly enormous amount of labour may be devoted to travelling and to transport. Richards has shown that this may well result in the people being too tired at the end of a day's work to prepare their food, so that malnutrition results, with its attendant reduction in the power to produce more food.

We must, then, be satisfied that, although the acreage of apparently available land may be immense, yet the people have a hard problem to select just those garden sites to which their labour may be most economically applied. This problem consists in the first place of deciding what actual area ought to be broken in. This depends upon the nature of the soil, upon the time and strength which the men can devote to the task, this in its turn being conditioned by the expertness with which other activities have been fitted in, and by the working power of the men, and still more the women, which is available for actual cultivation. Much planning and foresight are here needed.

The head of the household is the executive or leader in such matters, but it is clear that he can do little more than register the decisions of the members of his group, his own personal decisions doubtless being very effective among these. Should he, and the other men who help him, break up more land than the women will be able to use, they will be wasting valuable energy, and probably making extra inroads upon scarce food resources in consequence. On the other hand, should they break in less land than, as matters turn out, the women are able to cultivate, the result is a mixture of the women's labour and of land that gives results below the optimum. Land that might have been used, is not used; this may be partly compensated through the women paying more attention to that which is available, but this is not likely to make up the balance, for their technique does not reach to intensive cultivation.

The problem of selecting garden sites consists, in the second place, of some competition between heads of households for the securing of the best land. That this takes place is proved by the number of instances in which households have some of their fields near by but, this land being limited, others in more distant situations. Such a fact must, according to economic theory, give rise to something in the nature of a price for the land; that is, unless it is the custom for no land to change hands, or for the land to go to those men who show superior strategy and power in obtaining it. In practice, land frequently changes hands not by sale, but by the process of abandoning and taking up sites, while, as to power, there is but little evidence of "grabbing" as between Bantu subjects. That Bantu culture is perfectly capable of attaching the distinct equivalent of an economic price to land is shown in that community, the Kikuyu, in which the pressure of population appears to have broken down the underlying rule that land does not come into the market. Among these people the practice has grown up whereby any one family group, having a relative oversupply of land, is able either to sell it to another group or to permit members of other groups to come in as tenants, probably not paying a specific rent, but giving various advantages by their presence.

But, among practically all Bantu peoples, it is the custom, if not for land to change hands directly, at any rate for fields to be abandoned and new fields taken up in the regular course of events. This, suitable land having a relative scarcity, should with equal certainty give rise to a price or rent, in some form, payable for all lands except the worst in cultivation. The non-existence of money makes it difficult to distinguish this price or rent, yet we must be very careful before we say that it does not exist. Chiefs and sub-Chiefs have ways of helping favoured subjects in the obtaining of good land; these favours can well be secured by extra gifts or services rendered to the chief. These, then, though not formally distinguishable as such, con-stitute part of the price of such land. Further, a man who distinguishes himself by giving hospitality to his neighbours, or by making extra large contributions to communal expenses, will be in a specially good position for securing the land which he prefers, these disbursements, again, performing the function of the price or rent of the land.

There is yet another, most important, way in which land is paid for. It has to be broken in at the beginning of the season, and the labour required for this may be very great. This labour, it will be seen, *is in fact a price paid for the land*, and the man who can direct the best labour force to this work will to that extent secure the best fields. There can be no doubt as to definite evaluations being placed upon available pieces of soil. This is one of these instances in which the lack of a concrete money price must not be allowed to blind us to the existence of a real price. If a household cannot afford the appropriate expenditure, whether in presents to the chief, in shares contributed to communal expenditures, in labour in-vested in securing cultivable fields, or in many other ways, then it does not obtain the fields which it wishes.

Section IV

The Agents of Production

In all this physical production, we see the combining of the various agents. Of these, working power and land are primary; directive ability also is important; capital, in the sense of produced goods used to maintain the flow of production, is insignificant, but in the form of food, used both to maintain working power and to pay for additional labour, it is essential to the community. Units of these factors are applied in accordance with the ultimate valuations placed upon them by the executives of the various groups. These valuations secure in a quasi-automatic way that a certain proportion of scarce resources, especially food, shall be treated and managed as ultimate factors of production. This, given the exceedingly modest technical equipment of the Bantu, can scarcely be said to release the primary factors for a variety of round-about applications. We cannot say, therefore, that a fund of resources is created, capable of being managed by an entrepreneur, of being turned into productive equipment, and of being used to produce a variety of ultimate goods according to the demands of the consumers as anticipated by the entrepreneur. No great permanent supply of productive equipment is brought into existence; there is correspondingly little choice in the application of any such equipment.

There is, as we have seen, a surplus of consumption goods, but this is used to create or maintain only one real kind of productive instrument—the human frame. This, together with exceedingly crude and easily replaceable hoes, is the only capital instrument which is maintained; we can scarcely, in Bantu society, see a real choice as to what new capital instruments shall be created. We are thus brought to realize that we are dealing with a society which is virtually non-progressive, which corresponds in fact to such societies as have been assumed to exist in the works of economists. While there is capital in the sense of produced goods used for further production, and while this capital is obviously essential to any society, there is extremely little capital in the sense of new productive goods regarding which vital choices have to be made by entrepreneurs anticipating the demands of consumers.

It would be pedantic to insist that there is absolutely nothing corresponding to such goods. Some trace of their function may always be seen. The entrepreneur, whom we may for purposes of simplicity identify with the head of the household, always has some slight choice as to the class of goods into which he may direct the labour power under his command. He may decide to direct more or less of it into cultivation of fields or the tending of animals. The men or women of the household may turn their labour power into using a valuable local resource, such as a type of clay, into goods which they may exchange with other consumers. But such choices are so limited that, to give any valid description of reality, we must insist that though they differ in degree, rather than in kind, from the application of concrete productive instruments in Western communities, this difference in degree is so great that it may almost be treated as a difference in kind.

Management and the Entrepreneur

By treating it in this way, we may better bring out some of the fundamental relationships. In the first place, it is only in a society with a degree of progressiveness that the really burning question arises as to what form of new capital goods shall be created, and as to the uses to which they shall be put. There is no evidence that Bantu society, as such, is incapable of making economic progress along its own lines, but all available evidence points to the fact, correlated with a vast array of circumstances with which we cannot here concern ourselves, that the peoples all over Bantu Africa have existed in more or less set ways, making no noticeable provision for definite progress in the technical equipment by means of which they come to terms with their environment. This being so, the actual creation of additional capital goods has not been part of the peoples' activities. Hence we are driven to the conclusion, first, that the function of consumers to release part of their resources for further *general* production has scarcely existed, their state of knowledge not making this possible; second, that equally there has been little room for the function of the entrepreneur in managing such resources.

The Bantu, having the characteristic just described, have not arrived at the stage of using those units of exchange known as money. In the disposal of everyday resources, there is in the peoples' minds a definite scale of valuations performing one of

80

the functions of money. This is efficient enough to guarantee the effective economic disposal of consumption goods and of very simple capital resources. It is when long views are needed, and lengthy processes are involved, that people's powers of calculation must be supplemented by the instrument of monetary units. Without these, lengthy processes are indeed impossible. The members of Bantu communities undoubtedly make judgments of value, which reflect back upon the goods produced. In utilizing these goods they clearly visualize units and do so with a considerable degree of fineness. Extra handfuls of grain are noticed, and a variation in the value of cows' milk in a household will be quickly registered in accordance with the available supply over against the uses to which it may be put. There is no question of the *minimum sensible* being large. But, correlated with the extreme smallness of the supply of true capital goods, there is no general medium of exchange by means of which people may keep in mind the relative valuations of supplies of goods of different orders.

It is thus that there cannot be an effective supply of goods of a higher order, that is to say, of true capital equipment, for it is in the economic management of such goods that long views and refined management are necessary. There is no such thing, in any really practical sense, as a demand price for liberated resources which may be turned into such goods. This is the same thing as saying that there is no interest, considering interest as a distributive share. Consumption interest is seen in several ways among the Bantu, notably in the lending out of cattle. But entrepreneurial interest, the main type which concerns economic theory, is much better assumed to be non-existent.

It is impossible, however, to say that this type of interest is absolutely non-existent, and thus to discover, for the first time, an absolute difference between primitive and advanced economic systems. On the contrary, as we have several times pointed out in the course of this book, the head of the household may well be regarded as performing entrepreneurial functions. He may often be seen to reap an advantage in prestige and in the consumption goods at his disposal

F

from a successful exercise of economic foresight and combining of the agencies of production. The importance of this must never be overlooked. But it is still more important, in our view, to see that these entrepreneurial functions, and the rewards which are undoubtedly attributed to them, correspond to payment for management without corresponding interest. For interest is a share attributed and paid to the consumer who foregoes some consumption. It is virtually impossible to distinguish this in Bantu society, save in the fact that through there being a normal balance between production and consumption, standards of consumption are maintained. The entrepreneur, his management being practically confined to that of stable resources, cannot be conceived as paying interest, nor as being rewarded for the management of ultimate productive factors in a round-about economy. It is exceedingly difficult to think of consumers foregoing consumption with the direct motive of securing interest on what they save.

SECTION VI

The Attribution of Economic Shares

Having found it advisable to indicate these two vital differences between the primitive economy of the Bantu and the advanced economy of Western communities, namely, the non-progressive character of the former and the consequent absence of market prices by which surplus consumption goods can be turned into free capital equipment, it becomes necessary to point out that the much more fundamental fact of economic attribution does exist in Bantu society. The purposeful union of productive agencies most certainly takes place. Since these agencies are various and substitutable we have the fact of variations in returns. This is evident to our senses as we watch Bantu at work.

Further, we should say, there is a keen appreciation among the people themselves of the fact that each man, woman or child contributes something definite to the value of the final product, and should be accredited with this. They realize one of the fundamental problems of society, the sharing of work and of its proceeds, which is fundamentally a problem of economic management. They also realize the value of the contribution of owned factors, although the principal of these, land, is so definitely the possession of distinctive groups that the group as such almost automatically received the reward due to its use.

It is clearly to be seen that the physical result of any one person's efforts is no more measurable among the Bantu than among ourselves, but the formation of "market prices" which is essential to attribution, that is to say, to the apportionment of product according to the value of services rendered, does definitely extend to units of labour. As we have seen, in the absence of a monetary medium, this does not extend to the evaluation of goods of a higher order, and consequently these goods are scarcely brought into existence. But, labour being a most valuable agency in Bantu production, it is clear that there is some effective evaluation of its units just as there is of the units of consumption goods. This is made more difficult to perceive by the circumstance of the effective economic subject nearly always embracing the labour power of a group of individuals. The attribution, therefore, has to some extent to be carried out indirectly. As a rule, a group of men or a group of women will turn their attention to a given piece of work. But this by no means raises a new problem, for labour is habitually employed in groups in Western civilization. The solution of the problem is by the traditional method of regarding the marginal units of labour. A group of women will be hoeing a field; finding that the work is not going quickly enough they will appeal to the women of other households, very often giving rewards through the medium of a beer drink. The extra productivity achieved is very clearly valued. And so throughout the whole routine of work. A keen appreciation is shown of the energetic individual, or of the loss to the group when someone's labour is withdrawn.

To some extent the attributed shares are directly handed over to the economic subject. The clearest available example of this lies in the house of a single wife receiving ownership of the produce of her own fields. The skilful woman, who also makes a skilful use of her children and neighbours, receives a bigger share of the total produce of the household than does the less skilful wife. But, for the most part, and even within the household of the wife, the valuation of units of labour goes far enough to secure the economic application of that labour and, having done this, its main purpose is served. It is not nearly so necessary that the individuals within the group should each withdraw a share of consumption goods corresponding to the value of their contribution. This can safely be left to the organization of consumption, whereby each receives his share of satisfactions, though undoubtedly with extra prestige and sometimes gifts to outstanding personalities. The main object is the economic utilization of the labour power; this is always of the utmost importance; it is to achieve this, and not the giving of the correct share to each individual, that the evaluations of the society extend effectively to units of labour power.

CHAPTER VI

FURTHER APPLICATIONS OF ECONOMIC THEORY

SECTION I

The Essentials of Ownership

HAVING examined economic processes in Bantu society, it becomes profitable to indicate some of the economically significant aspects of ownership among these people. As has already been indicated in a reference to land-tenure, the sociological ramifications of ownership may be exceedingly complex. In the case of land-tenure, we decided that the whole set of relationships between the people and their land did not fall within our scope, but that our duty was to see in what ways these relationships acted as a basis for the economic management of the land. So it is with all other economic resources. The sociologist explores the vast network of relationships arising out of ownership; the economist, on the other hand, describes only the ways in which economic disposal is effected. To a great extent he takes ownership for granted, until it becomes evident that in the process of economic control certain characteristics of property rights become significant to that control. Ownership being, for our purposes, definable as the power of economic disposal, it becomes of real importance to see by whom economic resources are disposed of, for this will closely affect the valuations attached to them, and the choice as to the uses to which they shall be put.

The essential functions of ownership are dealt with throughout both the descriptive and the theoretical chapters of this book. The whole point in analysing the nature of the economic subject is to discover by whom ownership is exercised, and it will be recollected that we have come to the conclusion that ownership is practically always exercised collectively, even

85

when, on the surface, individuals appear to have control of it. We have seen that there is nothing mystical about this group ownership; that it is simply the resultant of the pulls of the individuals within the group. It has appeared further than this necessitates no departure from the use of abstract economic theory, since the formulations of this theory appear to be equally effective whether we assume an individual or a group to be the economic subject. We have further come to the conclusion that the consumption of resources for the satisfaction of human wants is also controlled collectively in a real sense, since the sharing of proceeds, the organization of wants, and the carrying out of those organized activities which in the main control the consumption of Bantu goods, are culturally determined. The culture lays down the value of certain activities, and goods are consumed in relation to these. In this way the individual derives the evaluations which are his incentive to work, from the organized activities of his group.

There is full play for his individual preferences, and even vital activities like initiation schools will be suspended when there is a scarcity of resources and other things are judged to be of more importance. This judgment must, of course, be made by individuals; the resulting confluence of their opinions leads to the new configuration of organized activities. Yet, no matter how these change, or even if some of them are abandoned, the fact remains that the whole of the resources of each community are still disposed of through their medium; whether the organized activity be a simple family meal or a great funeral feast, it and the other activities control the consumption of the community, and it is through this medium that individuals receive that share which is taken to be due to them. This control of consumption need not be regarded as a characteristic of primitive economies. Our own tentative opinion is that it is equally operative, though perhaps not obvious, in civilized communities. It certainly must operate in so far as the economic subject is any kind of group, for without it there would be nothing to prevent each individual seizing for himself whatever share of the group's produce he was able

86

to lay hands upon. We have seen that economic attribution can decide only the share of the produce going to groups, and not to individuals, among the Bantu. Therefore this further control of consumption is needed, to share out the produce within each group, to confer the ownership of this produce, only partly according to the services rendered by individuals, and partly also according to the wants of the individuals which must be satisfied if the group is to continue its life.

Having reviewed our conclusions about the economic subject, the units which exercise ownership, we are able to indicate some of the economic aspects of ownership among the Bantu. In the first place, we must consider the ownership of consumption goods. These being goods which serve enjoyment directly, having emerged from the employment of economic factors, it is clear that their ownership must, in some ultimate sense, be individual. The time must come at which the grain is in the bowl of a particular man or woman. Yet it is equally important to realize that it can be there only through the concurrence of other members of the group.

In Western communities it is possible to think, probably mistakenly, of an individual withdrawing his share of resources and disposing of them to his own enjoyment within only the limits of the law. Yet the limits of custom are no less effective even here; no matter on what a European may choose to spend his money, he must have some realization, however slight, of the consequences of his behaviour upon persons with whom he has social relationships. Should he choose to take a holiday, he may well take some of his family with him; should he merely buy some cigarettes, he will know that in practice he himself will not smoke them all, and he will probably spend less than he would wish upon cigarettes through a realization that he must leave money for the use of other members of his family. Even should we descend to trivial terms, it is still difficult to think of a European enjoying a purely individual ownership of his consumption goods; even when he buys an evening newspaper he will be careful to take it home to his wife, so that the economic subject purchasing the newspaper is really the man *plus* the wife.

All this applies with undiminished force to the Bantu. It means very little to say that they have individual ownership in their consumption goods; the point is that even this ownership is socially controlled. It is difficult for a Bantu man even to take a snack between meals without the concurrence of his wife. It may well be indicated to him that the odds and ends of food are needed for the children. Only when food is finally distributed to the individuals for their consumption is each receiving a share for himself alone. And even then he *must* consume his share; he may not, for example, obey an impulse to give it to a stranger and himself to go hungry, no matter how generous the impulse. As a member of the group he is under the strongest compulsion to treat "his own" food as the group thinks best. The food is one link in the chain of the individual's relations with his fellow members, relations which inevitably have their economic aspect. It follows then from our assumption of groups as the economic units that some modification is required in the economic practice which regards the ownership of consumption goods as necessarily individual. Ownership even of these goods must be by the subject, or group, and they must be applied to the physiological requirements of the individual in accordance with the valuations of the subject. The *having* of consumption goods must thus be regarded as being divided, though not in the same sense as that in which the ownership of production goods is regarded by economists as being divided.

The ownership of production goods among the Bantu appears to call for little modification of current economic concepts. With division of labour, ownership of such goods must be divided between the producer and those for whose wants he produces. We shall become well acquainted through the pages of this book with the rudimentary but real division of labour among the Bantu. We are already acquainted with the nature of their production goods, however slightly these may be differentiated from the consumption goods. It is owing to the existence of this division of labour and of these production goods that no one, nor any one economic subject, in Bantu society is exclusive owner of the means of production, whether material or personal. We have seen how there is no exclusive ownership of important factors such as land or accessories to production such as cattle. Always the ultimate ownership of such factors lies with the group which will dictate the mode of their employment. But the active ownership is in the hands of individuals within the group whose duty it is to secure their economic management. Land may belong to a household or sub-clan and, more especially, to a wife. But the management of this land is entrusted at particular seasons to certain men who must not only prepare it but must also see that the optimum quantity of it is prepared to be mixed with the available labour. These men, therefore, have the ownership of this means of production conveyed to them by the whole group of owners.

Production is carried out according to the evaluations of this same group acting as consumers. As consumers and as the primary owners of this land, these people set the pace of production, but this they do much more in their role of consumers. With the Bantu as with ourselves, production is carried out ultimately to meet the valuations of consumers. The specific type of conveyed ownership exercised by the men who control agricultural production is therefore a subsidiary type. Yet its reality has been noted by social anthropologists whose enquiries have gone deeply enough. They have found that a man will often state that a field is "his", while his wife will state that the field is "hers", and that no conflict arises from this. The economic explanation is that each one has had conveyed to him or her certain economic control of the field, on behalf of those whom, as economists, we must designate its true owners, those who are to consume its produce. In the same way, it might well be found, though it has not yet been noted, that Bantu men and women habitually transfer some of their labour power to the direction of others, who thus exercise a conveyed ownership of it in order to apply it, together with other agents, to the business of production.

89

Section II

Conveyed Ownership

It is in this way that we may see the factors of production being placed at the disposal of the persons who perform the duties of the entrepreneur in Bantu society. There can be no doubt that a definite evaluation is placed upon the units of these productive resources, and that the entrepreneur applies them according to these evaluations in order to produce goods to satisfy the demands of the whole group as final consumers. We cannot agree that a Bantu group is so unspecialized as merely to act as its own entrepreneur. A more intimate acquaintance with its workings soon shows that certain persons, notably the head of each household, have this function delegated to them. Yet we have seen that the entrepreneurial function is employed to a very much smaller degree among the Bantu than in Western society; that this is so because, that society being unprogressive and with a very limited technical knowledge, the accumulation of free resources to be used in further production is small. Hence the Bantu entrepreneur is without the control of any significant body of such resources. This prevents his being differentiated to anything like the same extent as in Western communities. He undoubtedly performs his functions, in a truly entrepreneurial way, in securing the economic application of such capital resources as do exist, and we must regard him as drawing, though in an unformulated way, an attributed share of the proceeds to himself on this account. The disentanglement of this share is made difficult to us through the fact that he is supplied with consumption goods only in the same way as any other member of the group, in the process of sharing out. Yet his share may be guaranteed by the fact that he personally is able to exercise an especially strong pull among his relatives on account of the directive services which he renders, and which are certainly appreciated. There can be no doubt whatever that typically in Bantu households the headman is the largest consumer!

But we are brought face to face with the fact that in Western communities it is only the entrepreneur who can bring about physical production from the purposeful union of productive resources, and that he will not do this unless he is satisfied with the share in the final product offered to him. It is difficult to visualize a Bantu headman ceasing to offer his services because of a satisfactory price for them not being offered. His real reward, even though he may himself be a hearty eater, is in increasing the resources of his household. It is this, and this only, which can reflect credit upon him and put greater resources at his disposal. Hence we can see a limited sense in which he is employed by his own group. His rewards being those of his group, he cannot really be dissatisfied with his entrepreneurial share. Should he feel that the returns to his services are insufficient, his whole household will share the feeling. This can be expressed in two ways, through a dis-integration of the group, with a consequent loss of its working power, and through a diminution in the quality of its land and personal resources. This may either spur the group on to greater effort or cause it to weaken; and so diminish the flow of new goods. The entrepreneur or headman will still have his fundamental problem of the disposal of such resources as are available, but, since he has no supply of really new capital equipment, the management of which would put him on a footing equal to that of a Western entrepreneur, we cannot imagine him slackening in his efforts through what he regarded as a too low evaluation being put upon those efforts. This fits in with the conclusion that, while Bantu communities have capital for the replacement of consumed goods, they are practically without that new capital which gives rise to interest. Hence, they have the functions of the entrepreneur in one sense only, that of a manager of resources in an unprogressive society.

We thus see that, considering the economic aspect of owner-ship among the Bantu, the purely individual possession of consumption goods must be questioned, not only because they are very seldom entirely consumption goods, but also because, even in so far as they are, they satisfy the wants, not of the individual as such, but of the individual as controlled by the economic unit. We are not satisfied that in saying this we have discovered any difference between primitive and advanced economies. Whether it would not be profitable to proceed on the same assumptions in applying economic theory to any society, is a question yet to be faced. As regards productive resources of various kinds, we find that they are all ultimately owned by the consumers according to whose valuations they are used, but that there is a distinct intermediate ownership, or economic control, vested in persons or groups who are specially qualified to use them. Ownership of productive means therefore corresponds closely to that in advanced communities, in that it is divided for the purposes of effective economic management, the ownership being brought together again when the ultimate goods are handed over to the people who are to consume them.

SECTION III

Custom and Economic Choice

We may proceed, briefly, to regard a typical Bantu unit, such as household or neighbourhood, as a market in which the economic subjects put forth their efforts and draw out the results, compare the values of units of different resources and consume and invest them accordingly, and strike a balance between the present and the future, by means of well-established customary control of consumption, yet with a very definite awareness of what they are doing. What can we say regarding the conditions of such markets? Is choice, on the whole, free? Is the number of parties to each act of exchange sufficiently large to make economic choice effective? Is life so largely dominated by large units of custom that the people merely habitually set aside so many beasts for sacrifice on a certain occasion, consume set amounts of food at family meals, make set and unchangeable payments each year to their chiefs? We must make it clear that, no matter what may be the answers to such questions, the formulations of economic theory will still apply. Even the last-named circumstance, that in which the *minimum sensible* is so large that all choice seems to be excluded, valuations could never remain fixed and steady, even though the disposal of the resources appeared to exclude choice to the uttermost. Valuations would have to change, if for no other reason, with the vagaries of nature. A bad season for crops would send up the value of units of grain as against units of cattle. Once we realize that such fundamental valuations cannot remain set, it follows that the disposal of resources cannot be conducted along the lines which old-fashioned anthropological books termed "customary". No matter how hard and fast, on the surface, custom might appear to be, commodities which become scarce must be husbanded, and we can conceive of no human society in which this would not be so, for society appears to be, in one of its most important aspects, a mechanism whereby the economic management of resources is secured. Always, in an unprogressive society, there may be the appearance of resources being disposed of in large, customary and unvarying quantities. The people themselves may often state that it is customary for them, on a given occasion, to contribute so many cattle, and further to give the impression that this number does not vary. But it is always the little more or less that counts, the marginal units, in fact. Bantu people are extremely well aware of these, and all our evidence points to the fact that a goat may be substituted for a cow, that handfuls of grain are carefully counted in any transaction.

The *minimum sensible* thus cannot be said to be large. Yet, even if it were, economic theory would still have a real significance for the society. No matter how large the units handled, the resources would still be disposed of in ways which would have to be regarded as achieving the maximum of satisfactions, and economic theory would have a new problem with which to concern itself. It would have to work out its implications in a society in which economic choice was at an absolute minimum. The Bantu, however, do not supply us with such a problem.

What of the number of parties sharing in each exchange? If each act of exchange could be conceived as being between merely two or three people, who, by some bonds of custom or law, had to deal with each other and with nobody else, then the degree of indeterminacy would be very large. At first sight, again, there is a tendency to think of savages as being limited in their dealings to their kinsmen, and consequently of economic choice being seriously limited. Yet, as we see elsewhere in this book, kinship imposes but few hard-and-fast limits of this kind. Indeed, it would appear that wherever kinship seems to show signs of depriving the people of effective economic choice, they have convenient ways of getting round the obstruction.

Take the example of the head of the household acting as entrepreneur to the members. This gives an important exchange relationship. If the members were absolutely bound to employ a particular headman in this role, they might have no clear way of deciding whether he was serving them efficiently, so that, for purposes of economic theory, the situation would largely be indeterminate. Yet even so its indeterminacy would not be absolute, for the people would be able to compare their situation with that of other households in the neighbourhood. It is perfectly obvious that this is done in practice. But, as will be seen from other chapters, there is often distinct competition for the role of headman. We do not mean that the actual head of a household is likely to have his position challenged openly on account of dissatisfaction with his economic management. There are less drastic ways in which he can be replaced. As he becomes too old, his younger brothers or elder sons will compete for his position and he may go into honourable retirement, in which he is likely to be consulted on all important matters. The size of Bantu households gives a very reasonable degree of choice as to which man shall effectively become headman.

But this operates even more distinctly in the right which each man has to take his own family away from the household and to begin a new homestead of his own. This is a right which is constantly exercised. It serves the double purpose of securing that that man who can best perform the functions of entrepreneur, shall perform those functions, thus yielding an effective competition between a fairly large group of potential business managers, and also the purpose that the size of the homestead, the main economic unit, shall approach the optimum.

Hunter, in particular, shows how effectively this is done among the Pondo. The size of the usual Bantu homestead is kept at or near such an optimum from the point of view of economic management, but, as we see in other chapters, associations of households through the neighbourhood principle, through the sub-clan, and through intermarriage, all widen the range of choice in this respect, so that we must conclude that in the important exchange whereby one man performs entrepreneurial services for his group, the range of choice is large enough to make the choice very effective. This has especial significance in that it is just in this exchange that we might have expected the principle of kinship to be effective in excluding choice and so introducing indeterminacy. It is thus unnecessary to repeat instances in which other exchanges take place, and in which the range of choice is not even on the surface dominated by a set necessity for one party to deal exclusively with another. It is difficult indeed to find definite traces of monopoly in Bantu society.

This concludes our attempt to indicate the ways in which the principles of economics apply to the primitive society of the Bantu. We see that even though these principles are tested out against a level of culture far below that in the minds of the people who formulated them, they still function in every essential particular. It becomes absurd to think of formulating new economic theories and, still more, new economic motives, for a primitive people. Whether the testing of economic formulations against the pattern of a primitive culture will result in the adoption of some new assumptions, or new emphases, into that theory, which may increase its relevance for advanced societies, is one of the questions arising out of this book.

PART II

CHAPTER VII

THE ECONOMICS OF PREGNANCY AND BIRTH

PRODUCTIVE activities are always related in the most direct manner to human needs. These needs give to productive activity its real meaning, for they dictate the values which will prevail in any community, and which will directly control production. In the meeting of these fundamental needs there is always a strong element of choice. A Bantu man will have to choose between an expensive or a cheap medicine to strengthen his new-born son. But if we think merely in terms of individual action we shall find it very hard to arrive at a fruitful application of economic principles to our Bantu communities, for while the man not only may, but must, choose between the more or the less expensive medicine, he will have virtually no choice whatever with regard to obtaining *some* medicine. The medicine may actually be harmful; European doctors may assure the man that it is poisonous; it may be physically harmless, yet merely magical; missionaries may try to persuade the father that he is acting foolishly, while practical men may deplore the fact that he is wasting his resources on such hocus-pocus. Experience today is showing how little effect such arguments have. To the Bantu father they are likely to be well-nigh meaningless. The magic, for which he gladly or grudgingly pays the market price, is dictated as a necessity by his own culture. The situation of birth is surrounded by dangers which the magic helps to control; this control will not be discarded by any wise Bantu. Nor is it secured in any haphazard way. It comes directly from the forces which, in Bantu thought, govern such events as the advent of a new life. The ancestors control conception; the magic may communicate with them. The physiological theories of conception often determine the nature of the magic.

Apart from this, the actual uncertainties and dangers in the processes of birth and early infancy are only too real, and the Bantu, in their deepest beliefs, identify these dangers with the lurking terrors of sorcery, against which magic must be purchased and employed.

Pregnancy and birth have the most direct bearing upon the economic life of the Bantu people. Native doctors specialize in the treatment of pregnancy and birth, and are rewarded accordingly. The supply of grain and vegetable food may be deeply affected, especially should the woman be confined at a critical season in the routine of agriculture; while special demands will undoubtedly be made upon food stores and, should the demand fall at a period of scarcity, the economic situation of a household is sure to be deeply modified.

There can be no doubt that pregnancy and birth have their economic aspects in these and many other ways. We must view them as vital events forming the core of a grouping of activities which ultimately governs the disposal of a large volume of resources. The choice of the individual must operate within the shell of these organized customs. He must make minor choices and adjustments in the light of his personal resources; but the culture in which he lives tells him that he must employ midwives, that he must make certain gifts to relatives on the occasion of the birth of a child, that he must procure medicines and charms, that, in fact, he must go through a considerable and expensive routine.

The primary need is simple. The safe birth of the baby must be secured if possible. But, from the nature of human culture, other more complex needs arise from the processes which satisfy the primary needs. The need for religious communication with ancestors at the birth of a child, and the need for protection from sorcery, become just as real, and therefore just as significant for economics as the need for safe delivery of the baby and proper feeding of mother and child.

There are many variations of custom among the Bantu peoples. But everywhere we find that pregnancy, birth, and the acceptance of the baby into the community are embedded in well-defined customs which the Bantu father and mother would no more think of neglecting than they would of neglecting to feed the child. Among the first of these is that of establishing legitimacy. This, from the very nature of the family, is an urgent need in any human society. It may take many forms, but the central need is always present, is closely linked up with the religious and physiological ideas of the people, and most definitely has its economic aspect.

Perhaps the first consideration in this respect is whether the child is likely to be an economic asset or the reverse, and whether a child of one sex is likely to be preferred on this account. It is clear that among the Bantu, at any rate until very recent times and in urbanized conditions, a child is an economic asset as well as a spiritual addition to the resources of its parents. From one end of Bantu Africa to the other, there has never, until very recent times, been an unwanted child.[1] The economic significance of this is immediate. Even if legitimacy is doubtful, as among certain tribes it often is, the child will be claimed rather than abandoned, and the only dispute may be as to which man has the right to claim the infant. The advantages of this attitude in a society in which life for the young is at best precarious need not be stressed. We are given the initial situation in which the child is definitely wanted, even though it may impose strains upon resources during its early years. We shall see shortly some of the economic effects of measures taken to decide whether a child is legitimate.

The sex of the child, too, may have much to do with the extent to which it is desired in any given culture. Superficial observers have been given to stating that girl children are much preferred by the Bantu on account of their being "sold" later in life. We shall see that, according to the fundamental principles of Bantu marriage, an exchange of wealth takes place in a direction opposite to that in European dowry. Wealth is given to the father of the girl. Nothing is easier than to suppose that this makes a father wish to have many daughters, especially as the wealth involved is really large, and, conversely,

[1] Only with such exceptions as those designated undesirable for superstitious reasons. They are certainly numerically insignificant.

the expense of marrying off a son may be great. It is part of the
work of an anthropologist to discover whether there is indeed
a stronger desire for girls, and for what reason. One of the
first indications that he would look for would be magic with a
sex-determining function. If such magic exists, and if it is
used to promote the birth of girls, then the anthropologist
would be disposed to conclude that the desire for the wealth
obtainable at the marriage of a man's children is a determining
factor. The anthropologist will further listen carefully to the
conversation of natives in order to determine their attitude.

Magic is reported from one or two tribes as being for the
purpose of determining sex. Yet there is not the slightest
indication that it is used to bring an excess of girls. Its use
is likely to be confined to balancing matters when any family
has had too many children of one sex. Among other peoples
it is reported that there are omens which indicate the sex of a
forthcoming child, but these omens, although they might well
be the foundations of magic, do not appear to be so used.

Bantu culture may clearly be seen to give a balance between
a narrow desire to accumulate cattle or other wealth on the one
hand, and a wider desire to build a complete family on the
other. The girls bring cattle; but they themselves will leave
the homestead when they marry. The boys, on the other hand,
will remain with their father. They will build their huts around
his. They will bring wives to add to the prestige and resources
of the establishment. The man who has many sons may have
difficulties in providing cattle for their marriages, but he will
have the much greater satisfaction of acquiring a large and well-
founded home. There is every evidence that this wider social
ambition, as it is expressed in the preference, or lack of preference, for boy or girl children, quite outweighs the direct desire
to accumulate cattle. When we find how very intense is the
Bantu's desire for cattle we shall realize how well balanced is
that desire by other socially dictated values. An acquisitive
attitude which might be disruptive is brought under control.
All children are wanted, boys and girls alike.

It follows from this that barrenness or sterility is one of the
greatest of curses. Smith and Dale show clearly the awful fate

of the Ila man who dies without progeny. His misfortune is carried on even into the spirit world. To the Bantu this represents a real terror. The childless woman is also one of the most unfortunate of creatures. Thus it is normal for pregnancy to occur within a few months of marriage. Should it be delayed, there is at once recourse, among Bantu tribes, to measures of one kind or another. These all involve the use of medicine, and medicine is always paid for, and sometimes very highly.

The first expense of a married couple may well be a visit to a medicine man to ascertain the reasons for delayed pregnancy. There are everywhere doctors skilled in this branch of medicine. Whether the wife or the husband is treated first will depend upon the physiological theories of the people. Among the Ba-Ila it is the wife who is treated first, while the husband takes medicine only if he has failed to secure offspring from a series of wives. Among the Lenge a divining doctor will be visited either by the woman or, more usually, by her parents. The parents of the woman are in every tribe directly interested, if only for the reason that if their daughter should prove barren they may have to provide one of her younger sisters in addition, and for very little extra cattle. The divining doctor of the Lenge may decide either that some ancestral spirit is angry and therefore preventing conception, or that the woman is actually possessed by a spirit of foreign origin which is taking the same action. In the latter case the woman herself may appeal to the spirit which is within her, offering it merely a prayer and a little water. Should, however, the mischief be caused by an ancestral spirit, an expensive sacrifice may be needed. If the ancestor is of her own line the expense will be borne by her family. If it is of her husband's line the expense will fall upon him or his family. A valuable animal may thus be at stake, and the burden be distributed according to the decision of the divining doctor.

A Bantu sacrifice is an expensive matter. No part of the flesh of the victim is wasted. All is eaten after the "spirit" of the beast has been partaken of by the ancestors of the worshippers. Yet a definite disposal of valued resources takes

103

place. The divining doctor may well obtain a part of the meat, and even the valuable skin. It is thus very much to be desired that the young wife become pregnant in the shortest appropriate time, for the visit to the doctor will be an expense even if he should not decide that a sacrifice is necessary.

It must be noted that repeated visits to the doctor, and several further sacrifices, may be necessary. Cattle-owning people will be particularly liable to find their wealth diminishing in these circumstances. Among the Lenge it is worth noting that the sacrifice may be merely a piece of cloth which is made into a garment for the wife. The doctor may be so reasonable as to see that she needs a new dress. But few Bantu peoples are lucky enough to escape in this way, and the doctor will in any case require his fee.

The first pregnancy having been achieved, if possible without the expense of a visit to a doctor or diviner, the normal course proceeds. There is no evidence of further great expense until the actual birth. But medicines are always taken by the woman during at least the later months, and very often by her husband as well, not to mention other members of the community. This medicine consists as a rule of decoctions from roots and it is probably easily obtainable in most districts. It is as the birth approaches that further expenses must be faced. Special diet must be found for the woman; special medicine may be resorted to to make birth easy; an ox may be killed so that the woman may eat the pancreas with the same object in view; a stock of firewood must be laid in; midwives must be engaged; possible recourse to specialists must be provided against.

It is clear that strains are put upon the food resources of the household in a special way. In the first place, the woman will have desires for special foods. In the second place, certain foods are in the great majority of tribes taboo [1] to her or avoided as a general practice. We have as yet exceedingly little detailed knowledge of these dietetic regulations, and must here content ourselves with remarking that in certain circumstances at least,

---

[1] Quite possibly such regulations will have sound physiological bases.

as when food stores are low, they must have considerable economic significance.

In one other way there is a minimum of strain upon resources. The woman is in practically all parts of Bantu Africa the hardest worked member of the household. Her duties, indeed, extend outside the household itself and embrace the fields which it is her duty to cultivate. It is clear that her valuable work is never dispensed with until the very last moment. Not only does she work until the first pains; she also may have extra work in preparing for the confinement. The collection of firewood is nearly always one of her heaviest duties, and she will lay in a special store for this occasion. This is especially noteworthy in that she can, on other occasions, obtain assistance in many tasks. Yet it is clearly reported that she performs this task, at this time, herself. The culture dictates that her work shall not be lost until the last moment.

A distinction must always be made between the first pregnancy and later ones. This applies in particular to the first pregnancy of any given marriage. The union of two people is in fact not complete, in Bantu law and custom, until the first child is conceived or born. We should thus expect special preparations, precautions, and expenses in connection with this most important event. While, however, the first child in a very real sense seals the marriage contract, it may do something more. Should it be the man's first child, that is, by his first wife, it carries him one stage further in his own development. Before being a father, he could scarcely be regarded as an adult. He would not be fitted for the duties of eldership until his son, perhaps some twenty years later, has in turn become a father. The principle of age sequence, or development, is of much greater importance among some Bantu tribes than among others. But always the stage of becoming a parent is an important one, and in some cases, as we shall see, has very distinct ceremonial expressions of the altered economic status of the new parent. In a polygynous society it will very often be the case that both parents do not attain that stage together. The man may have been a parent for some years before one of his new wives first achieves motherhood. In such a case the woman alone reaches a new stage in her development and, among one tribe at least, she goes through very definite ceremonies unaccompanied by her husband, ánd receiving as gifts an equipment with which to meet her new responsibilities. The first pregnancy or birth therefore must seal the marriage contract, and it may also mark an important step forward in the lives of the man and the woman, or of one of them. In each case the economic implications will be very definite.

It has already been mentioned that should the first pregnancy be seriously delayed, the consequences will be serious. A social loss is indicated, in that the woman is failing to perform her greatest function, and, despite the most expensive medicines, may continue to be barren. This social catastrophe has its economic aspect. The first probability among most Bantu peoples is that the woman's father will have to provide another of his daughters to be a second wife to the aggrieved husband, and will have to be content with a nominal return of wealth for this girl. The main loss thus falls upon the father of the barren woman. The second daughter having been supplied, and presumably achieving pregnancy in due course, there will be no question of divorcing her elder and less fortunate sister. There is not the slightest evidence of vindictive treatment of a barren woman. She may be scoffed at, but the attitude is obviously one of pity. In a society so often at the fringe of starvation the fate of any such individual may well be expected to depend upon her being able to perform other useful functions. There is no difficulty about her doing so. She will be able to till her fields and cook her husband's food. She remains not only self-supporting, but a distinct economic asset with the secure status and self-respect that this brings. In all probability a child in the household will sooner or later need a substitute mother, and this woman will look after the child. Divorce is occasionally mentioned in connection with barrenness; but the circumstances appear to be special. The main economic consequences of the misfortune are as we have described.

On the other hand, when the first pregnancy of a marriage does take place, there will in the vast majority of cases be extra payment from the happy father-to-be to his father-in-law. Bride-price is seldom given once and for all at marriage. The birth not only of the first but of all subsequent children may be the occasion of extra demands by the woman's father. The making of an extra payment at the first pregnancy or birth appears to be a well established usage.

Our clearest information on the point is from the Ubena people. Among these people a wife's first pregnancy is very clearly marked by a dance initiating her into the new period of her life, and is also the occasion for a definite payment from her husband to her parents. Further payments at subsequent births used to be customary and have now become virtually legal obligations. Difficult as it is to assess the value of payment without knowing the valuation of objects within the given tribe, it is yet made clear to us that these payments are considerable. Space does not permit us to list similar payments among all the tribes in our purview. It is enough to have seen that the first pregnancy has a special economic character, that its failure to materialize is a serious loss, that its happy achievement is one of the occasions for which the married couple and their relatives must mobilize a fair proportion of their resources.

The appointment of midwives is a main practical part of the preparation for any birth among the Bantu, and is supplemented by the calling in of other specialists when necessary. Very often, especially among the poorer people, the midwives will merely be female relatives, but it is clear that there is in this respect the nucleus of a specialized profession and that the services are always paid for. We may see entry to the profession by women following their mothers, and education for it by the admission of young married women to witness the processes of birth. Professional etiquette appears to be very definite. The practitioners specialize among themselves, some having reputations for dealing with special complications, while others possess the secrets of valuable medicines which they will disclose only in return for considerable payment. But most important is the light which the activities of midwives throw upon the relations between primary needs and more complicated or social needs. The primary need of securing safe delivery accounts, it is clear, for only a small part of the activities of the midwife, and it is highly probable that were this the only consideration there would be fewer specialists. The remuneration given to them would be correspondingly less, for their services would not yield the satisfactions which in fact they do yield, and consequently would not be produced in such quantities.

But the primary need of safe delivery is at once extended into two other needs, the satisfaction of which is just as important and probably more costly. The practical knowledge of even the best specialist is far from being certain to achieve safe results. The whole situation is one of danger. Tremendous hopes hang in the balance. Even the best Western knowledge cannot achieve certain results, and the infant death-rate among our Bantu peoples is often enormous. Magical control is therefore sought, and, whatever the expense, the midwives must supply it. A large part of their knowledge is not of the practical medical aspect, but of the magical measures necessary to ward off all surrounding dangers and to enable the people, especially the mother, to face the crisis with confidence.

A further social need is not less important. Legitimacy must be established. It is at the very foundation of the reproductive scheme. Should there be the slightest doubt about this important matter it is the duty of the midwives to clear it up. By means of omens, divination, and by playing upon the feelings of the mother at the critical hours, the midwives extract any necessary confession and establish the true fatherhood of the child. This is obviously no small part of their duties. It is a function in which the etiquette of their profession is exceedingly well-defined. They must use only certain means to extract confession; they must divulge the results only to certain people.

Let us watch native midwives at work. The first omen is a delayed or difficult birth. The woman is urged to confess, and promised that then matters will go easily. Or perhaps, as among the Zulus, the birth may be delayed through the anger of ancestors. The ancestors will be the woman's, and her parents will have to go to the expense of sending a goat or even an ox or cow to be sacrificed. Or it may be that a wizard has poisoned the woman so as to make birth difficult. Very definite medical symptoms are observed, but magical treatment goes hand in hand with practical medical manipulation. Should the birth be an exceptionally difficult one, the husband may be called in and he and his wife will perform a ceremony. This ceremony is performed among more than one South African tribe, and its main purpose appears to be that, should the child be legitimate, easy birth would follow.

The connection between protracted births and illegitimate births is brought out very clearly by the customs of the Thonga. So deep is this connection in the minds of the people, that a mother-to-be, should she know that the child is illegitimate, will very often confess to the principal midwife in order to secure an easy birth. Should this not be done, and should the delivery take too long, this midwife has a well-defined course of duties. She will send for the husband, and the rite, already mentioned, will be performed. If the husband is indeed the father, the child will come forth. But if this does not achieve the result the midwife will make it clear that birth can take place only after complete confession. Even should a child be born easily but in a particular position, it will be a sign of illegitimacy and a confession will be exacted.

Among the Thonga, as among all other tribes, it is necessary that the true father should be known. The Thonga midwives have very clear obligations not even to divulge the secrets to the husband unless they specially decide to do so. It is enough that they should know; the true father is known; to their primary duty of securing safe birth is added that of safeguarding the extremely important knowledge of paternity.

The midwives among several tribes may practise divination in order to secure this knowledge. This is of interest to us since divining is a profession in itself, and always a well-guarded and well-paid one. For these services midwives may be rewarded in beer, in fowls, or in any of the other means of payment used in such transactions. Space does not permit us to recount the further activities, of both a medical and of a magical nature, which they must perform and which often employ them for several days. It must always be kept in mind that these women will seldom be specialists in the full European sense of that term. That is to say, they will, unless very old, first and foremost be tillers of their fields and managers of their households. The price of their services must depend greatly upon the agricultural work which they have to forgo, or leave in other hands, while they attend a birth.

They are, however, women who themselves are past child-bearing age. The significance of this is that they will probably have younger female members of their own households to release them for their work as midwives. A younger married woman would probably be far too busy at most times in the year to carry on the additional activity of attending births for payment. This situation is implemented by supernatural sanctions which appear to dictate that only a female who is herself past the crises of giving birth, and indeed past all sexual life, is fitted to attend other pregnant women. The demands upon economic resources made by birth are much greater when complications set in, and when the parties can afford expert medical treatment. In addition to midwives, there are many medicine men and women who either themselves specialize in the treatment of difficulties at births, or who possess medicines which they will sell to midwives. Some midwives also add to their qualifications by further specialization, and by the ownership of drugs which they will sell to others. We have the instance of a woman among the Lenge who knows of medicine which enables children to be born in the right way and who will divulge the secret of its composition for a payment equal, in present-day terms, to about ten shillings. Her usual practice, however, is herself to use this medicine at births. Among these people also are midwives who are specialists in various details of difficult births. Another chief midwife among the Lenge is instanced as using a medicine at a critical moment, the composition of which was unknown to herself since its "owner" would divulge the secret for payment only.

ECONOMICS OF PREGNANCY

Following birth there is a period of careful diet, of abstention from work on the part of the mother for a period determined by the economic resources of the family. If the husband is poor, and has but one wife, a rite is provided whereby he acknowledges his fatherhood and permits the woman to set about her duties in less than the usual time. Among nearly every tribe there is at this stage a feast which performs several functions. It expresses the emotional release and thanksgiving that another member has safely been added to the household. It brings together the kinsmen, whose future duties to the child are thus expressed. It provides for the killing of an animal, ranging from an ox among cattle-owning people such as the Zulus, to a mere fowl among the Thonga. This killing adds to the available diet, and broth or other delicacies are provided for the mother. But of scarcely less importance, until very recent years, was the fact that the killing of an animal provided the skin in which the baby would henceforth be carried on its mother's back. This commodity, which we may call a sling, was always one of the compulsory expenditures, and controlled, as much as anything else, the value of the beast which had to be killed. A new sling had to be provided for each baby. It was strictly taboo to provide the skin before the child was safely born, this being on the principle that it is unlucky to "count your chickens before they are hatched". The killing had to take place at the prescribed stage, and thus serve the highly important purpose of providing the feast, with its nutritive, its legal and its ritual aspects, as well as the all-important sling.

Having seen the processes of pregnancy and birth, with their strong primary necessities and equally strong social necessities, we begin to see how, in a strictly practical way, values are formed in Bantu culture. The resources employed in these circumstances are a distinct drain upon the resources of the community, and they are used according to the judgment of the people, acting within the prescribed customary activities. Services are produced, resources disposed of, payments made, according to the valuations created by the whole cultural setting.

PRINCIPLES OF ECONOMIC SOCIOLOGY

REFERENCES AND FURTHER READING

How to Become a Witch Doctor (Art.). Rev. A. Burbridge. Nada, 1930.
Witchcraft and British Colonial Law (Art.). Gt. St. J. Orde Browne.
· Africa, 1935.
Marriage and Child-Birth among the Kanuri (Art.). R. E. Ellison, Africa, 1936.
Native (Bantu) Beliefs concerning Pregnancy and Child-Birth (Art.). P. W. Laidler, South African Journal of Science, 1931.
History of the Basuto. Ellenberger and MacGregor. 1912.
The Masai. A. C. Hollis. 1905.
The Bomvana. P. A. W. Cook.
The Social System of the Zulus. E. J. Krige. 1936.
Valenge Women. E. D. Earthy. 1933.
In Witch-Bound Africa. F. H. Melland. 1923.
The Baganda. Rev. J. Roscoe. 1911.
An African People in the Twentieth Century. L. P. Mair. 1934.
The Life of a South African Tribe. H. A. Junod. 1927.
The Ila-Speaking Peoples of Northern Rhodesia. Smith and Dale. 1920.
The Bavenda. H. A. Stayt. 1931.
Savage Childhood. D. Kidd. 1906.
Ubena of the Rivers. A. T. and G. M. Culwick.
The Essential Kafir. D. Kidd. 1925.
With a Prehistoric People. W. S. and K. Routledge. 1910.
Reaction to Conquest. M. Hunter. 1937.

CHAPTER VIII

ECONOMICS OF THE INITIATION CEREMONIES

OUR thesis is that in Bantu society the disposal of resources is governed by organized activities. Choice operates to the full within these activities, but only within them. There is a dualism which must be taken into full account. Organized society, carrying out a well-defined system of ceremonies, religious observances, and all kinds of activities which define its very existence, controls the behaviour of the individual in the most fundamental way, through forming his sentiments and thus controlling his values from birth onward.

Not the least of these organized activities among the Bantu peoples is that of holding ceremonies at or about the puberty of young people. By no means all of our tribes lay equal stress upon these ceremonies. Some of the most important are entirely without them; others have them for one sex only, or much more highly developed for one sex than for the other. Some perform them on only a family scale, perhaps for one boy or girl at a time; others make of them great tribal festivals. Some lay every stress upon the rite of circumcision, even to the point of carrying out an analagous operation upon girls; others perform the ceremonies in full without such an operation. Some important tribes appear to have acquired the ceremonies, or to have increased their interest in them, within recent times. Others, it is historically known, have either abandoned the ceremonies, or have discontinued some of their more striking aspects within recent times.

We cannot in this book concern ourselves with tracing the distribution of the ceremonies or of their details; nor can we account for changing emphases. What we can be sure of is that they are extremely prevalent among the peoples who form the subject of our study, and that wherever they exist they have very considerable, even extreme, importance.

Their significance from points of view other than the purely economic must be briefly indicated. Natives' statements vary greatly. One writer may report that they are regarded by the people performing them as essentially fertility rites. Another that they are for the purpose of strengthening the young people. Hunter records very clearly that the Pondo people state that the ceremonies must be performed for girls since otherwise sickness will come later. These same people, incidentally, scarcely perform them at all for boys. The true situation is, as usual, that the natives' own ideas help us only in the most limited ways. It is left to the anthropologist to discover the true function of the activities. He must relate them to the other activities of the people, to the social groups involved, and, above all, to the needs which must be satisfied if the society is to retain its integration.

In this case we may say that there is no *primary* need to be satisfied. A meal taken in common will satisfy the primary need of nutrition as well as a complex of social needs. In initiation ceremonies we shall assume that there is no corresponding primary need, but that they exist for the purpose of satisfying the no less pressing social necessities. In doing this, they draw upon economic resources just as definitely as if they were feeding and clothing the people. Indeed, the ceremonies do, as we shall see, help to regulate food and clothing and other material matters.

The social needs in terms of which puberty ceremonies must be evalued may be resumed as follows. They define and strengthen the group which carries them out. If on a tribal scale, they bring the tribe together, they provide an occasion on which the chief will exercise his authority; they enable him to levy taxes and perhaps to have his fields cultivated.

If the activities are carried out on a family scale, duties are defined and sentiments shaped; the father must provide the cattle that are needed at feasts, the mother has her contributions, and other friends and relatives play their part and thus help to build up a friendly feeling which will be of direct economic use in later life.

ECONOMICS OF INITIATION CEREMONIES

The ceremonies are not without their legal aspect, though this is never emphasized. They are really legal in the widest sense only, in that they emphasize mutual obligations. Artistic and recreational needs are well catered for; there are invariably special dances, feasts, and artistic creations. The supernatural aspect is always present, though there is little evidence that it is ever in the leading place. Some early missionaries speculated as to whether the ceremonies were a religious ritual, and we can well understand that at first sight they may appear to be so. Yet we must content ourselves by saying that a certain minimum religious element is always to be found. It may be that the initiates are regarded from that time onward as having souls, as being qualified, should they die, to take their place in the spirit world and so to influence the lives of the people on earth. On the other hand, the essence of Bantu religion is that the spirits which are worshipped are ancestor spirits, that is to say, spirits who became parents before they died. Since the puberty ceremonies certainly do not confer parenthood they cannot have this ultimate religious significance. Nevertheless, there is ample evidence that the spirits are never neglected.

The need for transmitting knowledge and traditions to young people figures much more largely in the initiation practices. They are, wherever found, educational in function. The initiates, whether boys or girls, are separated from the rest of the community for a time, whether some months or only a week or two. The Bavenda are the only people of whom it is recorded that they have a permanent school. During this seclusion, or separation, the young people are subjected to exercises and disciplines often of a very rigorous character, and they also learn dances and songs, and in many cases are lectured on the behaviour which, now that they are grown up, is expected of them. They are in a state of high emotional tension, and there can be no doubt that the instruction has a lasting effect. No matter how informal, or how non-intellectual it may be, it serves the supreme educational function of arousing the interest of the young people in the society into which they are to go out with full adult responsibilities. They go into the school children, and come out adults. If we were asked to state one principal purpose of the initiation routine we should have to say that it is educational.

The economic aspect, that is to say the aspect relating to the need to create, to administer, and to consume economic resources, is one which has escaped practically every writer on the African peoples. Several indeed have noted that the ceremonies are expensive to the people; many writers whose work is good in other respects have not even thought this fact worthy of mention. It remains for us to see that if these practices were removed, the economic life of the people would indeed be changed. We shall see that one of the motives for accumulating wealth would be removed; that its distribution would be affected; that the functioning of units, such as the tribe, would be changed in their economic aspect. The ceremonies are, among the people who practise them, really of extreme economic significance.

Beginning with the most definite point, the direct cost to the people concerned, we find definite evidence. Hunter tells us that in half the cases which came to her knowledge the women were not initiated until after their marriage. This is most unusual, and the reason is stated to be "the poverty, or parsimony, of the girl's father. It is not done because the father is poor. He waits for the cattle of the ikhazi" (bride-price). Here is economic choice in its purest form, together with the social pressures within which it must be exercised. The girl must be initiated; that is practically necessary. But the cost has to be met somehow, and it appears that in the changing economic conditions of modern times the father chooses, rather than to have the ceremony done with less expenditure of food and cattle, to wait until he receives the cattle due to him when his daughter marries. Hunter gives examples of the direct cost in animals killed to three families. These are but a part of the total cost. Grain also must be used for brewing on a large scale, while new clothes are provided, and much time is devoted to the activities, which would otherwise be used in producing useful things. We quote Hunter's list of animals killed:

ECONOMICS OF INITIATION CEREMONIES

1. *Kwa Soka.* 2 girls (unmarried) thombisa (rich umzi).
   Day of seclusion, 2 goats killed.
   Isibande, 2 pigs.
   Final killing (umgquzo), 2 beasts. Goat and sheep for amazibazana.
2. *Kwa Somponos.* 2 girls (rich umzi, royal blood).
   Day of seclusion, 6 fowls (by woman), 2 pigs.
   Isibande, 2 goats, 2 sheep.
   Umgquzo, 4 cattle. 1 sheep for amazibazana.
3. *Kwa Pethu.* 1 girl (rich umzi).
   Day of seclusion, 2 goats.
   Isibande, 2 sheep, 1 pig.
   Fourth day, 1 sheep.
   Umgquzo, 1 ox, 2 sheep.

Among the Kikuyu, we are told by Routledge, both marriage and death hold but a small place in the peoples' imagination compared to that greatest of all ceremonies whereby the boy becomes a man and the girl a woman. But the ceremony may be delayed for two or three years on account of the fees. Among the Bomvana a good season is followed by numerous initiation schools which last until nearly the end of the year. Vast quantities of beer are brewed and consumed; the boys' fathers may pay the enormous fee of three or four oxen. Among the Hehe, to go further north, it is reported that if girls are not initiated at the proper time, that is before puberty, heavy expenses for medicines will follow to overcome the super- natural consequences, so that the parents have good reasons to be willing to pay the fees.

Without collecting further instances, we may say that in every case the cost to the parents is so considerable that it is one of the major expenses to which they must look forward before their children join the adult community. They must meet it, or lose their position in society. They must plan ahead, tending animals and cultivating gardens, not so as to meet their primary needs for food and clothing, or to have a disposable surplus, but to have enough to meet this specific cultural requirement and others of a like nature.

What is the nature of the wealth involved in these practices, and to whom does it go? We must follow out the actual stages by which the puberty ceremonies distribute resources.

Varying greatly as one tribe does from another, we must take significant samples from such information as is open to us. Among the Bomvana, who perform the ceremony on a comparatively small scale, by districts, and whose schools rarely number more than twenty boys and sometimes only four, the process may be detailed as follows: the people co-operating build a special hut; this is built in one day's work, as so many African huts are, by the organized labour of all the men and women in the district which is to hold the school. The site of the hut is carefully chosen, being near the homestead of a wealthy man who is to look after the ceremonies. A miniature cattle kraal is then built. Then comes the first direct expense to the boys' fathers; they must kill a head of large or small stock, but poorer people may fail to do this. The initiation is not invalidated for them by their failure, they may send their son, nevertheless, but it is very clear that prestige, which counts for so much among these people, will make it most distasteful for them to omit the offering or even to make it a small one. The flesh of the offering is, of course, not wasted. Further, its skull is placed in a prominent position for future significance. Poor people, failing to show the skull, will have their poverty clearly marked.

Next, the wealthy man, already mentioned, chooses a victim from his herd; it is slaughtered, and the young men eat the roasted flesh. The circumcision is then performed, possibly in the miniature cattle kraal. The operator does not appear to be a professional man, but he may nevertheless acquire a reputation in that role and be asked to perform at many ceremonies. He will thus obtain payment for his work, though the form of the payment remains doubtful. The grain food for the boys for the next three weeks consists of old mealies, whose market value for any other purpose would be negligible, but which obviously must have been carefully saved, especially if preceding harvests were scanty, and in considerable quantities, for this occasion.

ECONOMICS OF INITIATION CEREMONIES

A special herd of cows is set aside to provide the boys with their milk, which they are likely to consume in large quantities as it is the main part of their diet. The herd consists of cattle contributed, about one from each, by the fathers of the boys. Since milk is a major element in everybody's diet, the strain upon the resources of the households must be something to be reckoned with. In a dry year, or in a year of cattle disease, both boys and their families must find their milk diet much reduced. The strain upon a family of sending one of its cattle to the initiation hut will be the more considerable if it has a baby at home. The abstracting of these cattle from the homesteads must necessitate considerable readjustment, even shortage. But a further direct expense is, in this connection, incurred by the wealthy man who supervises. He must provide a milk sac to be used by the boys. To do this he kills a goat or even, should the school be large and his resources plentiful, a head of cattle before the school begins. After the boys have recovered from the operation they are allowed to tend and milk their own cows, but for the three weeks previous to healing, this work has to be performed for them by other men, involving a definite amount of work.

Next, another goat is presented by the rich man, and the meat eaten by the boys. This has ceremonial significance, but will play its direct part in nutrition, both filling the stomachs and stimulating the spirits of the initiates.

In the old days the period spent in seclusion could be employed with some profit in hunting. Today, however, dancing is the main occupation, although the boys do tend their own cattle. Another factor to be reckoned with is that they have a certain licence to pilfer food from the people's gardens. It will always be impossible to estimate the extent of such depredations, but it is significant that in modern days, when needs press more heavily, they are discouraged.

The next, and by no means the lightest, item in this list of expenses is the large number of beer drinks given by the fathers of the boys. The fathers take it in turn to give really large beer parties which are attended by everybody in the district. They are the occasions of competitive dancing by the boys.

Some idea of the amount of produce and labour involved may be derived from the fact that each single feast must be big enough to accommodate visitors not only from the district which is co-operating for one ceremony, but from all parts of the neighbourhood. Beer occupies a high place in the Bantu scale of values; it involves an enormous amount of work on the part of the women, who already are not idle; it requires a large supply of valuable grain; and, correspondingly, it gives very great satisfactions. The circulation of this article of wealth among the Bomvana on these occasions must be really large. The father of each boy provides a feast big enough to be attended by anybody within reach, at a time when many people make it their business to travel long and far in order to attend these feasts and to share the appreciation of the dancing.

Not only is a large consumption of resources involved; a whole complex of satisfactions is yielded. The feasts may be given only by men who have sons at the school; thus their distinction is emphasized, and the preparation of a really creditable feast will test the economic adeptness as well as resources of the man and his wife or wives. They may dispose of beasts to obtain grain for brewing; they are sure to have cultivated extra fields [1] for the same purpose. It is on such occasions that they will test all their connections with relatives and neighbours, and the wife who is popular in the district will receive much valuable help which would be denied to a less capable manager. The man, likewise, begs and borrows on such occasions. His personal credit as a man of energy, able to manage things, is put to the test. To such a man much will be lent and given both in the way of help and materials, because it is known that he is the sort who will gladly return the services at a future time. The emotional interest in plenty, the prestige to be obtained from good economic management, never fails to be emphasized on such occasions.

Ornaments must not be forgotten, though there is no indication that they are of great value. Another way in which

[1] Not specifically, but simply more ground than would otherwise have been cultivated.

wealth circulates on a small scale is through the presentation of tobacco to the dancing boys as rewards from the onlookers. This tobacco is passed on to older men who are looking after the boys and devoting much time to the occupation. It, together with their share of the feasting, constitutes these men's payment for a very real service. A further part of their payment consists of new dishes which they receive from the mothers of the boys, who, together with them, make presents of bottles of brandy to their husbands. In this way the mothers also make public the fact that their sons are passing through the ceremonies. Further, the women must provide themselves with new skin skirts, as well as ornamental parts of clothing. A new skin skirt means that at least one beast has been taken from the herd.

The whole ceremonies may last some seven or eight months, the time depending entirely upon the resources of the community; a shortage of food, beer, and meat means a dampening of spirits, an unfortunate ceremony that people will look back on with disappointment.

As the ceremonies come to an end further definite rites are performed, and in some ways the most significant. The boys race each other to the nearest river, they wash off the paint which was part of their regalia; their old cloths are burnt together with the special initiation hut; on no account must they look back upon this hut while it is burning and they are leaving it. These parts of the ceremony are encountered in every part of Bantu Africa wherever the ceremonies are held at all. They mark the final casting off of youthful things and the start of manhood. But the new stage in life requires its capital equipment. As boys they possessed exceedingly little. As men they must have the wherewithal to face their responsibilities and must have the beginnings of the property which it will be their life's work to manage. Hence they are presented with the necessary wealth; it is now that they first own their own cattle, sheep and goats, as well as other objects symbolic of manhood such as spears. Thus they make their start in life.

It is impossible to make a survey of the cost of initiation ceremonies among every tribe known to us. These samples must suffice. The amount of resources involved obviously varies greatly from one people to another, but the two examples which we have given, the Pondo, as reported by Hunter, and the Bomvana, as reported by Cook, serve to give some idea of what happens. There is no indication that these are among the tribes which lay greatest stress on the ceremonies.

Having the foregoing description in mind, we may see how the tribesmen fit these large ceremonies into their economic year, and into their periods of scarcity and plenty. With regard to the year, they are always held after one of the main harvests and during a period when comparatively little work can be done. There is thus plenty of grain as well as plenty of time. With regard to the alternation of scarcity and plenty, it must be noted that practically no people hold the ceremonies every year, or even every so many years. When they involve only single families, with a mere handful of initiates, the resources of these families will be taken into account when the time for performing the ceremonies is decided upon. When the activity is held upon a tribal scale, the decision as to the time for the next occasion is definitely taken by the chief, or by some other authority. It is thus possible to announce a forthcoming ceremony when it is known that crops are to be good and grass green. Once again we see how the vital interest in plenty is reinforced by its expression in these organized activities. The people have every motive to work, and to husband their resources.

Nor must it be forgotten that a very large proportion of the wealth of Bantu communities is human. One of the main ways in which the people can see their wealth increase is in growing numbers of productive citizens. And the ceremonies mark and celebrate the reaching of full economic maturity by numbers of young people.

In certain cases initiation ceremonies are held upon a very considerable tribal scale. The clearest examples to hand are perhaps those of the Bavenda and of the Thonga. In such cases the chief plays a commanding part, the ceremonies seldom taking place, indeed, unless he has a son of his own who will lead the school. This son will be the first to be operated upon, and at all stages his importance will be emphasized. Should he be an actual heir to the chieftainship, the leading medical men of the community will be mobilized to attend.

Among the Bavenda there is a permanent initiation school, the only one which has come to our notice. It is reported by Stayt to be mainly a military institution; the actual ceremonies, however, are held periodically in accordance with the principles already described. The significance of the ceremonies as a means of enforcing the chief's authority and, above all, his economic position is indicated by the fact that nowadays, with military training losing its virtue, the schools are mainly a means whereby the chief obtains labour for the cultivation of certain of his fields, while so far have the schools adapted themselves to modern conditions that boys not wishing to work can make money payments instead. An additional source of revenue to the chief is found through parents of younger boys being willing to pay an ox to have their sons initiated, despite their youth, at a given ceremony rather than to wait until the next one. This also indicates something of the attitude of the parents. The ox is paid "to make the little boy big". The ceremonies require the attendance at the chief's residence, which is the capital of the Venda country, of very great numbers of people. Not only is it an occasion on which the chief augments his revenues, conferring adult status in return for remuneration; it is also an occasion upon which the wealth of the whole country is mobilized in a more or less effective manner. It is one of the occasions upon which it is emphasized that the whole country is an economic area of exchange.

Tempting as it would be to continue to review the economic significance of the organized activity of puberty rites, we must be content with the foregoing as having indicated their essential economic significance. When the rites are held at the capital of a chief they constitute an effective regulation of the economic life of the whole people. All, throughout the whole territory, must produce sufficient of the right things to enable them to play their part. They must also regulate the consumption of their resources, possibly for years, in anticipation of the initiation of one of their children. Not only must they produce and conserve these resources; they must have them ready at a particular time in order to meet the demands of tribal life. The very fact that they must take supplies of the various resources to the capital gives in the first place a valuable publicity which amounts to praise of the successful ones and disapproval of the unsuccessful; in the second place, a redistribution is involved. Not only are substantial transfers made to the chief; payments are made to other officials, to medical men, to operators, to attendants. The ceremonies are often a substantial source of income to such people, and, though we lack definite information on the point, we should guess that the ceremonies are often a mainstay of the medical profession. Many other activities are involved. Some are wholly economic in nature. An approaching ceremony creates a large demand for metal goods, for clothing, and for ornaments, as well as for accommodation as the capital.

The ceremonies may constitute the biggest single demand for the products of the iron industry. Spears, knives, metal beads must, among many tribes, be produced in large quantities. They are paid for either in grain or in small stock. Thus, were it not for these ceremonies, the iron industry would be much smaller, just as, almost certainly, the medical profession would be much smaller. Being small it would be less efficient. The skill which is developed in response to the demand created by the ceremonies calls men into the profession (for smithing is always a profession among the Bantu) who are available to make more utilitarian instruments at all other times. In studying these ceremonies we delve, so far as is humanly possible, to the very roots of demand. The organized activities fashion the sentiments of the people; the sentiments control their values; the values cause them to produce what they do produce and to dispose of their whole resources in the ways dictated by culture. Such ceremonies contribute only indirectly to the satisfaction of the primary needs for food, clothing, warmth, and the others. They arise definitely out of cultural needs, and being thus brought into existence, give tone and direction to the whole economic life.

ECONOMICS OF INITIATION CEREMONIES

REFERENCES AND FURTHER READING

Customs Governing Beer-Drinking among the Ama-Bomvana (Art.). C. S. Davies. South African Journal of Science, 1927.

Transition from Childhood to Adulthood among the Zulus (Art.). G. W. K. Mahlobo and E. J. Krige. Bantu Studies, 1934.

The Social Significance of Beer among the Balopedu (Art.). E. J. Krige. Bantu Studies, 1932.

The Circumcision Ceremonies in Fingoland (Art.). F. Brownlee. Bantu Studies, 1927-29.

Venda History.

Transvaal Ndebele Texts. N. J. v. Warmelo. Department of Native Affairs, Union of South Africa Ethnological Publications, Vol. 1. 1930.

Travels in Caffraria. Kay. 1833.

History of the Basuto. Ellenberger and MacGregor. 1912.

The Akamba. C. W. Hobley. 1910.

The Masai. A. C. Hollis. 1905.

Bantu Beliefs and Magic. C. W. Hobley. 1922.

Kaffir Laws and Customs. J. MacLean (ed.). 1858.

The Akamba. G. Lindblom. 1920.

The Ama-Xosa. J. H. Soga. 1931.

The Bomvana. P. A. W. Cook.

The Social System of the Zulus. E. J. Krige. 1936.

Valenge Women. E. D. Earthy. 1933.

In Witch-Bound Africa. F. H. Melland. 1923.

Among the Bantu Nomads. J. T. Brown. 1926.

The Baganda. Rev. J. Roscoe. 1911.

An African People in the Twentieth Century. L. P. Mair. 1934.

Hunger and Work in a Savage Tribe. A. I. Richards. 1931.

The Life of a South African Tribe. H. A. Junod. 1927.

The Illa-Speaking Peoples of Northern Rhodesia. Smith and Dale. 1920.

The Bavenda. H. A. Stayt. 1931.

Ubena of the Rivers. A. T. and G. M. Culwick.

The Essential Kafir. D. Kidd. 1925.

Anthropology in Action. Brown and Hutt. 1935.

With a Prehistoric People. W. S. and K. Routledge. 1910.

Reaction to Conquest. M. Hunter. 1937.

CHAPTER IX

ECONOMICS OF MARRIAGE

THE Bantu boy and girl are well provided with motives both for developing their productive efficiency and for sharpening their appreciation of economic valuations.

From almost incredibly early years, they find that prestige and credit come from skill in herding the animals or in filling the granary. Almost as early, they learn that wealth is exchanged, that resources, by some means quite outside their understanding, have values attached to them, and that satisfactions are derived from exchanging things according to these values.

At an equally early period of life they learn the next great economic lesson, that they do not merely produce and exchange in a continuous stream throughout their lives, making a deal or bargaining for a purchase whenever they think fit, but that there are certain great occasions for which they have to provide, for which they may prepare for years or see their parents prepare; that when these occasions come, they, the children, must be ready with the necessary qualifications, since otherwise they will be found lacking by their fellow-men. Initiation is one of these great occasions; marriage is the next. It is dangerous to think of Bantu life as being made up of a series of jumps from one ceremony to another. The ceremonial approach has been much overdone in anthropological literature, but marriage is much more than a ceremony. Not only is it the foundation of the family; it is also, in itself, an activity which may be prepared for for many years and which is made the occasion for very large exchange and consumption of resources.

Just as wealth is manipulated in Western societies by free investment in productive enterprises, so it is used among the

Bantu to carry out activities which result in the organization of such units as the family, which then become the really important economic units. The greatest possibility of increasing wealth among any non-Western people lies in natural fertility. If the soil and the seasons are good, the people have plenty. But not less important is human fertility. Children are among the greatest economic resources. An African community which failed to produce a steady supply of new members would regard itself as in the direst straits, as in fact it would be. It is only by having plenty of children that the parents are assisted in many ways, that they have an insurance against old age, that they can maintain or increase the yield of the soil. Not only would utilitarian resources of food be lost; the most prized objects of value, likewise, would disappear. Much has been written of how an African values his cattle; even more could be written of how he values the circle of huts, the growing family around him, symbolizing the things which he most desires from life.

This human fertility is connected in the most direct ways with the reproductive functions. A child, boy or girl, is an asset to the community in an ultimate way because he or she will beget others. Sexual life is therefore stressed and regulated, and the economic aspect of this is always of the utmost significance. Presents are exchanged even in the earliest sex play. When the first temporary unions are formed, resources change hands on a larger scale. In some tribes a man may mark out for future marriage a tiny girl, and the essence of his doing so is that he makes presents to her parents, helping to rear her. Among most tribes, wealth changes hands again should the temporary union result in a child born without legal sanction; this will take the form either of a fine or of a proper marriage payment. When marriage itself is to be accomplished there is practically invariably an exchange of valued objects, sometimes on an enormous scale. When children are born, further gifts are made. These gifts may continue for many years. At every stage it is emphasized, not only that the sex functions are one of the chief means of adding to the resources of the community, but that they are

127

the occasion for the mobilizing and transferring of wealth, and that the direct economic sanction is the most effective way of securing their proper regulation.

The absolute amount of wealth changing hands at marriage varies enormously from one people to another. But in every single people, so far as we can see, marriage and its correlated activities are the occasions for the biggest economic transactions known to the people. Malinowski has shown how among the Trobriand Islanders the economic activities controlling most resources, whether in the form of foodstuffs or of sentimentally valued objects, take place not only in connection with barter or trade, but as adjuncts to marriage and as the subject of ceremonial exchange. We can clearly see something of the same in Bantu society. Trade may be at the lowest minimum, only tiny surpluses may enter into it; the amassing of wealth simply and directly for utilitarian purposes may be very small. But great exchange of wealth there is, and it takes place in connection with such organized activities as initiation, marriage, first-fruits ceremonies, funerals and a series of others. All of these may have extreme economic significance, but marriage is the one which leads to the establishment of the most prevalent, most active economic unit.

To arrive at any understanding of the significance of gift exchange, whether in connection with marriage or any other activity, it is advisable first to analyse this mode of manipulating resources, which is, indeed, not unknown in Western communities, but is of such limited significance among them as to have received practically no mention in any economic writings. In non-Western communities its importance must at once be realized. In its essence it consists of resources given from one person to another, generally on prescribed occasions, and for an equivalent which we shall find to be very real but which is given in ways so roundabout that we should miss many important features if we attempted to reduce it to any terms of trade or barter. There may be no direct return of equal value to the person making the gift. In the Trobriands a man contributes largely, from every harvest, to the support of the household of a married sister. Gifts are made in acknowledgment, but merely as a kind of receipt. The real return to the man comes from his own household, in turn, being largely supported by a brother of *his* wife. So a great part of the economic resources of the Trobriands is manipulated in a kind of endless, or circular, exchange. The labour involved in transporting the food is considerable, but it is cheerfully undertaken. It is extremely difficult to find the characteristics of bargaining in this exchange. Rather is it true to say that a man strives to give as much as possible to his sister's household in much the same way that a man in England may try to support his family in the most substantial style.

At first sight it seems that this food exchange among these South Sea Islanders is indeed little but a waste of effort; that each man could better support his own family without the labour of carrying food to that of his sister. On close inspection we see that the practice has real economic value for the people of that culture. It widens the economic circle of exchange. The sister will probably live in a different district, and if one district suffers bad crops it will be relieved through drawing its food supplies from a very wide area, from every village from which any man has taken a wife. There are other considerations of this kind which we need not enumerate here, but there is something else. The exchanging is, in itself, a valued activity. To use a crude terminology, the people would pay to be allowed to do it. It satisfies a whole set of social values which give them self-respect and supply the motives for really good agriculture. Thus the manipulation of resources conforms to no definition of trade, yet is one of the main ways in which certain communities arrive at economic equilibrium.

This digression upon Malinowski's findings will help us to arrive at an understanding of the much discussed bride-price, bride-wealth, marriage transfer, or dowry, call it what we will, of the Bantu peoples. Bride-price, it must be emphasized, is not a social fact which stands by itself. It is often on a par with gifts at love-making, and it is inseparable from other payments made, or gifts given, perhaps long after marriage.

We are here deliberately abstracting it from its setting because it seems to us the best way to see certain of its characteristics.

Bride-price among the Bantu consists of an amount of resources, which may be cattle, or almost anything else, transferred in the direction opposite to that taken by dowry in European society. The goods go from the groom to, in the first instance, the father or brother of the bride. No practice among any African people has been discussed at such length or with, on the whole, such thoroughness and penetration. It is now finally established that this transfer of goods is the main legalizing act of Bantu marriage, giving legitimacy to the children and ensuring permanence, or a reasonable duration, to the marriage. As a legal act it may now be taken as definitely explained. The depth of its roots in Bantu society is also nowadays well appreciated, though perhaps not so thoroughly explained. Its persistence is such that even missionary societies, which for many years fought against it as a "sale" of the bride, now almost universally accept it, while some even enforce it in marriages among their converts. But its significance, its true correlation with other aspects of Bantu life, is open to further exploration. We shall find that only by understanding the full nature of African economic life can we properly evaluate this practice.

Every writer on the Bantu for many years has probed into the significance of bride-price, and there has resulted an economic explanation which is certainly that given by the people themselves, but which we shall find to be very little more satisfactory than native explanations of their own customs generally are. It is said that bride-price is a compensation to the father for the trouble and expense of bringing up the girl. This explanation is very widely reported, if not adopted, in the literature of Africa. It is based upon certain very solid grounds. With few exceptions the girl, in a Bantu marriage, leaves her father's house. His establishment is diminished. His supply of food will be less. To make good the loss, so runs the explanation, he must receive cattle or other valuable consideration. We may well believe that the people's own feelings, in so far as they can be expressed, take this form. Yet on closer analysis it seems to contain its own refutation. It is doubtful whether it ever is an expense to rear a girl. In losing her the family loses a valuable producer. That is to say, she has been earning her keep, and possibly something more, for a considerable time before marriage. If her father is indeed losing an asset, as we think he is, he may require compensation. But this is not compatible with the compensation being for the "expense of rearing the girl". We shall not be far wrong, if we say that that expense has been fully balanced by her work alone, not to mention the emotional satisfaction which her presence has brought to her father. In all probability her work alone, without the less tangible consideration, has paid for her keep, for, as we shall see in another place, a young girl performs extremely valuable services from a very early age. When we hear of a father in Uganda exclaiming "Do you rear girls for nothing in England?" we see him either as a greedy individual or as a man in semi-Europeanized community in which his daughters may begin to lead an entirely different life.[1] We should say that in the true Bantu culture, which is today a living force, economic reciprocity between children and their parents is just as definite as that between man and wife. That is not to say that it is perfect, but that the principle of economic balance does apply; the parents render services to the child and the child reciprocates. Her father is thus to be "compensated" not for his trouble and expense on rearing the girl, but on account of his losing a valuable member of his household.

But this idea also fails to carry weight; cattle received for the girl will soon pass on, in the great majority of cases, to acquire wives for the man's sons or for himself. The acquisition of these women is certainly the true compensation, and could take place just as definitely without the cattle transaction. We thus see bride-price as a transaction over and above the exchange of wives at marriage, as something which accompanies that exchange, but in no way alters its nature or affects its balance from the point of view of the community. It cannot be explained as compensation. How is it to be explained?

[1] Or, simply as giving a conventional explanation of his own people's customs.

The answer must be found in the need of the community for definite motives impelling it to produce, to muster, to count, and publicize its objects of wealth.

Of no less importance is the need to measure one kind of economic resource against another; it would be ridiculous to suggest that a Bantu man ever deliberately decides to exchange the grain-producing power of a daughter for the cattle, hoes, or iron rings that she may bring. Yet it would be equally futile to fail to observe that the man will be keenly aware that he is making such an exchange, at least until the goods are passed on to bring another wife into his homestead.

The problem of the roots of value once again bars our path. The cattle and other objects are objects of value; yet, apparently, they exist in the last resort only to be exchanged against each other. This is especially obvious in the case of iron and brass rings, ceremonial and quite useless hoes, ritual spears, and many other objects which have from time to time been used in this gift exchange. It is no less real, however, in the case of cattle and other stock. These animals may be said to have two distinct sources of value. They have their utilitarian value and their intrinsic or purely social value corresponding to that of the inanimate payments. Although these two values merge, as when cattle give extra prestige through being turned into highly valued food, they are really distinct, and our conclusion is that it is overwhelmingly on account of their social value that they are used in the marriage exchange. This social value, of the non-utilitarian type, can be explained only as a function of all other aspects of Bantu culture. It cannot be said to arise out of the fact that the objects are valued because they are used in the marriage transaction. It is equally true that they are used in that transaction because they are valued. The core of fact remaining is that Bantu life has such objects as an integral part of its very being.. The sentiments of children cluster around such things; they work in order to acquire them; they behave well so that their elders, as a reward, may present them with some of them. In adult life the people who own them derive deep satisfaction from doing so, and this satisfaction alone gives them the nature of wealth.

ECONOMICS OF MARRIAGE

It becomes one of the objects of life to possess such things, to enjoy the triumph of acquiring them, to bask in their ownership, to establish real power and prestige by being able to give them, and, in general, to enjoy the constant exercise of valuing and handling them. The utilitarian aspect is often present, as when a chief can acquire a good following through his power over this type of wealth. But to attempt to describe their functions on a utilitarian basis alone would give us a seriously defective treatment.

It is not surprising that the handling of these valued things is correlated at every stage with the main activities of the people. Two men do not meet and decide to exchange some of their cattle against each other for the fun of the thing. Nor do they have a circular exchange of the Kula type, although the result is much the same. They conduct the exchange, always, on the occasions which punctuate and integrate the life of the community. In this way they lend an extra interest and thus a powerful sanction to these vital activities. Whether the cattle, the rings, the other objects, are exchanged, as at marriages, or distributed in other ways as at initiations and funerals, the result is the same. The handling of the wealth is correlated with the vital activities.

The fact that people are definitely expected to muster and exchange valued objects on the occasion of a marriage is the means whereby the Bantu culture achieves a deeper relevance for that fundamental activity. Marriage is at the very root of the family. The family is the fundamental economic unit of Bantu life. The production and consumption of a vast proportion of the people's utilitarian resources are carried on within its limits. Economic choices as to the disposal of limited resources are made, as will be abundantly made clear, in conformity with the day-to-day working of this unit. Were marriage to lose any of its vitality, the family could scarcely continue to function unimpeded. Since the circulation of valued objects reinforces the whole structure of marriage, it also acts as a guarantee of the effective functioning of the family and therefore of the economic life of the people.

The value of non-utilitarian articles to the community as a

whole is thus defined. They do not feed or clothe the people, but they do make the society function and thus make possible the feeding and clothing of its members. Next we turn to the significance of the fact that these objects are invariably owned by groups of individuals. Seen from this angle they have two distinct uses. They give satisfactions in themselves, and, if only as a last resort, they may be exchanged for the necessities of life. Insignificant though exchange may be in any given area, there always remains the fact that the person with control of resources, of whatever nature, can exchange them, in case of need, for other things. The man with animals, with brass rings, with non-utilitarian hoes or spears, can buy the services of the doctor, of the priest, of poor people to labour for him, and, should famine occur, he may kill and eat his cattle or purchase grain from another part of the country. It is not surprising therefore that these objects supply a motivation for the activities of the individuals throughout life.

From the earliest years of his life, the boy learns that cattle will be needed for his marriage. He learns how they will be acquired. It is deeply impressed upon him that herds grow from careful tending, and even as he practises upon the goats his interests become shaped in such a way as to produce the skill of the herdsman. He is often rewarded in little ways for his industry. As he grows he sees cattle being taken from the herd and others being added to it. He learns that this is because his elder relatives are marrying. He develops a keen sense of the increase or the diminution of the herd. It becomes part of his consciousness that when his turn comes to marry he will need to have cattle in one way or another. He finds that these will be the more readily forthcoming if he stands high in the estimation of his father and others of his father's age. A Bantu boy cannot marry until either he has cattle of his own, or he has the confidence of his elders so that they will supply him in order to make him a full-fledged married member of the group. The difficulty of obtaining cattle for his first marriage is often real and is directly correlated with the relatively late marrying age of Bantu men. Thus the marriage gift-exchange provides the most direct incentive to the industry and general good behaviour of the boy throughout long years before the actual realization of his marriage. No less important, it defines his whole status, in an economic sense, within his community.

The same set of circumstances operate with no less force in the case of the girl. She is soon to realize the pride of a woman for whom much wealth is given. Her interests are aroused, and as she masters the many tasks of her daily life she becomes more and more aware of the cattle which will be given for her, possibly at a very early age, and which will entitle her to pride at her marriage and to a good social status long afterward.

Within a community which has not yet achieved the refinements of exchange contingent upon the efficient transport system of the Western world, the territorial circle of exchange is a matter of fundamental importance. Suppose that this circle is small, that it embraces merely the lands and property of one large family, such as a man, his wives, and two or three married sons with their wives. Suppose that this family simply rears its own animals, cultivates its own fields, and cherishes its own objects of wealth. At first sight it might appear that it would be just as well off as if it were carrying on the exchange of cattle and other valued things which we have seen to take place at marriage. It might even appear that it would be better off through avoiding the labour entailed in these exchanges. This appearance, however, would be entirely deceptive. The marriage exchange means that cattle and the other things are kept moving. Usually a man will marry a girl who lives within calling distance, but that may well be a few miles. The cattle move to the girl's village and may be used by one of her brothers to obtain a wife from yet another village, and so on without limit.

According to the psychology which very definitely underlies the transaction, the boy's people, who give the cattle, have pleasure in giving lavishly just as clearly as the girl's people have in receiving a substantial number. Thus when a marriage takes place between two districts, a definite redistribution of resources will occur, should one of the districts be thriving less well than the other. A district which is unfortunate, which has been struck by drought, or whose grass has failed to come as plentifully as before, will benefit from the exchange. If one of its girls is to be married, the cattle received for her will be a greater boon on account of the local shortage. They will often be the very greatest of boons in that their milk will keep alive babies which otherwise would have died. When the less fortunate district is acquiring a wife, there is ample evidence that the people of the girl will modify their demands to meet the circumstances. This may be an absolute modification, or, more often, a well-understood system of credit will be brought into play. The boy will acquire his wife in return for a minimum of cattle on the understanding that he will give more when he is able, or even that he will pledge the cattle to be received when his first daughter marries, many years later. The interdependence of districts is emphasized. From a Western point of view it might be more economic for the fortunate districts to go ahead and for the others to work and wait for recovery to depopulate. But in terms of Bantu life security takes on a much higher value. The enlarged circle of exchange provides benefits which become more apparent as we see more of the structure of the society.

A further effect of the marriage exchange is that emphasized by Smith and Dale and apparent from many other parts of Bantu Africa. Whether or not there is haggling over the amount depends very largely upon the district and the people. In one district it may be good form to bargain and even to browbeat; in another there may be a dignified statement by the girl's father and a strong effort on the boy's side to meet his requests; in yet another tribe the amounts may be so fixed by custom as to leave but little room for discussion. One thing, however, is certain; there will frequently be outstanding claims between the parties for past exchanges; there will often be set in motion a further stream of payments from the man to his father-in-law which may go on for years; and in a great many cases there will be other outstanding balances between the parties in respect of ordinary loans and services advanced in ways of life quite unconnected with marriage. The marriage transaction is the occasion for the raking up and discussing of all such claims. It serves as a "clearing house".

In Bantu culture the existence of some such occasion is of extreme importance. Goods and services are constantly being given and received; indeed we shall find that the many ways in which this happens run through the whole structure of Bantu society and that it is a main feature of its economic life. In the absence of writing, obligations have to be remembered, and witnesses and publicity are all-important. The considerable complexity of the debts contracted and of the services rendered provide one of the main puzzles of European administrators. While men often go visiting in order to collect their own debts, these individual dealings have but a limited function. The need for general discussions at which memories can be refreshed and witnesses consulted is great, but it is difficult to imagine that any Bantu tribe could deliberately arrange large-scale discussions for this purpose. The bride-price discussion provides the occasion. As is usual in Bantu life, as in any other life, needs are satisfied in clusters. The marriage transfer of wealth can be said to have, primarily, a legal purpose. But it satisfies many other needs, among them a whole set of economic needs, and not least among these is that for balancing accounts within the whole circle of exchange.

We thus see that although the marriage gift-exchange has its primary function definitely marked, it satisfies many other needs of which we have singled out and stressed the economic. The manipulation of wealth in this connection stands out from that involved in initiation, first-fruits, funerals and other organized activities, in that it does not involve the consumption of the main item of the wealth. It is simply exchanged, and this fact re-emphasizes all of the arguments which apply to the other activities. We are once again brought to realize that the administration of resources, from the Transkei to Uganda, depends upon personal choice which operates within the framework of organized culture. These two aspects are equally real. The culture provides the means whereby continued motivation exists. The individual may have but the haziest idea that he is making an elaborate series of choices as to the disposal of his resources, including the provision of capital resources which will enable his society to continue its life in future generations. But he is making the choices, and culture, through its own mechanisms, sees that he does so.

Other features of Bantu marriage are the exchanging of many other gifts in addition to the specific one which we have discussed, and the setting up of further streams of gifts, notably those from the son-in-law to his father-in-law as the latter comes to need help or to be in a position to demand it. Gifts take place from the first betrothal, or in mere infantile sex play. They always define the activity just as they do marriage itself. Once the marriage has been concluded, a continuous economic co-operation is set in motion between the two families which are thus united. More especially, the son-in-law by strict custom must help his father-in-law, and in addition, as we have seen, may continue to pay instalments of the bridal exchange.

One extremely important aspect remains to be mentioned. The Bantu family is essentially a polygynous one. The man who is economically successful is the one who has several wives who co-operate with him as one economic unit. The polygynous family has many economic advantages over that of one man and one wife. These will appear later in this book. In the meantime, it remains to say that marriage is the main culturally prescribed form of investment in Bantu society. By investing in additional wives the man acquires an economically superior establishment. But some means would always have to exist whereby certain men, and not others, would be able to acquire this. The resources necessary for each marriage provide the test. If a man succeeds economically, he has resources to invest. In other cultures he would have other activities open to him. In Bantu culture he is directed in one specific way. His surplus resources are likely to bring an excellent return if they are expended upon another wife. Thus we see the marriage transaction, in addition to all its other economic effects, guiding the investments of the community into the formation of economic units of optimum size. We see the activity of marriage, with its transfer of wealth, guiding the whole economic life of the individual, of his or her group, and thus we find it to be explicable in economic terms even though the economic is not its primary function.

REFERENCES AND FURTHER READING

Question in the Native Customs Examinations, 1923. E. G. Howman. Nada, 1931.

The Concluding Rites of Marriage (Art.). C. S. Davies. Nada, 1933.

The Importance of the Sib in the Marriage Ceremonies of the South Eastern Bantu (Art.). A. W. Hoernle. South African Journal of Science, 1925.

Bride-Wealth in Balobedu Marriage Ceremonies (Art.). Krige. Bantu Studies, 1934.

Some Customs Arising out of Bantu Marriage (Art.). B. H. Dicke. South African Journal of Science, 1930.

The Akamba. C. W. Hobley. 1910.

The Masai. A. C. Hollis. 1905.

Among the Zulus. D. Leslie. 1875.

The Ama-Xosa. J. H. Soga. 1931.

The Bomvana. P. A. W. Cook.

Among the Bantu Nomads. J. T. Brown. 1926.

The Baganda. Rev. J. Roscoe. 1911.

An African People in the Twentieth Century. L. P. Mair. 1934.

The Life of a South African Tribe. H. A. Junod. 1927.

The Ila-Speaking Peoples of Northern Rhodesia. Smith and Dale. 1920.

The Bavenda. H. A. Stayt. 1931.

Ubena of the Rivers. A. T. and G. M. Culwick.

Anthropology in Action. Brown and Hutt. 1935.

With a Prehistoric People. W. S. and K. Routledge. 1910.

Reaction to Conquest. M. Hunter. 1937.

CHAPTER X

THE ECONOMICS OF SOCIAL UNITS

SECTION I

The Family as an Economic Unit

So far we have written of organized activities. Now we come to deal with the social units through which these and other activities are carried out. By far the most important social unit is the polygynous family. We shall find that this organization far transcends the functions of procreation and the rearing of children, though these are at its basis, and becomes an economic unit, the circle within which, or by which, economic equilibrium is sought throughout Bantu society.

Our starting point may be the individual man or woman making choices as to how much of his or her labour shall be devoted to one occupation or another, or shall be reserved for enjoyment in leisure. No matter how definite the social setting of that individual may be, he or she may be skilful or clumsy in managing this economic problem. But these individual differences tend to cancel out. Society as a functioning whole requires its members to work within its frame. Hence we arrive next at the family as the most intimate and pervading unit. At once great differences become visible between the Bantu type of family and that to which we are accustomed in the Western world. In England or America we think of the family as a unit within which the housewife decides as to the disposal of her available resources, and which, largely on the basis of the results which she achieves, brings children to adult status and launches them into the world where they may found other families. The Bantu family has its primary function of raising children to adulthood. But it does much more. It is also the unit within which economic resources are brought into

existence. It is the unit within which Bantu men and women
find their life's employment. Within its circle the most fundamental economic choices are made, while when it co-operates
with other families it remains very much the key organization.
It is within the circle of the family that grain is grown, that
flocks are tended, that the proceeds are allotted to various
members and to various uses. It is in co-operation between
families that such great manipulations of resources as the
bride-price takes place, that the family of a chief is maintained by others, that families connected by marriage maintain
economic intercourse with each other.

So all-pervading is the activity of the family in Bantu life
its functions will be fully described only in the whole course of
this whole book. It is in dealing with land-tenure, agriculture,
and similar subjects that we shall see in detail many of the
economic aspects of family life. At the present stage we try
to indicate the main structure of the family so that we may
later on have a better appreciation of its many activities.

Bantu family life is essentially polygynous, patrilocal, and on
the basis of a group larger than the mere initial group of father,
mother and children. To deal first with this last characteristic,
it is rare indeed, if not unknown, to find a father and mother
with their children living alone in any part of Bantu Africa.
Wherever this is found it will be the clearest sign that these
people are Christianized and have abandoned their old ways of
life. Under changing circumstances the size of the group
living together tends to decline, and nowadays it may be
common to have four primary families living in one homestead, as in Pondoland, whereas formerly twenty would have
been a normal number. We shall not, at present, examine the
changing nature of kinship obligations which is responsible for
this change in the size of the group. It is enough for our purpose that when we speak of family we mean family in a wide
sense, as including perhaps a man and wife and two or three
of their married sons, together with a married brother of the
man, who himself may have grown-up sons living in the group.
The man at the head of this family will very probably have
more than one wife, unless one or more has died. His sons

will have probably only one wife each, since when they are able to have more they will, nowadays, tend to leave their father's household and to set up establishments of their own. By doing so they will not sever all connections unless they happen to go very far away. Their families may continue very close co-operation with the one which they have left, but the relationship will be modified by many practical factors.

The fact that the family is patrilocal is of great importance, as may have already appeared from the chapter on marriage. Girls leave home when they marry; thus they are much less important economically to their own families than are their brothers. It is when they join other families as wives that they achieve great economic significance. We shall see that married women retain fairly close and quite definite connections with their father's households, just as their husbands very probably continue to pay further cattle of the marriage exchange. It is through marriage that two families set up lasting economic relationships, but the fact that a wife is always "a stranger" in her husband's household is of fundamental economic importance.

To say, as we have said, that Bantu marriage is polygynous requires more explanation. It is often pointed out that in any polygynous society the majority of men, possibly the great majority, either have only one wife or are unmarried. It is frequently implied that monogamy is the really prevalent form, and that multiple marriage is some kind of extraneous development. This is further supported by the general statement that monogamy must be the normal form of marriage, since, in the long run, approximately equal numbers of male and female children must be born and survive.

In the present state of vital statistics we are often in some doubt as to whether equal numbers of boys and girls survive to reach adult status. Nothing is more certain than that the Bantu himself believes that there are, in his own society, more women than men. However this may be, Pitt-Rivers has shown that numerical equality is only one of the relevant factors and that what we may call the rate of circulation of the women is just as important. If it is the custom for girls to marry much earlier than men, this in itself may make the woman's married life perhaps twenty per cent. longer than that of the man. If, further, it is the custom for widows to be inherited and not to remain single, this also provides a means whereby many men can acquire second wives even if only in their old age. In addition to this, custom may provide that no girl who is physically sound will be unmarried after a comparatively early age, whereas a man may remain without a wife till considerably older. Custom does make these provisions to the full throughout Bantu society. Even if a man remains monogamous throughout his virile years, he will stand a good chance of inheriting a widow later, and it is by no means certain that she will be past her productive life, either as regards work in the fields or the bearing of children, for she may well have been taken to wife when she was but a girl by a man who was then past middle-age. The great majority of men who obtain several wives do so only gradually, and many years may elapse between the first and the second. Thus women who are taken as "little wives" normally become widows at an early age.

In view of these considerations it becomes clear that census reports showing the number of men with one wife and with more than one, give no true impression of the number of men who will be polygynous in the course of their lives. Thus if the figures show, for example, that fifty per cent. of the men at a given moment have only one wife, it is certain that a much higher percentage will be polygynists in the course of their lives. It is in this sense that Bantu society is essentially a polygynous one.

Further, we must ask whether polygyny is really an ideal which motivates the great mass of the people, or whether it is something unusual or belonging to one class only. It does belong to one class, that of the chiefs, in an especial way. A chief must have a number of wives. The economic effectiveness of his office depends upon them. But the practice is by no means limited to chiefs. It is the active ideal of every Bantu man. It is the measure of his worldly success and one of his main motives for economic efficiency. This is apparent from innumerable native statements and from evidence of all kinds. The circumstances in which a man achieves an extra marriage will be described later; in the meantime we must accept the fact that he does so whenever he can, and that any normal and industrious man has good prospects of becoming a polygynist.

There is another fact which makes polygyny yet more significant to our study. It is that even monogamists normally live in polygynous households. When a man takes his first wife, whom he probably obtains through the cattle of his father or an elder brother, he is extremely unlikely to leave his father's household. It is virtually unthinkable that a man with one wife should go and set up a homestead for himself. This would cut across the great working principle of Bantu life that the main social unit is the circle of huts, enclosing or sheltering the cattle kraal among the cattle-owning peoples, and embracing all those members of a family who continue their lives together. Thus even men with only one wife live in polygynous households. In these ways we see that the Bantu family is indeed based upon polygyny.

Sociologically it is not true that a polygynous family is merely a series of individual marriages. Each marriage is distinct. Each wife has her own hut. A man with two wives may be said to have contracted two marriages, each of which is as distinct as if it were monogamous. While this is true legally we shall find that, owing to the fact that a new social structure is created through the succession of marriages, vital economic differences are introduced. A new economic unit is created which could never exist under monogamy. To discuss Bantu economics as if monogamous marriage were at the basis of the society would be to employ a fruitless abstraction.

The Bantu family is the unit whose members have exceptionally close and probably lifelong exonomic relationships. There is usually a clear-cut division of functions between the men and the women, the men attending to the animals, to the obtaining and clearing of land, to the planning and building of the homestead, to the paying of tribute to the chief, and to a series of less important matters. The women are responsible for the actual cultivation of the soil, and in the main, for the sharing of food in the household. The head of each family, however, has a special function. He must co-ordinate the work of all the other members. It is this function which gives to him a distinctive economic responsibility and which gives to the polygynous household its specific economic character. Through it the household functions as a true economic unit. Each wife will have her own fields, but she will consult with her husband as to when cultivation is to start, how much land is to be cultivated in any given season, and as to what crops the various fields are to have. The man therefore focuses the work of all the women. We do not imply that the wives themselves would not share their work, but it is clear that the head of the household is an economic leader on whom special responsibility falls. With regard to flocks and herds, the man has a double duty. He must share out his total possessions of cattle, goats and sheep among the various wives, so that each one shall have enough, and not more than enough, at the expense of others for the needs of her own house. He has also to attend to the herding of the animals. He is responsible for finding pasture land, and for the work of the younger men and boys in taking the stock to the best land and tending them generally.

With regard to the disposal of resources, also, the man has a co-ordinating if not a final voice. Among the South-Eastern Bantu the main grain store is inside the cattle kraal, where no woman may go. The man is thus finally responsible for making the food last from one harvest to the next. Likewise, when any grain is to be sold, whether among the South-East peoples with their grain pits or among those further north with individual store-houses, the decision must be taken by the man in conjunction with that wife who is chiefly responsible for the grain. The working out of these principles will introduce many variations, but they can be said to exist with a surprising uniformity among all of the tribes within our view. It is clear that through their working the polygynous household has many economic advantages over any possible monogamous unit. A finer balance of utilities is achieved.

Looking at the Bantu family as a unit, from outside, we see that it functions in such ways as the following. It is the unit

K   145

to which a chief looks for his revenue, and in the old days it was the unit for "eating up"; it is the unit as regards land-tenure, both of arable and of grazing land; it is the unit which co-operates with others in such productive enterprises as building and sometimes field cultivation; it is also the unit which gives feasts, thus effecting a distribution of food over a large area. These activities are in addition to those of marriage-exchange, with its wide ramifications; to initiation ceremonies with their considerable effect upon the disposal of resources, and to other similar organized activities. Looked at from inside, the family organizes the growing and sharing of food; its members make such fundamental decisions as how much land shall be cultivated; they may well decide how much of their time is to be enjoyed as leisure; they make the extremely important decisions as to when valuable stock is to be killed.

REFERENCES AND FURTHER READING

The Kinship System of a Bantu Tribe (Art.). Rev. J. H. Seed. Nada, 1933.
Polygamy in Mende Country (Art.). K. H. Crosby. Africa, 1937.
Changing Conditions in Marital Relations and Parental Duties among Urbanised Natives (Art.). E. J. Krige. Africa, 1936.
The Black Woman (Art.). A. Sloan. Nada, 1923.
Zulu-Land. Rev. L. Grout. 1934.
Travels in Caffraria. Kay. 1933.
Story of My Mission in South-East Africa. W. Shaw. 1860.
History of the Basuto. Ellenberger and MacGregor. 1912.
Southern Africa. Flemming. 1856.
Travels in East Africa. J. L. Krapf. 1860.
The Akamba. C. W. Hobley. 1910.
The Masai. A. C. Hollis. 1905.
Kaffir Laws and Customs. J. MacLean (ed.). 1858.
Zulu-English Dictionary. Bryant.
The Akamba. G. Lindblom. 1920.
Western Civilisation and the Native of South Africa. I. Schapera (ed.). 1934.
The Ama-Xosa. J. H. Soga. 1931.
The Soul of the Bantu. W. C. Willoughby. 1928.
The Social System of the Zulus. E. J. Krige. 1936.
Among the Bantu Nomads. J. T. Brown. 1926.
The Religious System of the Amazula. Rev. Canon Callaway. 1870.

The Spirit-Ridden Konde. D. R. Mackenzie. 1925.
Hunger and Work in a Savage Tribe. A. I. Richards. 1932.
The Life of a South African Tribe. H. A. Junod. 1927.
The Ila-Speaking Peoples of Northern Rhodesia. Smith and Dale. 1920.
The Bavenda. H. A. Stayt. 1931.
Ubena of the Rivers. A. T. and G. M. Culwick.
Black and White in East Africa. R. C. and H. Thurnwald. 1935.
Anthropology in Action. Brown and Hutt. 1935.
With a Prehistoric People. W. S. and K. Routledge. 1910.
Reaction to Conquest. M. Hunter. 1937.

SECTION II

The Homestead

Specific organizations for economic purposes are not entirely lacking among the Bantu peoples, but for the most part the functioning groups are those which are to be discovered in any case. The neighbourhood, the age set, the tribe, the clan, the extended group of kindred, and, most important of all, the family; these are the main groupings of Bantu society; they function as legal, political, and religious as well as economic units. They are not specifically economic, but they are of the substance of economic life. Through them, individuals are organized for production and consumption; through them the people are guided in their main economic choices. The most ubiquitous, the most active, and the most uniform group throughout Bantu Africa is the family. Not only has the family a uniformity of structure, from Uganda to the Transkei: it has a character of its own, marking it off from family organization in almost any other part of the world.

Certain principles indicate the size which the homestead or family group is likely to attain. If it is too big it will be clumsy. There will be quarrels inside. The people will be too far from their fields. The headman will have difficulty in co-ordinating the efforts of all the men and women in his group. Thus, in the case of commoners it is seldom found that a homestead has a total of more than twenty huts. On the other hand, even among people who have adopted Christianity

147

and practised much economic individualism, it is seldom that the minimum group of man, wife and children will ever be the effective one. As we shall see, Bantu life in its very essence requires co-operation on a household basis, and requires that the household shall be large enough to provide a basis for the co-operation.

On approaching a Bantu village, by which we mean any group of homesteads in close neighbourhood, the first impression upon our senses is made by the buildings themselves, and we shall begin our study of the family by describing these, for they are by no means mere technical structures; they are erected to meet the needs of the people, their spiritual as well as their material needs. An understanding of why the huts are placed as they are gives at once a deep insight into the people's culture, and when we learn not only of the form of the huts but of their purposes, we probe into social life and begin to appreciate the economic aspect of that life.

No matter in what part of Bantu Africa we may find ourselves, so long as we are not looking at the homes of Christianized Bantu we shall find the huts to be grouped, roughly but definitely, in a pattern representing a sector of a circle. This pattern is perhaps most pronounced among the cattle-owning people of South-East Africa, where the cattle kraal is in the centre of the circle, but it is no less definite among peoples who are either without cattle or who do not attach the same importance to them as do those of the South-East. Where the cattle kraal is not the centre of the homestead, the place for meeting, and for sacrificing, is.

In South-East Africa, with its extremely powerful cattle-cult, the cattle kraal is in many effective ways the centre of the homestead. In the old days, when homesteads were moved more often than they are today, the new site was chosen very largely as an ideal place for the kraal, and, this supreme condition fulfilled, the huts of the people could always be grouped around it. It had to be, if possible, on sloping ground and facing east so that the cattle would receive the early morning rays of the sun. This was considered necessary if they were to be healthy and to give much milk. But the cattle kraal was much more than a place in which animals were kept at night. It was, and still is, the place in which chosen beasts are sacrificed, so that it is the shrine, the religious centre of the group. Quite possibly, the head of the homestead would find his burial-place within the kraal, wrapped in the skin of one of his favourite cattle.

But one other consideration, a purely practical one, weighed in choosing the site for the kraal. Somewhere inside the fence the grain pits had to be dug. The soil for these pits had to be very carefully chosen, for if it were of the wrong sort, and not well drained, the grain would become musty; the store, upon which the life of the group might well depend, would be lost. Once the pits were dug, and filled after the harvest, their mouths would be covered with flat stones and soon many inches thick of manure would conceal their exact whereabouts. No thief would think of entering the cattle kraal with evil intent, for many curses would at once operate against him. Only in case of war would the grain be lost. But a more immediate and practical control over the grain was established through its being stored in the place of the cattle; no woman may enter the cattle kraal. Thus, whenever the pits were to be opened it must be by the men of the homestead, under the orders of the headman. In this way ultimate economic control of the family resources was firmly placed in the hands of the male elders. This is the more illuminating as we find that in many parts of Bantu Africa where the grain pit is unknown, even to legend, this ultimate control of the family resources is still definitely in the hands of the men. Today, with the grain pits disappearing in many places and being replaced by the white traders' store, it is still the man who has ultimately to decide what shall be sold to the trader and what retained for home use.

The cattle kraal is seldom an elaborate structure. There appear to be no traditional materials of which it must be built. Usually branches loosely put together to make a circular fence will serve the purpose. But it is on record that it may be made of stones and mud, and it appears that when big game was dangerous it was an infinitely stronger structure than is ever to be seen today. In East Africa today, when cattle kraals are built out in the pasture lands and away from the homesteads, they are built very strongly indeed, quite capable of keeping lions and even more destructive animals at bay. It is of more than purely historical interest for us to use records of earlier times which tell us that until perhaps midway through the nineteenth century homesteads were moved very much oftener than they are today, and that at each moving a really substantial cattle kraal had to be built. For, this being so, we see that men, until comparatively recent times, had sets of duties which they are no longer called upon to perform. A change of this nature may have considerable importance, and we believe has, in setting men free for other kinds of work.

The cattle kraal is invariably circular. It has no standard size whatever. It may be just big enough to house the two or three beasts of a poor man, or several acres in extent to take the herds of a chief. But in either case it is constructed with one gate, and that opening uphill. Further up the hill, facing this gate, would be built the chief hut. This is the hut, not of the man who is head of the household, but either of his mother, of his one and only wife, or of his principal wife. The man himself usually has no personal hut, although this is not a rigid rule. Each hut is attached in a vital way to a woman who is its mistress and who manages her household in and around it. The little children may sleep in the grandmother's hut; the young men and young women may have huts in some other part of the semi-circle. But the essential huts are those of the married women. As the head of the household acquires more wives with his increasing years and status, each is given her hut on one side or the other of the main hut. So the segment grows, and it is the ambition of all to come as near as possible to making a complete circle around the cattle kraal. One younger brother will have the huts of his wives in another part of the circle; another younger brother will have his family in another part, and so on. Wives who are married later will have their hut further from the main hut, except that all the huts of one man's wives will invariably be together.

In this way the household is constructed, and when we see a collection of huts we know that it corresponds to a very live reality.

REFERENCES AND FURTHER READING

Zulu-Land. Rev. L. Grout. 1864.
Wanderings in the Interior of South Africa. A. Steedman. 1835.
Kaffir Laws and Customs. J. MacLean (ed.). 1858.
An African People in the Twentieth Century. L. P. Mair. 1934.
The Life of a South African Tribe. H. A. Junod. 1927.
The Ila-Speaking Peoples of Northern Rhodesia. Smith and Dale. 1920.
The Bavenda. H. A. Stayt. 1931.
Ubena of the Rivers. A. T. and G. M. Culwick.
Black and White in East Africa. R. C. and H. Thurnwald. 1935.
Anthropology in Action. Brown and Hutt. 1935.
With a Prehistoric People. W. S. and K. Routledge. 1910.
Reaction to Conquest. M. Hunter. 1937.

SECTION III

The Homestead at Work

Let us first take a brief glimpse at the homestead at work. It may consist of three huts or of three hundred; these huts may surround the central cattle kraal as in South-East Africa or, lacking this core, may keep more loosely to the circular design. The form varies throughout Bantu Africa, but the day's work shows a remarkable uniformity. A young woman rises before the others; she takes a pot, carries it perhaps a mile or more, fills it with water and returns; she revives the glowing embers and perhaps warms up some food left over from the evening meal. By this time most of the other members will be up and ready to go about their tasks. Who was the young woman? Almost certainly, she was a wife, probably new to the homestead. Her duties are arduous. There may be other women of about her age in the homestead, but their behaviour is very different. It is the wife who works, especially the youngest wife. It is well understood that, especially in the first few years of her married life, her work will be very hard. The unmarried daughters of the family have less heavy burdens, and the married daughters who have returned to visit their parents will work much less on their holiday, though they will not be idle.

The morning is still young, but the homestead is now at the very brief morning meal and soon the routine of work will begin. Already, however, the behaviour of the young wife will have shown, to the keen observer, part of the framework of economic obligations within the circle of huts. Whence did she take the food for the morning meal? To whom will she give it? This particular wife has the obligation to prepare food for her own children, for her husband, and for any guests whom her husband may be entertaining. The guests at the morning meal will almost certainly be limited to those who happen to be staying with the family. Other wives cook other dishes, but the young wife, whom we assume to be responsible for this meal, will now have taken food from her own kitchen or from her own store. Her own private resources will never be confused with those of other wives or of her mother-in-law. Within the homestead the houses, in the sense of each being the sphere of a wife, are units of the most definite nature. Therefore if she took left-over food from the kitchen of another woman it would be only with that other woman's permission. More normally, she herself would have cooked some extra food the previous evening to supply the morning meal, while on other days other women would make that provision.

To whom does she give this food? In the case of this simple morning meal it will go to everybody in the homestead. But even here some few differences will be apparent. Her own children, if any, may well receive some slight preference, for the bonds between a woman and her own children are always closer than between her and the several other groups of children who may well be living in the same homestead. For example, her co-wives will have children; children of brothers of her husband may be living with them; there may be other young residents. Ideally, perhaps, all of these should receive equal treatment. But, practically, differences will show. Much will depend on the personality of the woman as well as on the standing of the children themselves. Thus an orphan child may not receive the best of attention. These matters will appear in more detail when we come to the more elaborate evening meal. In the meantime we see the food more or less hastily consumed, especially if it is at a season when there is much work in the fields. It is even possible that some members of the homestead will have been in the fields all night and that, unless they have cows near them to supply them with milk, a little food will now be taken out to them.

The actual ways in which the members of the family will set out for work will depend enormously upon the season and upon the kind of district in which they live. Yet here again a surprising uniformity may be seen throughout Bantu Africa. Whatever stock there may be will now be the care of the boys and men. Little boys may drive the goats to pasture. Older boys will take the cattle out of the kraal and skilfully lead them to the best available grass. Very young boys may stay to play in the homestead or may be carried to the fields by their mothers. All of the women, excepting any who may be in extreme old age, will now go to the fields, for even in the period just after harvest there will always be some work to be done there, some root crops to be tended, some preparations to be made. Even very young girls will accompany their mothers and often have their own corners of fields which they feel to be their own. Children will play about on the edge of the fields, while others may be left in the homestead with but a slightly older girl as their nurse. This work of nursing is definitely recognized, and later in life the nurse may well receive some fairly substantial acknowledgment from the children whom she once tended.

This daily routine is by no means unvaried. There are times when the men have much to do in the fields. Sometimes they have clearing, sometimes ploughing; in many districts they have fields of their own. When the men's share of the work is less pressing they are able to travel, to take an active interest in the affairs of the tribe and to attend the hearing of cases at law. There will be problems of raising bride-price;

debts will be contracted and repayment demanded. Distant relatives will be visited, and consultations held as to the disposal of valuable family property. The wives, too, have variations. Household furniture may need to be replaced; dresses to be renewed; visits must be made to their fathers, who still have important obligations to supply these needs. More accurately, the furniture and clothing may be claimed in their fathers' homesteads, but actually from the wives there, who in their turn replenish themselves by visiting *their* fathers' homesteads!

In this way there arises one of the systems of the circulation of resources which is so characteristic of primitive communities. It would be so much more directly economical, by saving the energy and time spent in travelling, for each homestead to supply its own needs in these matters, and in fact, as we shall see, husbands have obligations to supply their wives' clothing, yet the exchange, or rather the circulation, goes on. One homestead takes from another and that other from yet another. Since in the first homestead there will probably be several wives, whether of the same man or of two brothers, and since each of these wives may well have come from a different homestead, it will be seen that each group of huts may draw upon a considerable number of other establishments for its needs in household equipment. The wives will also visit for the sake of visiting, and this is a privilege very precious to them. They may provide some little excuse, as when a young Pondo wife leaves a broken pot when she goes to visit her father's homestead. The broken pot is a sign that she has broken something and must go to her home to replace it. The fiction is well understood.

But there are other variations in the woman's routine. She does not always dig her own fields by herself. When the hoeing or weeding is ready to be done she invests in a working party. She first prepares beer, as much as she can afford, for this is one of the main attractions. If her husband is well-to-do, he may kill a head of small stock. It is here that the wife in a large homestead has an advantage, for a poor man will not be able to kill for her work-party. She lets it be known that on a certain day the beer will be at her home. That is the invitation for the people of the neighbourhood to assemble. They perform the work in her fields, then they feast. If exceptionally lucky they may get some food to take back to their own homes. The feast is part of their payment, but only part. The rest of the return will be made when they themselves call work-parties. In this way variety and companionship are achieved in what would otherwise be very tedious work, and it is not to be wondered at that individuals today are not too keen on adopting up-to-date methods, since these almost invariably mean that co-operation with neighbours is broken. The institution of the work-parties is very definitely a means of organizing the labour resources of a district and of applying them in an economic manner to work which has to be done. Thus the wife on one day may have much beer to prepare for a coming work-party; on another day will have that work-party to go through her fields; while on other days, again, sometimes even in the busiest seasons, she will go to work with parties on the fields of her neighbours. In the season after harvest the routine, naturally, will be different. Initiations will provide much work in their preparation, and much festive and pleasant occupation. Funeral feasts will be held when the pressure of work permits. Not least, marriages, with their infinite activity, will tend to take place when the pressure of field work is relaxed.

Toward evening the next stage in the day's routine may be observed. Again, much depends upon the season, yet many features persist throughout the year. The cattle are brought home to be milked. This, far from being a simple technical operation of no interest to the sociologist, has the clearest implications for the structure of the family group. The first point is that although all the cattle belong to the homestead, they are definitely apportioned within the homestead. Each wife has cattle which are part of the resources of her house. One or two beasts may be her personal property in that she brings them with her at marriage or obtains them in some other way, as in the form of a gift from someone who has an obligation to her. The gift from a child, which he makes when grown up to the woman who nursed him, will provide an example. The woman is definitely entitled to the ownership of all the produce from this stock. Its progeny belong to her; she will have the major voice in deciding whether it is ever to be killed; when it dies, its meat is part of her food resources, although, of course, it will be eaten at once by all the people who are customarily entitled to share in the meat diet of the homestead. The skins of the stock are likewise the property of the woman, and the fat from its carcase may become a valuable possession to her. Her ownership is evident at the daily milking. The milk must go into her calabashes, or, should there be a milk sac for the whole homestead, she will claim an amount out of this equivalent to the amount which her cow contributed to it. Thus the sharing out and ownership of the milk at once shows that the cattle are not really a homogeneous herd owned communally by the family group. The woman, when she has this private stock, very clearly has extra resources which she must dispose of economically. That is to say, she herself may be specially requiring the milk, as when she has a young baby, or some other woman in the homestead or neighbourhood may have need of the milk, and a loan or exchange, or even purchase, will result.

Whether or not each wife has some such resources as privately owned cattle, she will certainly, if her husband has any cattle at all, have one or more of these beasts allocated to her, so that while the herd as a whole belongs to the homestead and is under the ultimate management of the husband, the cows are shared out among the houses, each house being the establishment of a wife. The husband may reserve certain cattle for himself, but these must always be potentially available for distribution among his wives. Each wife is keenly interested in the economic resources of her own house, and it is with regard to property that jealousies arise. The finding of cattle to obtain another wife for the homestead, either for the husband himself or for a son, must be done by collaboration between the husband and the wife or wives, who may be able or willing to invest part of their resources in this way. The full economics of this mode of managing cattle resources will be discussed later. It is enough at this stage to see that the milk from practically all of the cattle belongs, not to the homestead as a unit but to the various houses in proportion to the amount yielded by the various cows. This often leads to inequalities as between wives, for if one wife's cows happen to be ill she is without her usual supply of milk. It is thus important to note that mutual exchange is the normal practice. The actual terms of exchange will depend upon the relative values of goods within the homestead; but the fact of exchange is always present.

Whatever the season, probably some food, much or little, grain or tubers, will be brought home in the evening. The treatment of this food will again show the economic realities underlying its production and utilization. The tubers, sweet potatoes, or whatever they may be, do not have to be stored in the homestead. They are dug up as required; their store is the earth in which they grow, and this earth is always owned by one woman, so that there is no doubt as to ownership of these goods. Grain, on the other hand, must be stored. There are many varieties of grain, several of them important. The arrangements for storing correspond to the uses and to the value of the grain. Special stores are generally to be found for the grain which is staple to the diet of the people for the greater part of the year. It is this which must have permanent store-houses. It is this which has the storehouses which may be almost as prominent in the fields or in the homestead as the huts in which the people live. It is this which, among the cattle-owning people of South-East Africa, was, and still is, in the more conservative districts, safely stowed away in the pits beneath the cattle kraal, but which now tends to find its way to the traders' store, to be kept by him at what appears to be an exorbitant cost and returned to the people as they require it.

The main economic characteristic of this grain is that it appears to be, more than the other food, under the control of the husband. The placing of the grain pit within the cattle kraal both symbolized and made complete this control. But this control is never divorced from a practical share in administration invested in the wife. It is quite impossible to say that it is the duty of the wife to grow the grain and then to hand it over to her husband. The day-to-day administration is in her hands. It is when the husband thinks that she is being too liberal, not eking out the grain sufficiently with tubers, or perhaps feeding too many children besides her own, that he expresses his concern lest the homestead be left too short before the next harvest. Often, after harvest, there is some choice as to what may be done with the surplus or apparent surplus. The wife may feel herself entitled to some ornament, and disposal of grain to purchase this must be a matter for discussion between her husband and herself. At the evening meal she uses some of the food just brought from the fields, some from the stores, and the milk to which she is entitled. If there are many wives they do not all, every evening, have to do an equal amount of cooking. They take turns in the main responsibility, so that work is shared. But usually each wife will cook at least some little dish, and in the homestead with many wives there will be a plentiful evening meal without undue work to any of them. Each wife sends a dish, whether the main one or only a tit-bit, to her husband. She provides other dishes for the young children and possibly yet others for the older children. She herself may eat in her cooking hut or wherever she pleases, but will not usually eat her main meal with her husband, although she may join him afterwards in a tit-bit when he is free from his guests.

The number of guests will depend largely upon the amount of food available, that is to say, upon the husband's and the other menfolks' skill in managing their cattle, and upon the number of wives and the skill of each one in producing from her fields. The amount of food regularly available for the evening meal is of supreme importance. It is this which gives the homestead its physical nutrition and its standing in the neighbourhood. Strangers passing through the district are told that there is always food at such and such a household. Relatives, visitors from the chief, friends and neighbours, are welcomed where there is plenty. It is thus that the headman of the homestead becomes powerful and can further increase his resources. He is able to follow lawsuits which may add to his wealth. He is able to lend and borrow among a wide circle, and often to sell or exchange advantageously.

Taking the homestead as the unit, we have seen how it is made up essentially of a series of houses, each house being the establishment of a married woman; how these women are grouped around their own husbands, of whom there may be but one, although more probably there will be two or three, in the homestead. Always one man, either father or grandfather or eldest brother, is definitely head of the whole establishment. His sons, with or without their wives, must consult him in all major and most minor economic problems. He in his turn must consult them. While each family within the homestead is a clear economic unit, the homestead as a whole is just as definitely economically one. Throughout all our studies the homestead, the family, and the house of the wife, will feature as the decisive establishments, since within these inter-personal comparisons must take place, to produce the final economic choices.

REFERENCES AND FURTHER READING

Native Foods and Culinary Methods (Art.). J. R. Duncan. Nada, 1933.
Problems of African Native Diet (Art.). Sir J. Orr. Africa, 1936.
On the Food and Nutrition of African Natives (Art.). E. B. Worthington. Africa, 1936.
A Dietary Study in North Eastern Rhodesia (Art.). Richards and Widdowson. Africa, 1936.
The Southern Basotho, Photographs and Descriptions in the Bantu Tribes of South Africa. A. M. D. Cronnin. Vol. 2. 1928.
The Vathonga in the Bantu Tribes of South Africa, Photographs and Descriptions. A. M. D. Cronnin. Vol. 4, Section 1. 1935.
Minutes of Evidence taken before the Select Committee on Masters and Servants Law (Transvaal) Amendment Bill. 1913.
Zulu-Land. Rev. L. Grout. 1864.
Wanderings in the Interior of South Africa. A Steedman. 1835.
Story of My Mission in South-East Africa. W. Shaw. 1860.
Zulu-English Dictionary. Bryant.
Among the Zulus. D. Leslie. 1875.
Kaffirs of Natal. J. Shooter. 1857.
The Life of a South African Tribe. H. A. Junod. 1927.

The Ila-Speaking Peoples of Northern Rhodesia. Smith and Dale. 1920.
The Bavenda. H. A. Stayt. 1931.
Ubena of the Rivers. A. T. and G. M. Culwick.
Anthropology in Action. Brown and Hutt. 1935.
With a Prehistoric People. W. S. and K. Routledge. 1910.
Reaction to Conquest. M. Hunter. 1937.

SECTION IV

The Homestead and Its Neighbourhood

It is next to be noted that no homestead is isolated. It may be five minutes' walk from two or three other homesteads, or it may be a mile from the nearest. Much depends upon the country, but always there is real co-operation between neighbours, and neighbourhood is seldom fortuitous. For example, in the old days rather than at the present moment, a rich man would have not one homestead but several. Today among many peoples this is the effective practice of chiefs, but not of commoners. The principle, therefore, is important. A chief is, after all, often but the member of a certain lineage who succeeds in amassing resources. When this happens the man may well find many advantages in having more than one home. His original homestead will be the centre of the neighbourhood. The fields of his wives will occupy a great part of the cultivated land. Their work-parties will set the pace, and even in a sense organize the agriculture of the district. His herds of cattle in particular are likely to be great even in country where other men have little but goats. Thus his cattle may have to go further and further away for their grazing. It will not do for him to occupy all the grazing land of the district. Besides, diseases are dangerous in large herds. Therefore another homestead is indicated, if only for that reason alone. In addition, his wives may have to walk further and further in order to get good fields, and also they will prefer to be relatively near to their fathers' homes. Thus when a new wife is taken she may be given a new establishment altogether, and one or two others may join her. Or on one of the occasions on which he decides to move his homestead, and moving is everywhere fairly common, the man may decide to break it up and so spread his enterprise over a larger area.

The essence of the arrangement is that the man will now supervise, and visit in turn, his homesteads instead of managing only one. No principles are changed. In each homestead will be found houses functioning exactly as if the headman were living there the whole of the time instead of part only. Though this arrangement may have virtually ceased to exist except in chiefs' families, it is at the base of the institution of chieftainship. It will be seen that the man, either when he acquires extra stock and wishes to distribute it among his wives, or when he wishes to dispose of stock which he will have to obtain from the resources of one or more wives, will have a far larger range of choice for his operations. It is in such circumstances that considerable inequalities may appear as between wives.

We must be careful not to suppose that in the ordinary homestead there is substantial equality in possession among the married women; actually, where there are but two wives, one may be a much better manager than the other, and this may show itself in her food stores, in her cattle, in the nourishment of her children, and in many other ways. Yet within a single homestead of average size it is difficult for one wife to make great economic advances upon the others. There are too many calls upon her to support the children of the others; it is understood that the husband, while he has not in his disposing of property to bring all wives to an equality, must tend, on the whole, to give to those who lack.

With scattered homesteads this principle will not entirely disappear. It is, indeed, one of the advantages of having several establishments that when one is unfortunate it may be replenished from the resources of the others. But when the homesteads are some miles apart, and when they may be in districts of different type, it will probably be only on occasions of distress that one will receive assistance from the others. In ordinary circumstances it will be the duty and interest of each homestead to make the most of its own resources and to stand up for its own economic rights against the others when need be, just as within any homestead each house insists on its own claims as against the others. In the case of a series of home-steads, each will definitely be ruled by one elder whose authority will be second only to that of the head himself. This elder will usually be a younger brother of the head. He also, as well as several other brothers and male relatives, will have his family within the particular homestead, the huts of his wives being further toward one of the ends of the semicircle, beyond the huts of the headman's wives which are toward the centre, facing the entrance to the cattle kraal.

In the case of a rich man's homestead, whether it be his only one or one of a series, its neighbours will stand in a fairly definite relationship to it. That is to say, they will either be dependants or will be people who stand to gain by co-operating with the economic leader of the district. In some cases these poorer people will actually have their huts within the headman's homestead. This is purely a matter of convenience. Large homesteads are often difficult to manage, mainly through there being too many contacts between the wives. Equal or greater efficiency will usually be secured through the main homestead having at most the huts of one or two dependants within its circle, while other people with whom it co-operates live in the neighbourhood.

The ways in which a neighbourhood of homesteads tend to co-operate with the leading homesteads are multifarious. The rich man may well have more cattle than can be economically managed by the group of families within his own circle of huts, and will require outside labour to herd them. Or, to state the matter differently, his cattle will give a supply of milk, part of which he would like to dispose of in exchange for other things. One never hears of surplus milk being sold to neighbours; it is not impossible that this may happen, but the usual practice is for the rich owner to allot certain of his cattle to his poorer neighbours, who then tend them and are rewarded with the milk, usually also with part of the progeny, with the meat of those that die, occasionally with a beast which is given them to kill as a sacrifice, and, directly important in the old days and of some monetary value today, with the hides of those that die.

Much litigation may arise from this practice of employing neighbours to herd surplus cattle. At the death of the owner their position may well be uncertain. The herders may try to claim as many as possible for themselves, yet, in spite of this, the system works. But we have as yet seen little more than one side of it. The great advantages of having cattle in one's possession, even though they belong to someone else, are not adequately paid for only by herding these cattle. In addition, the owner will be entitled to call upon his neighbours, who are, in a way, his employees, to perform other services. Sometimes these will be specific, as when the men of the dependant families give some days of labour in the fields of the economic leader. In other ways the services will not be specific but will function none the less, for the dependent homesteads will be those which invariably send their women, and very often their men, to the work-parties of the wives in the chief homestead. In addition, constant lending and borrowing of food and household utensils will proceed. In the agriculture of the district the fields of the chief homestead will tend to get the best attention and hence to set a standard. The neighbourhood is yet another effective economic unit; it is not necessarily under the leadership of one main homestead, but it very often is. Even when it is not, when the homesteads may have more or less equal resources, there will still be much economic give-and-take.

It has been mentioned that, except in the case of chiefs, or of potential chiefs, it is now unusual for men to have more than one homestead. But now we must note a tendency which unites both the principle of a series of homesteads ultimately under one management and of co-operation through neighbourhood. This is, that when any homestead shows signs of becoming too large it is not necessary that its own head shall branch out into another. It is enough, and indeed very common, that a member of his family should do so. One of his younger brothers or of his sons will feel that it is now his turn to have a homestead of his own. There are no rules as to where this will be established, but in practice it will exceedingly often be in the same neighbourhood, within co-operating distance. It thus becomes one of those homesteads which most normally co-operate economically with the original one; it is also, and this is the important point of principle, still ultimately under the leadership of the head of the family. To the extent that this is so, many of the same results are achieved as by the head of the family setting up a new homestead of his own. The two principles, of economic co-operation between kindred, and of economic co-operation between neighbours, are jointly achieved.

The authority of the head of the kindred, which in some books is at this stage given the name of "lineage", is by no means the same as it would be if he had wives of his own living in each homestead. But we lack information as to the precise differences. It is certain that the head of the kindred will give help to his brothers and sons, should they require it, in obtaining land for their gardens and for grazing. In many cases, indeed, the head of the kindred will be the actual head-man of the district under the chief, and as such will be ulti-mately responsible for the sharing out of lands at the beginning of each season. This alone will establish him in an effective though not necessarily intimate control. Further, a certain degree of control will result through the dominating position of the work-parties of his wives, for they, having probably the best land and almost certainly greater means of giving feasts, will have the most important work-parties. They are also able, by giving more of these parties, to cultivate more land. This means that in time of need it is they who will assist the wives of less favoured homesteads. All these circumstances maintain the reality of some central control over the homesteads by one family in one district. But the other side of the picture must not be forgotten. Each homestead regards its own economic interests as extremely important if not paramount; there is always the tendency to claim advantages at the expense of one's kindred. Yet this only brings into full relief the main fact of co-operation.

How real this co-operation is, is one of the main questions to be answered. It suffices to note now that the principle of reciprocity is at its basis. When we speak of the head of a kindred as economic leader, or of the chief as economic leader, the implications are not quite the same as if we were using that term in a European society. There can be extremely little possibility of his conducting matters to his own advantage. His sons and younger brothers will consult him before disposing of any valuable piece of property, but equally he will consult them in a similar circumstance. Before the head of the kindred sells a beast, or gives bride-price for a new wife, or provides bride-price for a son, or possibly gives a cow to a niece whose father is poor, he will just as certainly consult other members of his family who are within reach as they would consult him. Such groups are held together, on the economic side, by the solid advantages of co-operation. It is the easiest thing in the world for one member, should he be dissatisfied, to move his homestead to another district and to co-operate with people there, to try to get better results. On the other hand, each headman will by his effective leadership try to gain new adherents. Free choice is nearly always effective, for it is traditionally easy to move a homestead and, except in a very few places where acute land shortage has recently been created, new homesteads are welcomed in any district.

In dealing with the economics of the family we have passed imperceptibly to those of other social units, in particular to the kindred or lineage and to the neighbourhood. This is as it should be, for the family is not a hard and fast unit, but shades into these others. We have seen that the smallest unit, and a very effective one, is the house, the establishment of a wife, while the largest economic unit is the tribe. But in between these is another form of grouping which has received very much, if somewhat uncertain, treatment in writings on Africa: this is the clan. For our purposes the clan cannot be regarded as an effective economic unit in its own right. That part of a clan which may dominate any given district is, however, on quite another footing. It is simply the kindred or lineage about which we have already written. This is the part of a clan which is effective. It is the part whose members trace actual relationship and who live close enough together to co-operate. Beyond these, other people stated to belong to the same clan can very often be traced into other districts. These larger groups are not without something in common. They have names in common; they have food and ceremonial customs in common; above all, they forbid intermarriage between their members, and there can be no doubt that this is effective, even despite any Westernization of ideas, even at the present day. But economic co-operation seems to be much more problematical. It may be that when people travel in distant parts they tend to receive hospitality from people of the same clan who may live there. On the other hand, it seems just as probable that they will go to men who are famed for giving hospitality, while nowadays this must be of even less importance than formerly, because hospitality tends more and more to be paid for. This applies, of course, to hospitality to strangers. That between neighbours is on a different footing since it is part of their general give-and-take. It would appear that if a man wants to borrow a cow and has to choose between asking two complete strangers, one of whom is a fellow-clansman, he may prefer to ask him. But this indicates a very minimum of economic co-operation and may be taken as a true measure of the clan's value as an economic unit.

Two points relating to the clan remain, however, to be discussed. One is that the people themselves may very often stress the clan in speaking of their economic lives. The other is that in each kindred, in each homestead, even in each family, members of more than one clan are, owing to the practice of exogamy, to be found. What significance have these points for our study?

When a Bantu man speaks about his clan he thinks chiefly of those members of it whom he actually knows and to whom he can trace his relationship. This brings no new fact before us, but we must note the man's point of view. He almost invariably, unless notably lacking in ambition, visualizes himself as the potential founder of a new "clan". That is to say, he dreams of his wives and children becoming numerous and of his grandchildren spreading over the land. This group will then be known as So-and-So's clan, and may even spread far beyond its original district. In mythology, a living reality which appears constantly in conversation with Bantu people, this is how clans were founded, while in actual fact this must have been so in a good many cases. We mention it now as showing an extremely important ideal in the lives of Bantu men. It serves to illustrate and confirm that attachment to the ideal of a complete circle of huts, embracing those of his own wives and of his dependants, which we described earlier in this chapter. This household is visualized not merely as becoming substantial in itself, but also as spreading, and it is significant that when we treat of the Bantu kinship system in its economic aspect we discover the same tendency at work as the Bantu himself presupposes. The tendency, in fact, does actually work, though not in any ideally perfect way. We have to assume it in order to give us the necessary basis of uniformity without which scientific treatment is impossible.

REFERENCES AND FURTHER READING

The Development of the Military Organisation in Swaziland (Art.). H. Beemer. Africa, 1936-37.
Kaffirs of Natal. J. Shooter. 1857.
Western Civilisation and the Natives of South Africa. I Schapera (ed.). 1934.
The Life of a South African Tribe. H. A. Junod. 1927.
The Ila-Speaking Peoples of Northern Rhodesia. Smith and Dale. 1920.
The Bavenda. H. A. Stayt. 1931.
Ubena of the Rivers. A. T. and G. M. Culwick.
Reaction to Conquest. M. Hunter. 1937.

CHAPTER XI

A SURVEY OF ECONOMIC UNITS

SECTION I

The Transkei Peoples

IT is now necessary to survey the structure of the economic units throughout certain Bantu tribes, bringing into relief their economic aspects.

The missionary writer Steedman tells us that when the first plough was introduced among the Xosa people of the Transkei the men said: "These *Abafundis* [1] have brought a THING into the land worth more than 10 wives." European influence began early in this district, three important chiefs embracing Christianity in 1833.

The plough is one of the few elements in European agricultural equipment which has been readily adopted by Bantu people. We shall find that its adoption has been quite consistent with a refusal to adopt almost anything else in the way of European methods. The ready resort to the plough may at this stage be taken to indicate that the people in the Transkei have no objection to enlarging cultivated fields, to employing youths and cattle in ploughing, and to lightening one part of the women's work. At the same time it must not be supposed that even today land is ploughed universally in the Transkei. Ploughs are common, but the women still have their full routine of agricultural labour.

Writing of the Transkei peoples, Steedman tells us that their homestead sites are chosen on the sides of fields with a view mainly to the welfare of the herds. This establishes, together with all other observations on the point, the fact that among these peoples the love of cattle is a ruling motive in life.

[1] Teachers, *i.e.* missionaries.

168

Steedman noted that cultivation was relegated to scattered plots of all sizes and shapes. He found the soil to be rich, and gardens to be made on the flats near rivers and on convenient patches upon hillsides. Pumpkins, melons, a small species of millet called "Caffer corn" and also maize, grew to unusual heights. The neighbouring Pondos had large quantities of sweet potatoes or yam. Tobacco grew throughout. The missionary observed that there were differences between the Pondos and their Xosa and Tembu neighbours, in that the Pondos were more interested in cultivation, their men taking a regular part in field work, while the Xosa and Tembu men confined themselves to their interest in cattle.

Boyce, another missionary writer, described the Pondos as he found them. The country which he knew "abounded in population". The homesteads were larger than in the other parts of the Transkei, and the people were supported chiefly by tillage; there were few cattle, a result of the wars. Boyce estimated that within two or three miles of chief Faku's headquarters there could not be less than seven or eight thousand people.

Mr. Shepstone counted, from one hill near Faku's place, one hundred homesteads each with twenty to forty huts. We know that even today cultivable land is plentiful in Pondoland, and we are entitled to speculate that the large size of the homesteads a hundred years ago was correlated with plentiful and good land, and a lack of necessity to find pasture for large herds. Both sexes were found to be "very industrious compared with other tribes"; here for the first time the missionaries perceived an indication that the people "understood the value of time"; it also appears that they knew the advantage of exchange, for one woman said "Pay me now for my milk, for it is time, I want to work in my garden". Mr. Shepstone was "quite enlivened after seven years in Cafferland". The people also were willing to conform in dress in deference to the missionaries' feelings; a hint was sufficient; this was "no small comfort". But all was not idyllic. At one place Boyce reported that some two hundred people were seeking roots for food, and that in consequence of continued scarcity many men were driving from their homesteads the least valued wives, who were the old and infirm.

Kay wrote of the Transkei country occupied by Tembus. The Tembu chief Pato's headquarters evidently bore no comparison with those of the Pondo, Faku. The hamlet of the former consisted of four or five miserable huts and a large cattle fold. Pato, however, may well have had more homesteads than this, for at another place Kay discovered land with plenty of grass and a good situation for cattle which had been the old chief's "principal grazing farm some years before". Kay tells of how these essentially cattle people would very easily move their homesteads when streamlets evaporated or were lost by absorption in sandy beds. The headman would remove, with family and herds, to a new place, and in a few days would be quite at home there with his huts erected and his cattle fold made. The great object of the missionary was to turn the people's attention more fully to agricultural life, so as to attach them to the soil. It was then a country of broken land with numerous small homesteads. Corn and milk, however, were offered for sale to the missionaries. The homesteads consisted of from six to a dozen huts; except for a few thorn branches thrown around the hut to prevent the cattle tearing off its grassy roof, it seldom had a fence of any description. The houses of nobles and of the most indigent showed no material difference; at the most, the houses of the rich may have been a little neater; they were not more substantial. Chiefs had more huts owing to their greater number of wives. Each wife was required to make her own hut, the missionary reports, not quite accurately. The king's wife herself was not exempt. She had more assistance, but was alone responsible. There was little labour involved in building the huts, and their destruction seldom gave uneasiness to the occupants. The homestead was simply from six to a dozen of these huts and a cattle fold or two. The latter was usually by far the most prominent. Whatever the state of the houses, the cattle kraal at all times had paramount claims upon the attention of the owners and was always in much better repair.

When it was a question of choosing a new site for a homestead the main question was whether it was suitable for the cattle kraal. This had to be built so as to ensure the maximum of sun in the early morning. The cattle kraals, the missionary noticed, were always right in the midst of the houses, under the owner's eye, while gardens or cornlands were scarcely ever attached to the hamlets, possibly not being within sight of them. Large herds were the people's most valuable riches; cattle were the subject of the daily study of every native from the time he was capable of engaging in the affairs of life to the very last moment of his earthly career. Tears were scarcely ever shed excepting when the chief laid hands upon some of the "horned family"; this was real grief.

Kay gives the occupations of the men mainly as tending the cattle and the cattle kraals, when they are not visiting for soliciting presents and journeying in quest of news. The building of a cattle kraal, although this was more substantial than a house, is stated to have involved but little work. Thorns and small branches were used, and in colder weather the interstices were filled up with mud. The cattle were brought home every night, and the people were extremely anxious that the herd should lie as dry and warm as possible, hence the location on sides of hills facing the rising sun. Another reason for the cattle kraal having to be as comfortable as possible was its being a place of general resort for the men.

Another man's occupation was the erection of fences around the cultivated gardens as the blades began to make their appearance. These fences were extremely slight. It is evident through Kay's account that the people had not to cope with the more dangerous sorts of wild animals. Only a few years earlier, he might have found that the men had much heavier work. After the harvesting of the crops, the slight garden fences were torn down and the cattle grazed, communally, on the stubble. Here we have our first glimpse of the fact that traditionally even garden-land is grazing at one time in the year, a fact which to this day militates against a Bantu man and woman fencing their gardens permanently and so shutting themselves off from their neighbours for the sake of improving their agriculture.

171

In Kay's book the function of the man as economic leader among his wives is fairly clearly indicated, although the implications are not studied. Thus, it is pointed out that at a certain season the man has to make the decision to kill numbers of cattle, providing new cloaks for his wives as well as flesh food at a time when this was needed. Grain pits are mentioned, as being invariably in the cattle kraals and dug by men. Although, it is stated, these storehouses were frequently exposed and the kraal deserted for weeks or months together, they were rarely or never broken open. The missionary did not perceive the religious sanction explaining this. Other, and more practical sanctions, must not be forgotten, however. Vital stores were kept in these pits for long periods, and to break one of them open would be a deliberate and major crime. An earlier traveller, Varrow, is quoted as asserting that wheat will keep in these pits for fifty years and millet for a hundred. Kay's own experience is that in the estimation of the people themselves the grain is kept good for two or three years only. It is a fact that grain is very liable to take on a musty flavour after only a short time in a pit, and that this flavour, when too bad, is unwelcome to the people. This alone may go some way to accounting for the fairly rapid displacement of grain pits by traders' stores.

Kay makes a few observations directly upon the family system. They are interesting mainly as showing what an observant missionary saw, and how little attention he gave to the routine of the family structure, as against witchcraft and other sensational features, which occupied many pages of his book. He tells us that the matrimonial bond in that part of the country is a "commercial contract", five to ten head of cattle being given for a wife.

A headman near seventy years of age is described deliberating over whether he should invest in another wife. He proposes to the girl's parents and offers a price. She is escorted to his place by her female relatives; on their arrival the old man grumbles and reckons up the cost in excellent cattle if he should retain her. He gives grave deliberation to the matter. He orders a hut to be prepared for his guests, but the prospective bride has to be supplied with food by her relatives until he finally makes up his mind. The old man came to a decision which he announced by slaughtering a beast. The news immediately spread in every direction, and within a few hours there was an amusing scene. Crowds of men, women and children came toward the spot, some driving milch cows, other carrying milk sacs, young boys and girls came laden with baskets and calabashes. Feasting was general for several days, everyone contributing. Meat, however, the grand dish, was supplied by the bridegroom himself, and several beeves were consumed. On the last day of the feast more cattle were slaughtered and there was an ox race. The bride emerged from seclusion and went through a ceremonial, after which she was led to a hut which she was to occupy until able to build for herself. Thus was she formally placed amongst the wives, publicly announced mistress of a certain division of her husband's house.

Thus the missionary, although his account is short, gives us excellent information about several important points. The man was old and was very deliberately making a considered investment. The girl would soon be a widow and in all probability would spend the prime of her life as mistress of a house in the homestead of a younger man. In the meantime she would be a junior wife, a rafter, possibly assisting an older woman in work which she was no longer able to perform with ease and efficiency. The old man would recover in household service and in abundance of food what he had lost in cattle. Nor must we omit to mention the enormous sanction of publicity; there could be no doubt whatever as to the new status of the girl. The feasting is yet another matter. We should say that quite a substantial part of the most valued diet of these people is taken on the occasion of ceremonial feasts, and that these are of particular importance as giving significance to special groupings of people, in this case the neighbourhood who were interested in the marriage, and that it is upon these occasions that people chiefly bring themselves to face the enormous economic charges of slaughtering valuable animals. It is almost exclusively on such occasions of heightened emotions and special meetings that beasts are taken into the cattle kraal for the last time for the killing.

The Cape Colony Commission on Native Laws and Customs (1881-1883) made excellent efforts to unravel the true nature of the family as an economic unit. The questions put by the Commissioners may appear to be crude, but they did succeed in eliciting information. Thus one European witness was asked, "Are women looked upon as having any civil rights?" The answer was that a few, such as wives, widows and daughters of chiefs, had some rights. The next question was, "Would you interfere with that custom by giving a woman rights?" The witness was inclined to think that such a drastic step should not be taken until it was called for "by the improved condition of the women". He pointed out, however, that when a wife by her industry produces corn enough to maintain her family, and with surplus to barter for a cow, that cow with its increase is looked upon as her property, separate from the estate of her husband.

The next question was whether in view of the woman herself being considered as property, and of cattle being given at her marriage, "she is virtually indentured"? The answer was "Yes, perhaps so, but her husband can't sell her again, as he could a chattel."

Native witnesses were questioned and, with special reference to the Fingo people, asked whether polygamy was a custom which they wished to be continued? They replied that it was, that "a man who marries many wives does injury to no one, and merely adds to his own stock of corn (importance)". The significance of the woman's own house as an economic unit appeared later, when it was asked whether a man may hold property in his own right apart from his family? The answer was, "There are instances among us; for instance, my father is dead. My mother is alive. Certain cattle who were attached to my mother's house are reserved and kept apart by me. They are peculiarly my property; when I die they descend to my eldest son, and are treated by him in the same way." We have not yet described one most important aspect of the Bantu family system, which is that the sharing out of property between wives almost automatically provides the system of inheritance. In fact at every point the polygynous household acts as an economic unit not merely at any given moment but continuously through time.

The Bishop of St. John's gave written evidence to the Commission and showed an excellent understanding of the economic aspect of the people's family life. Bride-price, he said, might with advantage be regulated by law, "but its ramifications are so intricate and extensive that any hasty or unwise legislation might create evils which do not exist now." The natives, he remarked, could always render regulations nugatory by an understanding with each other. With regard to the structure of the household, the Bishop pointed out that the man is the head of the homestead. "He has property of his own, and has a voice over the whole property of the kraal [homestead], but not absolute power over it for his power is limited by the rights of the houses and of the several wives, which may be asserted by their friends if he refused to regard the expressed wishes of the houses."

Other European witnesses were questioned, mainly about the position of wives other than the first. It was pointed out that in the case of a man having several wives, in one of the districts referred to, each would have her own house but they would also be grouped under two main houses, those of the great wife and of the right-hand wife. The next wife would be a rafter to one of these, and any other wife also would become a rafter to one of the two great houses. This is an aspect which hitherto we have not sufficiently stressed. Always, throughout Bantu Africa, one wife, usually the first, has an outstanding position. The details vary greatly, even neighbouring districts differing, for example, on such points as whether the first wife will always remain the great wife, whether there will be a left-hand wife who will have a special position second only to that of the great wife, and whether other wives will be relatively independent or will always be regarded as in some way within the household of a senior woman. In the case of the Xosa people the rule is for the first wife to be the great wife, the second to be the right-hand wife, and for the third possibly to be known as the left-hand wife but always attached as a rafter to one or other of the first two.

The term "rafter" is expressive. The motivation to take an additional wife must, from the form of the family structure, often come from a senior wife who wishes to have an assistant. The cattle to obtain the new wife must come from the herds of the other wives, and in practice they tend to be supplied by one senior wife in agreement, of course, with her husband. The older woman thus makes the investment in quite as full a sense as does the man; it is done by agreement between them. But the wife whose private herd is directly depleted looks for a direct return. It comes, in the first place, through the working power of the new wife. This enlarges the food resources of the older woman, giving her a more powerful standing within the homestead, and greatly increases her ability not only to grow enough grain for beer but also to cope with the laborious work of brewing. Since beer is second scarcely even to meat as an ingredient of feasts, the woman's status is closely affected by her power to produce it, and the man's by his power to dispense it.

The same witness was asked whether the head of the homestead has the power to decide upon the status of each wife. He answered, "He would not decide upon the status of any house without due deliberation, and would consult with his relatives." The answer shows an incomplete appreciation of the normal way in which houses get their status, but it led to another question which produced a useful answer from a native who was present. The question was as to whether there were any instances of a man attaching more rafters to his right-hand house than to his great house? The answer was to the effect that if the great wife is really unpopular the smaller wives may appeal to the husband to be transferred to the other side of the circle of huts, that is to say, to the right-hand wife. In this way the right-hand house could become more important than the great house, but, it was added, the practice was unusual.

The native witness went on to say that the principal wives had a good deal of authority over the rest. "They would be like a family, the great wife being a mother, and the other wives would assist in the work going on, for instance, in the garden. They would go to the great wife and say, 'Where is the seed, as we will dig in the garden.' Most likely the great wife would be there also."

When a wife is newly married, cattle will probably be apportioned to her at once. If she were attached to the great wife's house a cow or two might be taken from that house and given to her for her support; thus the great wife, before a subsidiary can be taken, must have not only enough cattle for the greater part of the bride-price, but must also have enough to spare to give the new-comer the necessary milk, and, in the old days, skins for her clothing. The investment, it should be noted, would be expected to bring in a further long-distance return as well as the immediate result from the new wife's work; some sixteen to twenty years later, it might be hoped, a daughter of the new wife would be married and would fetch cattle to replace those taken from the great house. The advantage of these cattle might go to the son of the great wife if his mother were old or had died in the meantime. The economic balance is kept in adjustment through the generations.

Acquisitions to the cattle of the homestead, as they came to be made, would be apportioned according to simple rules. Those acquired by the wives would remain the assets of their own houses, while a senior wife might allocate a beast acquired by her own skill to one of the juniors in her house. It would thus not be lost to her, and she must help to see that the wives under her are properly equipped. Cattle acquired by the man would be allocated to one of the houses, whether of a senior wife or of a rafter, according, ultimately, to his judgment as to which would make best use of it. If the allocation is not made when the beast is acquired, and made publicly, it is assumed that it has been attached to the great house. "If the husband merely drove the cattle into the kraal without apportioning them, then they would be taken for granted as belonging to the great house." That is, of course, unless it was known that they were in return for the daughter of some one house, and consequently needed no allocation. A native witness gave an illustration of what happened when he acquired some cattle.

"For instance when I returned to my kraal with two head of cattle from a son-in-law, I called my sons and wives together and said, 'This red cow goes to the right-hand house, and the other cow I give to the rafter of the great house.' My great son, the universal heir, who was present, approved of what I did." The native witnesses here disagree with the Bishop of St. John's, who had regarded the man as having unallotted cattle.

The greater number of cattle will go to the great house, but that house has greater obligations to fulfil in return. Despite the great powers of the wives over cattle which have been apportioned to them, much ultimate power rests with the man. Thus if he is fined he must go round his wives' houses and decide from which he will take the cattle to pay the fine. He must balance the claims of the various houses. Only very recently it has been urged at the Transkeian General Council that when a man has to collect cattle to pay a fine he should not be distrained upon for those which his wives brought with them at marriage from their fathers, since these are in a peculiar sense their personal property, distinct from those allocated to them by their husband, and necessary for their food supply. Every woman, excepting only the very poorest, takes a cow from her father's herd to be the foundation of her own house. This is only one of the many ways in which the traditional practices of the people, retaining their vitality, influence behaviour at the present day and so make it essential for us to understand the roots of these practices.

Continuing our examination of the evidence given by native witnesses, we find these witnesses being asked whether many disputes arise through a man neglecting to make the allocation of cattle. They were asked whether the chief would step in and remind him of his duty. We presume that the commissioners had in mind some purely suppositious case of a man keeping so many cattle undistributed that it would be obvious that the great house was not entitled to them all. The replies give more valuable insight into the workings of the system. They are to the effect that not the chief, but the man's relatives, would say to him that he must share out the cattle. Asked what would happen if a man left his home in Tembuland to buy cattle in Cape Colony but died on the way back, the witnesses answered that the son, that is to say the son of the great wife, would go and fetch the cattle which his father had bought. The distribution would rest in his hands. "In most cases he would allot the cattle just as his father would have done. When the son succeeded to his father's place in the kraal, in all probability the chief himself would go and visit the young man and give him advice, or there would be an assembly of councillors, and men in the neighbourhood, and the young man would be told that he is now in the place of his father, that he must remember he has great trust reposed in him, and that he must look after the children left by his father." If the son persisted in keeping the cattle for himself, his uncles would step in and remonstrate with him. If, still, there should be difficulty, the family would appeal to the chief. The chief might intervene to the extent of dividing the cattle equally between the houses, but this would not be probable, since the needs of the various wives might be different. One might have many children and another few. The chief would be more likely to order the relatives of the deceased father to settle the matter.

The Commission then branched into a discussion, with the native witnesses, of some of the consequences of local missions having interfered, among their converts, with the practice of giving bride-price. We cannot here devote space to this very interesting episode, but it is well worth our while to note that the upshot was that the witnesses declared that there was more immorality on mission stations than in the kraals. The missionary member of the Commission expressed his surprise, but the witnesses stuck to their point and, apparently, actually gave names of some girls on mission stations who had become mothers without being married. We can only hope the immediate consequences were not too serious; the important point for us arising from the discussion is that the natives one and all insisted upon the control over his daughters which a father had through bride-price, and that once this was removed anything might happen. We thus see it made clear that the father's function as economic leader of his homestead includes and is reinforced by his duty of controlling bride-price. Clearly he would always co-operate with the girl's mother, yet his ultimate responsibility stands. It is he who arranges bride-price for the sons, who receives it for the daughters. When it is given in instalments, he must claim these when he thinks he can pay them as best he can. Thus he must keep himself aware of the economic position of his debtors and creditors over marriage bargains. The responsibility is great, and presumes that he will have sufficient leisure to travel and see people. Since he is in this way the main controller of incoming and outgoing cattle with regard to his homestead, his economic control is assured.

REFERENCES AND FURTHER READING

One Hundred and Fifty Years of Economic Contact between Black and White (Art.). H. M. Robertson. South African Journal of Economics, 1934-35.
Cape Colony Native Laws and Customs Commission. 1881-83.
    Appendix B. Hon. C. Brownlee's Notes.
    Replies by the Hon. C. Brownlee.
    Replies by the Bishop of St. Johns.
    Memo on *Native Laws and Customs of the Basutos.*
    Code of Native Law administered in Natal.
    Replies by T. Liefeld.
    Notes by Rev. Chalmers.
Wanderings in the Interior of South Africa. A. Steedman. 1835.
Travels in Caffraria. Kay. 1833.
Story of My Mission in South-East Africa. W. Shaw. 1860.
Kaffir Laws and Customs. J. MacLean (ed.). 1858.
History of the Abambo. Ayliff and Whiteside. 1912.
Hunger and Work in a Savage Tribe. A. I. Richards. 1932.
The Life of a South African Tribe. H. A. Junod. 1927.
Reaction to Conquest. M. Hunter. 1937.

SECTION II

The Bomvana

All of the principles which we have enunciated receive interesting illustration in Cook's book on the Bomvana. These are a typical cattle-owning Bantu people. A survey of Cook's material will serve to illustrate many important points.

SURVEY OF ECONOMIC UNITS

It is first made clear that the Transkeian peoples do not live in villages; the term "village" is misleading, in fact, in almost any part of Bantu Africa. It is so frequently used, however, that a slight passing reference may be made to it. In some cases a kind of village may be said to emerge when homesteads are closely grouped. Such a grouping may be found, though seldom, in almost any part of the territory of which we write. On the whole it is not good to think of such agglomerations of homesteads as units. They seldom function in a way much different from the more scattered homesteads which are so much more common. New principles of government, law, or economics never seem to be discoverable merely when several homesteads happen to be placed close to each other. Cook points out that as a rule Bomvana homesteads are dotted about the tops of ridges; they nearly always do cluster into a situation suitable for residence and for cattle; but, as Cook points out, the Transkeian peoples do not live in villages. The same has to be said of the very great majority of the Bantu peoples.

Another sense in which "village" may be found from time to time in Bantu Africa is that the homesteads of chiefs and other very wealthy men may become so large that for all practical purposes they are villages. But even here the principles of the homestead function almost without changes.

Among the Bomvana, Cook uses the term "house" to designate "the wife or wives and their children who are ranked together". Thus the great house will include the great wife, her children and any supporting wives and their children. It is further shown that a man may have several homesteads, and that in this case it is left to him to decide in which the houses are to be grouped. Thus, although it is common for minor wives to be within the houses of the more important wives, he may, for example, have both the great and the right-hand wives in one homestead, and minor wives in another. These minor wives still belong to the houses of the more important wives, but obviously cannot be under their economic leadership in the same way as if they were in the same homestead. Whether they are effectively under their leadership in field cultivation, we are not told. This is quite possible, for normally members of different homesteads may work fields which are grouped together.

As in the case of so many Bantu peoples, we are told that homesteads are smaller to-day than formerly. The Bomvana have now only two houses, as a rule, in each family, the great house and the right-hand house. It appears that in other days it was usual to have not merely extra wives, but specifically named houses for these wives. Every example drives home the point that the Bantu homestead is not, and never has been, a mere agglomeration of wives. It becomes clear that whether the number of wives per man was small or large they were invariably organized into groups, each with its own organization, enabling it to function as an economic unit.

Among the Bomvana the principle of rank is active in the grouping of houses as well as of wives within each house, so that the great wife of a homestead is the senior wife of the senior house. Her hut is usually the largest, and to it, that is, to her private establishment within the homestead, is attached the greatest amount of property. Her establishment also has an especial significance from the fact that her eldest son is heir to the leader of the homestead. This son, as we shall see more particularly in dealing with other matters such as inheritance, has always, even before he is adult, a peculiarly powerful position. In some ways his economic leadership may be more effective than that of his father. No other male in the homestead can challenge his position; some of his half-brothers may be older, but even they are junior to him in rank.

Cook tells us that the great wife of a chief is usually the one whom he marries when quite an old man. Commoners almost invariably have the first wife as the great wife. In the case of the great wives of chiefs a new principle is introduced, for they are paid for, not by the chief himself, but by the whole people. This, again, is a practice widely distributed throughout Bantu Africa, giving the whole of the people a direct interest, through their economic contribution, in the great wife of the chief, the mother of the future chief.

It is emphasized that among the Bomvana the great wife receives treatment which "varies but slightly from that received by the other wives". Always the wives in the Bantu family, with the very rare exceptions of those in the households of the greatest chiefs, of whom there are a mere handful on record, form a co-operating unit in which all are more or less on equal terms. There is no sign that the great wife ever stands apart to direct the activities of the others in a managerial way. She always has her own fields, and tills them until old age with her own hands. The point is important, for the managerial function, so far from being lacking, is very much in evidence and is exercised by the husband.

Very frequently among the Bomvana, according to Cook, a wealthy man will build separate homesteads for the great house and the right-hand house. The deciding factor in the building of a separate homestead appears to be the number of cattle. If a man has a large herd he must have separate cattle kraals, hence separate homesteads.

The houses of supporting wives tend to have significance from the fact that their sons become heirs in the event of the senior wives being childless, or of their sons dying. Apart from this, the main element in the position of a minor wife is that she is a "rafter" to a senior wife. Yet the fact remains that in a few cases the Bomvana have the supporting wives not attached to the more important houses but all placed together in a separate homestead. Within such a homestead, again, one of the minor wives will inevitably be senior and will have her position so marked by her hut being in the centre of the semi-circle, opposite the gate of the cattle kraal. The fact that minor wives can be grouped in this way shows that there is no fundamental distinction between them and their seniors, who, in their own homesteads, manage day-to-day affairs while the juniors carry out exactly the same routine in their separate establishment. Once again, we do not know the precise extent of economic co-operation between such homesteads. It is very possible that all of the wives co-operate in field labour; it is also highly probable that their essential co-operation consists in the fact that the cattle in each homestead are under the ultimate management of one man, that all of the women also are under his management as regards the routine of their agriculture work, the amount of land which each will cultivate, the sharing out of the crops as food and for sale, and the innumerable other ways in which the family, in this case a group of homesteads, co-operate economically.

Cook gives interesting reflections upon the parts played by various members within a typical homestead. Brothers, particularly elder brothers, are interested in the lives of their sisters and take an active part in such matters as bride-price and the selection of husbands. This active interest, or control, is reflected in the behaviour of brothers and sisters who, as they grow up, associate less freely and show respect towards each other. But the most interesting part is that played by the son of the great wife. He is leader of his other brothers, even though these may be half-brothers who are older in years than he. He becomes leader, the "younger father", and often much more practically interested in the affairs of the family, at least in their everyday aspect, than is the father himself. There is great cohesion among brothers, since they grow up in very close contact and, through the principle of age-grouping, so active in all Bantu society, do not associate with their elders. In day-to-day labours it may well be the eldest brother in each homestead who is consulted about cattle and about food; the father, especially as he becomes older, is regarded as "the repository of law and order". His sons and daughters may stand in awe before him. His ultimate economic control is unquestioned, even though he may delegate management to his heir.

Coming to the relatives by marriage, the mother's brother is important. He does not play a part in the current management of any homestead except his own, but he remains important in that homestead into which his sister has married. He is in a way her ultimate guardian; should she suffer a charge of witchcraft, he is her refuge; similarly, should her sons need help they will go to him. "He cannot refuse food or aid". His attitude is friendly and is symbolized by gifts and by beasts for sacrifice. He ought to give his sister's son a beast or other kind of present at his coming out from the initiation school. If this son is sick his uncle may sacrifice for him at his, which is also the boy's mother's, homestead.

The mother-line is not forgotten. Economic co-operation of a distinctive type is maintained between homesteads united by marriage. Further, we must again emphasize that in a polygynous society, in which the prosperity and happiness of a wife depends upon her fair treatment among other wives, it is of great advantage for her to have one man of her own generation who is peculiarly interested in her welfare and in that of her children. Her husband is interested in all his wives and their children; each wife's brother, outside of his own homestead, looks after her especial interests. A further security is given not only for the active distribution of resources between homesteads, but for the active maintenance of the status of each wife and her house, upon which her economic efficiency may depend.

REFERENCE AND FURTHER READING

Social Organisation of the Bomvana. T. A. W. Cook.

SECTION III

The Pondo

By far the most complete and expert analysis of Bantu social life in modern literature is that made by Hunter in her book, *Reaction to Conquest*, a study of culture contact in South-East Africa with special reference to the Pondo people. Our survey of Hunter's work must be brief, evaluating only such information as other writers usually do not produce. The Pondo system is typically Bantu, conforming to all of the tendencies which we have described as normal in Bantu Africa. We thus need devote but slight space to elementary description. Each house consists of a woman and her children; it has its own property in cattle and the right to till certain fields; "but all the members of the Umzi (homestead) eat together and work together". The women take it in turns to cook, the work being fairly equally shared. The work of cooking is not sharply separated from work in the fields; according to the season, one wife will leave the fields early and cook for the other. Thus the women's work is regarded more or less as a whole, and co-operation is secured on this basis. Hunter mentions a feature to which we have not as yet given attention, but which is found throughout all the Bantu peoples, namely, that a young wife spends perhaps a year in a kind of apprenticeship. During this year she cannot have her own stores of food, for her new fields will not yet be yielding. Correspondingly with this situation, a house is not built for her during that year. Not contributing to the homestead's food, she does not have the full status of a wife. The young Pondo bride "cooks for her mother-in-law" for about a year; she sleeps in a storehouse, with her husband, if she is an only wife. The date at which she is supplied with a house of her own is not strictly determined by custom. Hunter gives a most illuminating example of the kind of circumstances which influence conduct within a Bantu household. Although it is usual for a woman to take her own house after about a year, or when her first child is born, an example is given of a homestead in which five wives, married to three sons, still live with the mother of these men. The reason given was that they had no elder children to look after their babies, so found it easier to leave them all in their mother-in-law's hut.

The freeing of a young wife from her apprenticeship is on the initiative of her mother-in-law, but the wife "cannot but be satisfied if her mother says that it is right that she should go". The elder women thus have power to regulate the positions of the younger. The moment of decision must come at harvest. It is then that the young wife can collect food of her own growing, from her own field. The mother-in-law says "go and get meals from your own field, and cook in your own hut". The young woman takes on new responsibilities; there may be children other than her own, who must be fed, and her mother-in-law calls the children of the homestead and says, "You and you will go and get food from So-and-so's hut". The transition of the wife to a higher stage is marked also at this time by the important allocation of a cow to be milked for her house.

The sharing of responsibility for making food last through the year, between the man and his wife, is clearly stated by

Hunter when she tells us that normally it is the woman who arranges the menu and decides upon the quantities of food to be cooked, but that the men control the store-pits in the cattle kraal, and that they complain if they think that the food is being used up too quickly.

Hunter emphasizes well the human basis of co-operation within the homestead. Each mother and her own children are bound by emotional ties which make them a clear unit within the larger unit, and never lost in it. These emotional ties extend to the property of the woman's house, in which she and her children have a vital interest. "Often there is rivalry between two wives of one man to secure property for their house." Much emphasis is laid by the people upon the duty of a woman to feed children other than her own, but Hunter points out that this very emphasis reveals the special interest of the woman in her own children. The same problems of securing co-operation between groups are evident in Bantu Africa as in Europe. There is the same larger economic interest of the whole group, opposed by the willingness of its components to benefit at each other's cost. Competing economic interests are real, and the group can function only when its own emotional ties are sufficiently strong to override those of sectional interests.

As with other peoples, the Pondo have the problem of deciding upon the best size for the homestead. This, of course, will never be the best merely from the economic point of view. In the old days defence may often have kept homesteads at an uneconomically large size; to-day it is possible that personal feelings and family ideals have the same effect, though this remains to be investigated. Hunter makes it clear, however, that removals of homesteads are not unusual and, this being so, we may assume that they break up into their component parts as readily as need be. The frequent removal of homesteads is another very prevalent habit almost throughout Bantu Africa. Especially among cattle-owning peoples, removal must be normal, for a cattle kraal cannot stay many seasons in one place unless the people have a regular method of clearing it out, and this, so far as we know, is lacking. The tendency to move homesteads fairly frequently is strongly confirmed among the Bantu by their supernatural beliefs. The actual reason for a move will usually be something of a supernatural nature, an association of witchcraft with the place, the displeasure of spirits, the death of several members without obvious explanation, or of the eldest man.

Hunter, giving us more information about the factors determining the size of the homestead than we get from any other writer, shows that as the homestead grows it tends to split up. A large homestead may be unmanageable for purely human reasons, its members failing to agree personally; the resulting economic loss from any such state of affairs must be considerable, and the obvious remedy lies in changing the size of the unit. This may be done in one of two ways, depending upon the situation. Thus if one man has a considerable number of wives he may put a number of them into a new homestead. Hunter makes it clear that this is uncommon among the Pondo, although chiefs used to use it as a means of controlling outlying districts, and she states that there is no evidence that the practice was ever really common. On the other hand, it is very easy for a homestead to divide up by one of the men in it going elsewhere with his family. This is the normal process. The ease with which it is carried out, especially when homesteads are in any case not regarded as permanently located, indicates that there should be no real difficulty in a homestead having approximately the most advantageous size. We must always remember that a homestead normally has several brothers in it, each with his wives, and that each of these men is actuated to some extent by the ideal of having his own circle of huts.

The strength of the ties binding a house, that is to say a woman and her children, is well illustrated by the fact that among the Pondo a son, when he comes to set up his own homestead, not only usually has his mother to live there with him, but can actually demand that she live with him, even though this involves her leaving a second husband who has given bride-price for her. This man cannot demand either her return or the return of his cattle.

The consultation between father and son on economic matters is shown by Hunter to indicate very close economic co-operation. Even when a son has set up his own homestead, which is not likely to be far away from that of his father, father and son will continue to consult about the disposal of property. If the son proposes to sell a beast or even part of a surplus crop he must of course co-operate with the wife, but will also consult with his father. When Hunter wished to buy a second-hand barrel, worth ten shillings, from an elderly man, this man would not close the deal "until he had consulted a son living in his own *umzi*, a mile away". Many illustrations serve to show the significance of a group of homesteads, linked by kinship, by intermarriage, by simple neighbourhood. The homestead is certainly the key economic unit but it is not the ultimate one. It may be regarded as midway between the woman's house, on the one hand, and on the other, the district.

The working relationships between father and son are of the essence of Bantu economic life. We know of the father's ultimate responsibility for the feeding of an unmarried son. He must apportion cattle so that the boy's mother has a sufficient supply of milk; he must see that she has enough fields cleared, and that she receives all the assistance to which she is entitled in cultivating them; should the boy's own mother be unable for any reason to maintain him, the father is responsible for seeing that he is kept by some other woman in the homestead. These responsibilities are shared at every point by the boy's mother, yet in fact and in the outlook of the people the father has the key position, which is further emphasized by his strong obligation to provide the cattle for his son's first wife. The return obligations of the son are no less real, and are directed specifically to one parent or the other, with little confusion. He will keep his mother when she is old; he will help her always to fight for the rights of her house. But it is to his father that he owes assistance in all men's work and, in the old days, his prizes from war and hunting. The strength of these obligations is shown by their persistence under very different circumstances at the present day. In South African law the native father is regarded as controlling the labour of his sons

189

and as being responsible for their actions and torts while they are minors, so that under the Master and Servant law it is assumed that when a native man contracts to give service to a farmer he also contracts the labour of his sons. Hunter shows also that when a boy brings his wages back from European employment he is expected to hand them over to his father.

The economic co-operation of father and son receives, as do so many of these vital elements in Bantu culture, strong sanction from the people's religion. When a son is ill in his father's homestead, his father is responsible for sacrificing in order to restore his health. As will be seen later, a sacrifice among these cattle-owning people may involve an economic decision of the first order. But even when the son has gone to his own homestead he and his father will consult before either of them will offer a sacrifice. Their economic co-operation is confirmed and strengthened by the requirement of their religion. Were it merely a matter of consulting about selling a little grain or a second-hand barrel, the consultation might fall into neglect; the sheer necessity, however, of consulting over vital matters such as sacrifice, involving the slaughter of precious cattle, keeps the practice alive and vital.

The part played by the father's brothers in a homestead or in neighbouring homesteads is well described by Hunter. She shows that the father's brothers frequently live in the same homestead as the child and may have as close a daily contact with him as his own father. The economic relationships between the boy and his father's brothers are, however, very unlike those with his father. He will inherit nothing from him; he is most unlikely to receive any of his bride-price from him, unless the father is poor. Yet the uncle may be consulted in important matters such as the sacrifice of an ox or cow. Further, the father's brothers all have the same father, the boy's grandfather, and this holds the group together in important ways so long as the grandfather lives. He is regarded as "the source" and is consulted about the disposal of property even by his grandsons.

A father's economic relationship with a daughter is of less day-to-day importance than that with his son. The daughter spends by far the greater part of her adult life in another homestead, quite possibly in a different district. Yet the economic relationship is perfectly definite. The father owes the daughter maintenance while she grows up, until her contributions to the resources of her mother's house becomes substantial. The father receives her bride-price, but, as we have seen, this may not imply much, if any, nett gain. On the other hand, he and his wives have the clearest obligations to the daughter all her life, even after she has gone to her husband's home. Her father has first to provide her with a wedding outfit, a heavy outlay, then, among the Pondo, to dress her all her life. He must also provide gifts for her in-laws, while the maintenance of her house in domestic utensils provides another example of that sort of circular transfer of resources which appears to be a feature of primitive societies, and which we shall now examine.

The Pondo wife, wishing to acquire new household goods, visits her father's homestead and helps herself to such goods as she wishes, at the expense of the wives there. They do not protest, and Hunter even gives an example of a young woman who bought a new dress from a trader then soon afterwards appeared in rags. She explained that the dress had been taken by one of her husband's sisters who had visited the homestead. The wife visiting her father's home may take what clothing and household utensils she wishes. The sufferers are the wives in their homestead; their remedy is clear; they in their turn visit their father's homesteads and take what they need. Although this system of transactions is carried out without ceremonial, it appears to have much in common with the circular exchange of the *kula* and *urigubu* of the Trobriand Islanders reported by Malinowski. From a directly utilitarian point of view the transaction is nonsensical. Yet, as Malinowski has shown, it may have great cultural value.

Without pressing further the parallel between the Trobrianders and the Pondo, we may see at a glance some of the ways in which this custom may have great economic significance. In the first place, it marks the responsibility of the man and his household to continue their active interest in his daughter even after she has gone away; the man has, after all, received bride-price for her; in native opinion this is to her credit, and entitles her to something in exchange, even though the cows may have gone to get a wife for one of the girl's brothers; they were acquired on account of the personal value of the girl. In the second place, the circulation of resources, with the contacts which this entails, is in itself something of value in Bantu sentiment; nothing could be more foreign to this sentiment than the ideal of each man and wife simply producing things and using them at once without the thrill of exchange and the satisfaction of vital social contacts far beyond the close family circle. It provides one of the means by which social ties are maintained so that they may be economically efficient; the family groups who exchange household goods will almost certainly co-operate in bigger enterprises. Further, Bantu women work very hard and require holidays; such a simple explanation of their visits to their father's homesteads is not to be overlooked.

On their visits, Hunter reports, they are definitely honoured persons. If the things which they want are not there, the wives will scatter and find them. The visitor will help in the fields, but by grace and not by obligation. Her whole position in her father's homestead is shown to be quite unlike that in her husband's, and it is clear that her life would be poorer had she not these two settings between which to oscillate. In the place where she is a wife she is not without honour, but, especially when a young wife, her work is hard. A mother-in-law in Hunter's book calls her son's wife "the bell", because now that she is here she will just call and get things done as a white mistress does. The new wife is an economic asset, invested in for economic reasons. When young, she has more work than honour. But no one will deny her her visits to her father's homestead, where her standing is different, for here she is a woman whose bride-price has brought cattle to the kraal.

We return to the central point, which is that the polygynous family is the means whereby the Bantu man for the most part exercises his economic interests. Through bride-price he is able to invest his surplus capital, which it is the great interest of his life to acquire. The increase in his herds may come from skilful tending, clever bargaining, from good fortune aided by magic; through his wives, under his direction, producing surplus food for sale. The whole process links up at every point with the smooth working and effective application of labour in the household. The people do not labour merely to have food and clothing. Their culture provides them with a complex apparatus wherein many needs are satisfied beyond the primary ones, and in which the satisfaction is attained not merely by increased stores or herds, though these are vitally important, but also by a general feeling of plenty which enables the people to satisfy social as well as material desires, to strive for the complete circle of huts round the cattle kraal, for the family, as we have seen, is the central institution in the administration of economic resources, of the material and the human energy at the disposal of the people.

REFERENCE AND FURTHER READING

Reaction to Conquest. M. Hunter. 1937.

SECTION IV

The Zulus

Krige begins her study of Zulu homestead life with a passage which we shall quote. Note that she uses the term "village" as equivalent to our term "homestead": "Though the head of the village often has a large number of wives, things run very smoothly in a Zulu village, because each woman is independent. She has her own hut, her own fields which she cultivates to supply the needs of her own household, and also cattle appointed to her hut for its own special use. These cattle are inherited by her eldest son, and once they have been apportioned, do not strictly belong to the husband any more. Each wife is expected to grow sufficient food to supply her own household, and though she cooks for the inmates of her own hut only, she must always send food to her husband."

N   193

The economic independence of each woman's house among the Zulus, and they are a typical Bantu people, is further illustrated by Krige when she shows that husbands may arrange to live at the huts of each of the wives in turn, and that they will have their meals in the hut in which they are staying; food will, as usual, be supplied to the man by all of the wives, and any left over will be returned to the one from whom it came. The rules regarding the supply of food are important both in themselves and in their defining the more general economic situation. Rights and obligations with regard to food symbolize more important rights and obligations; the right of a wife to have returned to her the food of her own supplying, which has not been used, is one of those daily matters which constantly keeps before the minds of the people the economic status of the wife. But the food in itself is important; it is a large part of the people's economic resources, and at certain periods of the year a very large part.

Krige also shows how in a larger homestead the houses of the principal wives, embracing the houses of several lesser wives, may become economic units of a special kind. In such a homestead only the wives within the house of the great wife may at one time send food to the husband, that is, when he is living in that part of the homestead. This applies when the great wife's house is large and may, for practical purposes, be regarded as detached from the rest of the homestead. In certain circumstances, as when there is a first-class supply of suitable land within easy reach, there may be no need for a man with many wives to split up his homestead. Nevertheless it appears that the parts which might become separate homesteads function with a certain independence.

The economic value of children's labour is well illustrated by Krige. Little girls of six, she tells us, may often be seen nursing their smaller brothers and sisters, while the "little girls are as busy as their mothers, helping them at home or in the fields". The leadership of the head of the homestead is recognized even in the routine of milking, for when milking time comes, his cows are milked before anyone else begins the process. The differentiation of the spheres of activity of men and women among the Zulus is emphasized. The sexes have different spheres and never encroach upon each other. "This differentiation is carried into the minutest detail of their daily life". The whole code of manners emphasizes the fundamental distinction, and the significance of this for the economic aspect of the people's lives can never be overestimated. It is a commonplace that the main division of labour among primitive peoples is by sex, and it is just the details of this division which most often draws adverse criticism from superficial European observers.

It is essential, however, to realize that upon this elementary sharing of work rests the whole structure regulating the economic aspect of life. Any change in the economic functions of men or women—and such changes are consistently made, for custom is never a rigid thing—involves not merely a change in the actual performance of work, but a rebalancing of obligations all along the line. In a relatively undifferentiated society, the primary differentiations provide the basis for economic organization. Rank is second in importance only to sex, or equally important in different ways, and we have seen throughout our study of kinship that the principle of rank constantly functions in economic matters. The head of the homestead is economic leader; his wives are arranged according to rank, the great wife being economic leader in the woman's sphere, unless the man's mother is still active. The brothers and sons of the head also have their rank, with economic responsibilities corresponding to it. Age is another natural fact which gives a basis for the sharing out of economic functions. The youngest boys and girls herd goats and nurse babies; the oldest men and women become responsible for the telling of folk tales, a not unimportant contribution to the economic life of the homestead. Between youth and old age is the prime of life, which itself is divided, for we have seen that the young wife has not quite the same responsibilities or privileges as her older co-wives.

Krige shows that the head of the homestead in Zululand exercises all the economic functions which we have found him to exercise elsewhere. She does, however, add to our analyses by showing the amount of solid work involved in his responsibility for law and order. He must hold many consultations and keep in touch with many relatives and neighbours in order to know exactly what is best to do. It is not hard manual work, and it is always carried out in an atmosphere of ease and hospitality, but it is just through the man's success in his management of human relationships that the economic welfare of his dependants will grow or decline.

The relationship between homesteads united by marriage among the Zulus is well illustrated in Krige's book, and has a very wide applicability through Bantu Africa. Krige tells us that in former days marriage created a very special relationship between a man and his wife's people. This is true not only of former days but of the present day, and is one of the facts to be reckoned with in treating of Bantu economic life, even under conditions of extensive Westernization. A man among the Zulus is reported as being under constant obligation to assist his father-in-law. Each time the father-in-law obtained a wife for one of his sons, the son-in-law would contribute a beast. Any time the father-in-law needed help he could demand service from his daughter's husband. A son-in-law is called in Zululand "the handle of the hoe", the hoe being the most important implement owned by the people, and with ritual as well as utilitarian significance. The procedure of the Zulu father-in-law in asking his "hoe-handle" for assistance in finding bride-price for a son is illuminating. He would first of all send an ox to the son-in-law, which would become the young man's property even though he sent nothing in return. But he would send as many cattle as he could afford back with the messengers who brought the ox. This shows clearly that bride-price is something which can extend into a chain of economic exchanges, involving the disposal of considerable wealth over long periods of years. In relationships between homesteads linked by marriage economic co-operation is a most essential feature. Much has been made by writers of the so-called antagonism between such families; Krige indicates this antagonism at the time of marriage, but shows that it is definitely ended at the wedding feast and that thenceforth an interchange of presents seals the bonds. In our opinion the antagonism before marriage is predominantly ritual. It very largely takes the form of competitive display of wealth. This display is of great economic importance, for it publicizes the standing of the parties. That lasting economic co-operation is established is clear. This may be of even greater significance if the intermarried families live so far apart that they would not otherwise be economically linked. The psychology of the situation must not be one simplified in any one direction. There is strain between the two families, and this is represented in bargaining. There is fundamental co-operation; this is the reality which must function, otherwise there could be no bargaining; new economic relationships are set up and maintained by the social fact of intermarriage.

References and Further Reading

Zulu-Land. Rev. L. Grout. 1864.
A Journey to the Zoolu Country. A. F. Gardiner. 1836.
Zulu-English Dictionary. Bryant.
Among the Zulus. D. Leslie. 1875.
Kaffirs of Natal. J. Shooter. 1857.
The Social System of the Zulus. E. J. Krige. 1936.

Section V

The Thonga

Junod, in his unsystematic but highly illuminating way, throws considerable light upon the economic aspect of Bantu family life. He writes of the Thonga people in Portuguese East Africa, and every fact adduced bears out the essential similarity of these peoples to all other Bantu peoples in these vital points. Junod makes it clear that nowadays marriages take place at a much earlier age than formerly, since now by working for Europeans the young man can get enough cattle or money for his bride-price. This bears out the analysis which showed that bride-price is the capital which the man has to accumulate in order to establish and expand his homestead. With it becoming easier to obtain, we should expect to find fundamental changes in Bantu family life. Junod also shows that in former times it was the boys who had to be fully grown before they could think of marriage; he gives twenty-five as the accepted age. Girls, we know, married much younger, thus providing one of the essential conditions for the polygynous household. About the economic significance of polygyny Junod leaves no doubts. "Conclusion: the greatness of an African is before all else a matter of pots, and the matter of pots is closely connected with polygamy." He gives picturesque accounts of successful polygamists beginning with an arc of huts, extending this into a semi-circle, possibly into a complete circle, and dispensing hospitality to the countryside, so achieving all the power and prestige that is of the essence of the Bantu ideal of life.

Junod makes it clear that the wife may be little more than a servant during her first year of marriage. She must cook at the fireplace of her mother-in-law. She has not yet her own pot, and cannot have, for she has not yet the mealies of her own garden, having cultivated the previous year in the gardens of her own father and mother. If she is her husband's first wife he is not yet a "lord", but if he is rich, or heir to a rich man, he will soon have a second and third wife. Most men do not achieve a complete circular homestead; "Three or four huts, a wretched quarter of a circle is all that they attain to."

The value of the work of daughters is well illustrated by Junod. The young girl may stay for a time with her grandfather, then will return to her mother and work for her; "the mother needs no longer to crush her mealies, neither to go to the well nor to the fireplace". But after the daughters are married the mother again has to do her own work. In agriculture everyone in the family has his or her own field, the mother's being largest, but each girl has her plot. The amount of cattle which the girl will bring into her father's household at her marriage will depend very largely on her reputation for working; more cattle may not actually be given, but her father will not let her go unless the whole bride-price is paid at once if she is known to be very industrious. "But old and decrepit women are despised. As long as they can still till their land, they are treated with consideration, but when they have lost their strength and must be fed by their children, they are looked upon as troublesome burdens. I must say that, as long as she still has an atom of vigour, a Thonga woman goes to her field and tills it. During all her lifetime she has contracted such an intimate union with Mother Earth that she cannot conceive existence away from her gardens, and she crawls to them with her hoe, by a kind of instinct, till she dies."

Junod indicates that Bantu marriage has its own emotional structure, and on his examples we may indicate the great significance of this for the people's life. Husband and wife, says Junod, have little intimacy. We shall find that this is correlated with their economic co-operation. A friendship and intimacy between a man and wife, if carried too far, would be incompatible with the carrying out of their economic function even in a monogamous family, but would still be more out of place where the ideal is that a man co-ordinates the work of several wives. Junod points out that polygamy is uniformly practised all through the Thonga tribe. This does not mean that every man has several wives, but that, as we have shown, it is an ideal toward which all men work, and that a great many men do have more than one wife in the course of their lives, while all, even those who remain monogamous, live in the homesteads of men who are more successful and thus take their place in an economy regulated according to the dictates of the system. Junod points out that the people's laws of succession necessitate polygamy, since a younger brother inherits the widow of his elder brother. The two are, indeed, intimately correlated. Not the least difficult problem in changing the structure of Bantu family life would be that of adapting the laws of succession. The general economic aspect of polygamy is further emphasized by Junod when he says: "This is the regular method of becoming a rich man, an ideal which is by no means confined to the black race."

Further light is thrown upon the structure of the family by the evidence given by Junod of the peculiarly important position of the first or great wife. He takes this to confirm the hypothesis of a primitive monogamy. We see its significance in her functions of economic leadership. Junod, we should add, wrote as a missionary very much opposed to the principle of polygamy. This leads him to put undue emphasis upon certain aspects, yet his passion for truth makes his study of the greatest value. He gives a list of the reasons for and against polygamy. These, for the light which they throw upon economic matters, are well worth summarizing. The reasons for are as follows: A proverb says, "One woman does not build (constitute) a village"; to have many wives is the glory of the headman; he can practise a generous hospitality; if one wife dies he is not left alone; if one is ill he still has food; there are many hands to do the work, for the wives help each other; there are many children; the women could not "find money to buy their clothing" unless they married. The first reason against polygamy is that it creates jealousy. This jealousy is clearly shown to be in connection with the sharing of resources; the aggrieved wife may refuse to cook or to get in the harvest. The children, we are told, are taught to hate each other and to hate their father. Here we must enter a protest; the truth of this could never be substantiated. The indication of this difficulty is, however, valuable. One of the problems of the husband is to secure co-operation among his wives in their work. Skill in this may count for as much as anything else in promoting the welfare of all; it is the main ingredient in the people's economic efficiency.

Junod's next reason against polygamy is that it encourages drunkenness, a reason which does not conflict with the general conclusion that the man has more resources, including, essentially, grain and women's labour with which to make beer. Further, it is against polygamy that "It develops pride in the heart of the polygamist". Junod's next reason is a more practical, entirely revolutionary one, namely, that polygamy is expensive as the husband must pay a tax of one pound for each wife. One of Junod's informants suggested that polygamy destroys a man's strength, but this was rather laughed at by the others. Junod, despite his bias, illumines many of the most vital points.

Junod's description of the circular homestead reinforces a

number of important points. These homesteads, he says, show a remarkable uniformity all through the tribe, being built on the same plan even in districts which have not very similar physical surroundings. They may, however, be with or without strong circular fences. In the case of homesteads without them, tactics in case of war required immediate flight, not the defence of the home, showing an essentially pastoral trait. But all have fences, even if only fragile ones. Their purpose may be almost entirely the supernatural one of excluding witchcraft. We have hitherto not included this factor in our analysis of the Bantu homestead, but it is important. Witchcraft simply represents inexplicable misfortune; if things go wrong for discoverable reasons there is no impulse to pick out some unfortunate being and to accuse him or her of exercising supernatural powers of malice. But inexplicable misfortune is always present; witchcraft is even today often given as a reason for abandoning a homestead; while an accusation of witchcraft is frequently the reason for a man and his wife leaving one homestead and setting up a place of their own. It is simply the case that things have not been going well and that he or she has in consequence been charged with witchcraft. The outer fence symbolizes protection against this supernatural enemy; it simply expresses a desire to exclude misfortune. It is significant that Junod reports homesteads today as being, on the whole, smaller than in former times and that the natives give witchcraft as the reason. Witchcraft, they believe, has considerably increased in later times and the result has been the breaking up of many homesteads. The phenomenon can doubtless be explained in terms of the difficulties which the people encounter in adapting themselves to the new ways of life.

But even apart from this, it is clear that there never was a tendency for homesteads to grow indefinitely. In Junod's words, "Generally speaking the Thonga village cannot long remain of any considerable size; it tends to fall to pieces." Junod gives three main reasons for the breaking up or moving of homesteads, which two events he regards as identical. The first is purely supernatural. If lightning strikes a homestead it will probably have to be moved, though not certainly. Lightning has a peculiar significance in Bantu culture. It appears to be invariably a communication from the most potent powers in the supernatural world, probably from some very incompletely formulated Supreme Being; the beast which is struck by lightning is the only one which is never used as food. Among the Thonga, then, there is a presumption that a homestead struck by lightning will be abandoned. But a way out may be found, presumably if the site is still good and there are no practical reasons for moving. A doctor is called in and he "treats" the place which was struck. Should he be able to find in the earth a certain kind of bird, it is a sign that the homestead may be allowed to carry on. Only when this bird has been discovered and removed are the people allowed to stay. Otherwise "the mysterious power of heaven inside the circle of huts would bring disaster". The lightning thus has at least the economic significance of incurring a doctor's fee; it may involve the expense of moving a good homestead; or it may be the occasion helping the people to make up their minds to move a homestead which was due in any case to be moved soon.

Junod's second reason is the death of the headman. This has significance for us as bringing into relief the sociology of the establishment and the ever-present mixture of practical measures and of their supernatural accompaniment. When the headman dies, his homestead must be abandoned. It was he who founded it, performing the vital rite at its inception. Upon his death his mystical connection with the homestead is broken. But it is not abandoned at once. There elapses a year of mourning which may be well occupied with the processes of inheritance, the sharing out of widows and property to the heirs. This completed, the homestead ceases to exist. It is only on the death of the headman himself that this happens, for he is the only person with rights in the whole circle of huts. When a lesser person dies, his or her own hut is destroyed.

The next reason is purely practical; the exhaustion of the gardens. These people had few cattle when Junod lived amongst them, so that they moved not to seek new pastures but to obtain better food supplies.

SURVEY OF ECONOMIC UNITS

Junod's extremely detailed and valuable account of the many rites involved in building and moving homesteads need not detain us. They are, however, of very great significance. The homestead is not a homestead without their full observance. The extra labour which they involve may be considerable; their efficacy in strengthening the emotional ties of the family well recompense this labour. It is no more to be neglected by an economist than is that of a purely utilitarian type.

The economic authority of the Thonga headman is based upon a well-defined co-operation and sharing of responsibility. He has much authority over his younger brothers and his children, his duties being to protect the family property and to secure the best disposal of resources. Thus in modern conditions, with young men enjoying sources of income which would not formerly have been theirs, the head of the household may, according to Junod, confiscate their money if they are addicted to drinking and may ruin the household property. The headman is responsible for all claims against the inmates of his homestead. He may be called upon to pay a debt contracted by any of these. This payment is, however, regarded only as a loan to the person, to be recovered in time. Yet so strong is the reality of economic responsibility within the homestead, that children inherit the debts of their deceased parents, being expected to pay them even if they inherited no valuable property. It is a Bantu maxim that "a debt never dies". Younger brothers in a homestead are by no means without economic responsibility, each in his own sphere. They have the full right to enter even into the very large bride-price contracts. Such a contract applies simply to the man, and his wife or wives, who make it. The acquisition of the extra wife is the achievement of that family, not of the whole homestead. It may be a further step toward that man setting up a homestead of his own, and we have no evidence that any obstacle is ever placed in the way of a man wishing to do this. It is, indeed, a specific right of the man to leave the homestead should he be dissatisfied with the reciprocity between himself and the headman. This exactly corresponds to the right of a man to leave a chief whom he regards as unsatisfactory, and

203

which constitutes one of the main sanctions for the efficiency of chieftainship even today in many parts of Africa. The analogy between the head of a homestead and the chief of a tribe can be carried still further, and is so carried by Junod. The headman has the right to demand work from the men in his homestead for homestead purposes. When the cattle kraal needs to be rebuilt, or when weeds must be removed from the meeting place, the headman gets the young men to do the work. It is essentially a repayment for the benefits which they derive from his management and is precisely similar to the "statute" labour which chiefs may impose. But in Bantu society neither goods nor services are given for an abstract return alone; the headman must be careful to take only the necessary amount of service and then must pay directly in the form of food, not mere day-to-day food with only nutritional value, but beer and meat, the rare and valued festive foods. The feast, looked forward to after the work, is also one of the main incentives. The more detailed co-operation of men and women in agricultural and other work will be described later. We may conclude our analysis of Junod's description of the family with his interesting example of another kind of special payment. After the man has done his share in clearing fields, and in other ways assisting his wives in their agricultural work, the wives prepare a special kind of beer "to thank the husband". This is in no sense an ordinary payment; Junod believes its significance to lie in its indicating to the husband that the harvest is now gathered. We believe it to indicate also that the fields are the women's special sphere and that the man must receive a token payment for stepping into that sphere.

REFERENCE AND FURTHER READING

The Life of a South African Tribe.   H. A. Junod.

SECTION VI

The Ubena

In coming to the Ubena peoples of Tanganyika, we find a people living in physical conditions almost as unlike those in

South-East Africa as could well be discovered in the same continent. It will suffice to mention that only the chiefs have cattle and that rice is the staple food. We find, further, that they are described by anthropologists whose training and outlook bring them to notice features not yet fully analysed in South-East Africa, except by Hunter. The Culwicks, however, state that they studied "a typical Bantu tribe", and we agree with them. Different though the circumstances are, the culture is fundamentally the same as in other parts of Bantu Africa.

The Culwicks describe the Bena head of a household as giving serious thought, by about the end of October, to the rice stores of his family. These by now begin to be depleted, and very likely the man takes the announcement that no more must be made into beer during that season. The ultimate control of the headman is made clear. Should stores be really low he will very probably go further and announce that more land must be cultivated for next season. He not merely makes the decision, but goes to work to implement it, clearing and burning the lands which he intends his wives to cultivate. This further confirms the position of the man as economic leader, and there is every reason to suppose, although we lack definite information, that he has this same key responsibility among all Bantu peoples. We thus see the man's duty of clearing the land not merely as a contribution to agricultural work, but also as a means whereby he regulates the amount, the locations, and the numbers of fields to be cultivated by the members of his homestead. This may be taken as the centre-piece in the productive life of the family. The clearing of the land is universally men's work among the Bantu. Its indirect, regulative aspect is just as definite as its direct, utilitarian one.

The Bena man apportions the land among his womenfolk. Each wife is entitled to enough for the purpose of her house, which include the feeding of the man and his guests, and in return she must make the best use of the land so as to pay her share in the household outgoings, such as ceremonial expenses, and taxation. The Culwicks perform the valuable service of showing that garden lands are apportioned among wives in much the same way as are cattle.

The collaboration between men and women in the routine of agriculture is much as we should expect. An important point mentioned by the Culwicks is that work-parties for the fields can be organized by people who have enough resources to make beer as a reward. This, again, is typically Bantu, as is the nature of the payment. This is essentially twofold; the helpers are rewarded for the most part by themselves receiving help, in turn, at another time. Yet their immediate reward consists of the beer and the social enjoyment of the occasion. No doubt is left as to this reward being regarded as valuable, for it is the rich people who can afford to give it. The controlling power of the headman again comes into evidence. Whether or not the family will have enough beer at the exact times that help is needed, when, it should be noted, beer is scarce and precious, will depend upon the skill and foresight which the man has shown in the production and husbanding of the household stores. "A well-to-do man will call for labour and organize a beer drink on quite a large scale perhaps two or three times a year, and his humbler fellows may also do it in a small way." ~

The Culwicks make it clear that with few exceptions all the property of the family belongs to and is in the last resort controlled by the head of the house, and always with a view to securing its most economic disposal for the benefit of the whole household. When husband and wife consult about the disposal of a surplus, the ultimate decision is with the man; his wife can but safeguard her right to a fair reward for her labour. The more evidence is accumulated about the economics of the Bantu family, the more significant does the economic leadership of the husband appear to be. According to the Culwicks the position of the wife is little more than she is able to claim payment for her labour. Her income appears to be very largely an income from labour; the income from property appears to belong to her husband. This is shown conclusively by the customs at the death of the husband when the heir who inherits the wife inherits, as a matter of fact, her field and crops, which, however, remain hers only if she stays on her husband's estate. Should she choose to return to her home, she loses the field and crops. The actual situation in daily life will be modified by the interplay of personalities. The wife also has the support, a most important consideration, of her own family. Should she regard herself as not getting a fair deal, her relatives can make matters very uncomfortable for her husband.

A very clear distinction is made between the crops of the wives. This is an elementary principle among all Bantu. Among the Bena it is stated by the Culwicks that the individual right of the wives in the produce of their own houses takes two forms, first as to the sharing out of food for everyday purposes, and second as to the reward of each wife out of the sale of the surplus from her crops. It appears, however, that the wife is not automatically given her share of goods obtained by the husband in exchange for her surplus. The husband would seem to exercise some choice as to the proportion of these goods which he will keep for himself and the part which he will give to the wife. The wife's share will usually take the form of new clothes and ornaments, this being the recognized way in which the commodities are obtained. It is general in Bantu Africa that the husband is responsible for clothing his wife or daughter, and also that the wife gets a considerable part of her ornaments from the proceeds of the sales of her surplus crops. In South-East Africa the provision of clothing was, until recent years, connected with the management of cattle. The man killed cattle and made the skins into clothes. This has been entirely changed in recent years, but the adaptation among the South-Eastern Bantu leaves the man responsible for buying his wife's clothes out of the resources which he sells. Among the Bena the point is made clearer through there being no cattle. It would appear that the husband has the ultimate responsibility for marketing the produce of his whole household and then of providing clothes and ornaments for his wives according both to their needs and to their claims, which are based upon the amount which each contributed to the disposable surplus. Instead of controlling the disposal of cattle, the man controls the marketing of goods.

It is scarcely possible to lay down any principles according to which food is taken from the huts of the various wives to be consumed in the homestead. Among the Bena, as among all African peoples, there is the conflicting tendency for a wife to enlarge her importance by contributing as much as possible, and at the same time to conserve her own stores as much as she may without incurring the stigma of meanness. According to her own character she may feed her own children first and foremost, or may treat them very nearly as in no way apart from the other children who eat in the homestead. The Bena people are never far from actual hunger, so that if a woman feeds children other than her own it will be in response to powerful incentives; there may be great credit attached to doing so; or more immediate significance may be the consideration that the other wives reciprocate; while there is no doubt that in a Bantu household the child which is likely to be rich when it grows up will receive better treatment from its co-mothers, whom it may richly reward in later years. It is clear that in a Bena household one wife and her children will not starve while others have enough. This minimum condition is definite throughout Bantu territory. But, at the other extreme, the industrious and skilful wife does expect to be richer than her less successful colleagues. Giving the husband more food and more stores to sell, she is able to claim a corresponding reward. She and her children will be better clothed, better fed, will have richer ornaments and more power in the homestead; in short, they will have those things that constitute wealth to the Bantu.

The Culwicks make a very useful attempt to estimate the economic advantages of the polygynous household. Complete accuracy is of course impossible, but certain facts do emerge. "One thing is plain; the bigger the household, the bigger the balance " (of advantages). The expenses of the household rise with each additional member, nevertheless the people are justified in regarding an industrious wife as the greatest asset. The rich man has many social obligations, which prevent his accumulating wealth, but they are in themselves the substance of his wealth. An interesting example is given of a very rich household having unexpected calls made upon its hospitality, with the result that at the beginning of October it was left with only one month's supply of food to see it through until March. The head of the household was able to balance matters by carrying out a trading transaction with European traders. The example is taken, rightly, to show how near even the richest people are to actual starvation. The same applies to very many Bantu tribes, though by no means to all.

At this stage we may summarize the main principles already elaborated. The family, as the basis of the homestead, is at the root of the people's economic life. The homestead itself is the main economic unit. It is clearly indicated that economics is only an aspect. Nothing could be more fantastic than to describe the family or the homestead as "economic institutions". They are institutions which enable the people to cope with all their variegated needs; their activities have as many aspects as there are needs. The economic is but one of these aspects; but it is an important one, and is more directly linked with family and homestead than it is with family and home in Western society. Among ourselves, family and home, for the most part, control the distribution of resources after these have been drawn from outside activities. Among the Bantu the complete cycle in the disposal of resources is managed within the homestead. The decisions governing production as well as consumption are taken thereby, the members co-operating according to well-defined rules of behaviour. It is the family or homestead which supervises the economic use of the time and labour power of its members. It is within this circle that expenditure—day-to-day expenditure on ordinary meals, or great expenditures for weddings or funerals—are decided upon. The homestead co-operates with other homesteads, again according to the norms of the society. In this way a very large amount of co-operation is achieved. This co-operation we are finding to be just as intricate, as well adapted to making fine economic choices, as anything in Western society. The first step towards understanding it is to see clearly the social structure through which it functions.

CHAPTER XII

TILLING THE SOIL

SECTION I

Food and Knowledge

THE economy of all Bantu peoples is obviously able to shift its balance between the two main sources of subsistence, between agriculture and the herding of live-stock. At the present day far more utilitarian satisfaction is obtained from the tilling of the earth. This was obviously not always so. Even today it appears that curdled milk is a mainstay of Zulu diet. Much evidence shows that various peoples now attach much greater importance to tillage than formerly. Cattle in the olden days, and in conservative areas today, supply a variety of commodities whose productive yield shows signs of declining. Not only daily food in the form of milk, but also flesh food for festive and other important occasions, in addition to precious fat, and the magically valued contents of the gall bladder, as well as skins for clothing, were, and to a great extent still are, yielded by the four-footed, self-transporting store of resources. However these productivities may have declined in value, the many secondary or social needs satisfied from live-stock still give cattle a very great value, so that, as Hunter reports about the Pondo, even though the mass of the people's utilitarian requirements are satisfied by agriculture, their emotions may play much more actively around their cattle.

We need not be surprised at this. It is common for people to be much more attached to the ornaments and so-called luxuries of life than to its "necessities". The Bantu do not hold great competitive festivals on the occasion of their harvests, as do the Trobrianders. These latter people have elevated one of their food crops into a position of ceremonial importance. The Bantu achieve by far the greater part of their ceremonial expression through the medium of their cattle.

TILLING THE SOIL

Yet the tilling of the soil, especially today, and possibly far more in the future, engages a truly enormous proportion of their interests. These may represent dull toil rather than pleasurable social activity, but whatever the mental attitude, there is no doubt that agricultural activities are the centre point for the disposal of a vast part of the people's resources in land, labour power, accumulated capital such as it is, and economically directive energy.

It is most important that we should not lose ourselves in a maze of technological description. To the man on the spot, this is, no doubt, of great interest. In particular, efforts to change Africans' methods of cultivation must be based upon the knowledge which the people themselves wield. Field reports in the future will probe deeply into this knowledge. But, for our purposes, technique, and the knowledge with which it is associated, are no more than two of the infinite number of considerations which determine the economic aspect of Bantu agriculture. The economist must ask, not so much what type of implement is used to turn the soil, as, what proportions of the people's time and energy are spent in wielding the implement; what knowledge determines these activities; what other activities they must give up in order to do that work; how much choice their culture permits them as to the amount of work which they will perform; to what extent each labourer consumes the fruits of his or her own work, or how, in a distribution of resulting commodities, the value of each person's share may be computed. We must examine the division of labour and the functioning of specific groups not as technical problems, but as concerning the ways in which people invest their energies and draw out their rewards. We shall find, in fact, that in analysing the economics of social units we made the bulk of possible discoveries about the economics of agriculture, for agriculture is carried out entirely by these units, and in seeing how the disposal of resources was governed by them, we virtually arrived at the principles controlling agriculture.

As in so many other departments of Bantu life, striking similarities exist between the agriculture of practically all the peoples from the Transkei to Uganda. Rice is a staple in very limited areas of suitable ground in East Africa; bananas become a staple in Uganda and are important in other fertile regions such as Kenya; in North-West Rhodesia, the people virtually choose as their staple either maize or eleusine. Over by far the greater part of Bantu Africa, however, the staple crop is maize; it is supported by other cultivated grains of varying importance such as millet, sorghum, and variations of these; while everywhere root crops are of great importance. Fruits, also, ranging from the highly cultivated bananas of Uganda and Kenya to the vast number of wild growths which are resorted to by children or in time of scarcity, are everywhere essential to the local diet. Given such a range of similar products, and a social system of such fundamental uniformity, we should expect to find the economic aspect of Bantu agriculture conforming to similar principles throughout our whole area. This is, in fact, the case. The main cycle, the main forms of grouping, are found from South to North-East Africa.

For us, as for the people themselves, the effective start of the agricultural cycle may be taken to be the decision to clear lands for the coming gardens. We find no African people among whom clearing is not a major annual operation, although it is often carried out to prepare a field for many years of cultivation, and sometimes only for one or two years. The first stage, when it is known that the time is due for clearing to begin, is to decide which ground is to be cleared, and how much. This involves the all-important question of the people's knowledge of the types of soil. That this knowledge exists, and that it is expirically established, there can be no doubt. It must be reckoned as an important part of their capital equipment. It is all the more significant to us in that the great majority of investigators into African life have seen fit to take the systems of knowledge, whether meagre or well developed, for granted. Thousands of pages have been written on trivial agricultural rites, as against a few dozen lines on the all-important knowledge which, through technique, influences Bantu agriculture at every stage. We should be the last to complain of a full treatment of agricultural magic. This, too, is part of the essential equipment. Resources are invested in magic; magic plays its part in controlling both the work of agriculture and the distribution of the product. But we can imagine the people cultivating the soil without magic; we cannot imagine their doing so without knowledge. The principles upon which they argue that a given piece of soil will be fertile or infertile are just as much part of the whole equipment for the successful carrying on of agriculture as are the principles upon which they decide to give so much, and no more, work to a given field. The body of knowledge is quite as much a part of their capital as is the land itself. Many are the examples in Africa today of Europeans endeavouring to make good a diminution in the extent of the soil possessed by Africans, by increasing the extent of their knowledge regarding the soil.

There is, however, no evidence whatever of property existing in agricultural knowledge. It is rather a free good, quite unlike knowledge in medicines and magic, which is very definitely the property of individuals and is bought and sold. There is extremely little evidence even of knowledge of agricultural magic being private property, with the very important exception of rain magic. Hunter, indeed, gives us details of magic performed for the benefit of fields, and states that everybody tends to have his or her own formula and to apply it in an individual way. Agricultural knowledge, not being private property, finds but little specific formulation. It remains the factor which determines the evaluation of soils, and is thus at the basis of the economic aspect of Bantu agriculture.

Krige is the only writer who tells us that her people, the Zulus, have little knowledge of the fertility of soils, and we must attribute her statement to an accidental oversight. Other writers show, not only that their people have a good, if limited, knowledge of what a given type of soil will grow, but also that they apply well-understood principles in discovering whether a given land is likely to be fertile. Hunter tells us that "The silt on the banks of the large rivers is known to be the most fertile land, and the next best that where the bush has grown. For this reason bush is often cleared to make fields, even when open grass-land is available. Where there is no bush the richness of the soil is judged by the type of grass growing there." Definite principles are here indicated. If the soil will grow one type of grass, then it will grow a certain type of crop. So definite is the knowledge, and so clearly is it trusted, that the people will undergo the labour of clearing bush sometimes in preference to using grass-land. We do not say that such knowledge is profound; we do say that it is in itself part of the people's capital equipment, and, further, that it guides them in a very direct manner in the economic disposal of their resources. The limits to this knowledge are indicated when Hunter tells us that, although the fertility of disused homestead sites is known and made use of for the growing of tobacco, the people have not deduced from this the significance of manure for their soil. Casalis gives us similar though less detailed information about the Basutos. These people are well aware of the suitability of different soils for different purposes, but, again, fail to realize the economic value of manure, so that, as with practically every Bantu people, this product is not of economic value, simply because of limitations in the people's knowledge. Smith and Dale tell us that the Ila people select "a piece of land, preferably in the bush, that commends itself to him and his wife, arguing very sensibly that if it will grow timber it will surely grow grain". This shows us once more that the laborious work of clearing is undertaken at the instance of the people's definite knowledge and of their belief, unformulated and crude though it may be, in the uniformity of Nature.

Beyond this we can go but a very little distance in our examination of the African's knowledge of the soil which he works. For the rest, his more detailed knowledge can be deduced only from his activities, which will be more than sufficient to show how wide and effective that knowledge is. The possibility, however, of the European's tapping rich strata of well-formulated principles is indicated in the following quotation from a book written, not by a professional investigator, but by a practical colonist who did not disdain a native's advice:

"I myself visited several Kaffir mealie fields, in order to find out the reason why they invariably produced better crops than most of the fields, in the same district, which were cultivated by white people. Noting an old Kaffir, with his pick, breaking up new veld to a depth of three or four inches, I imagined that only the laziness characteristic of his race prevented him from digging deeper. The soil appeared to be very fertile; and was from ten to fourteen inches deep. I took the pick from him; and in my own way and according to my own idea at that time, I began to turn over the soil to a depth of eight or nine inches. The Kaffir immediately stopped me, saying, 'Na, Baas, na mealie-dig deep'; and he expounded to me the whole art and mystery of successful agriculture as practised by the Kaffir race. His premises were as follows:

(a) that most moisture came from below:
(b) that, if the soil were loosened to any considerable depth, air and the sun's rays would be admitted:
(c) that, if hard solid ground remained below, the mealie roots would penetrate it:
(d) that the admission of air and the sun's rays below the mealie roots would cause evaporation of moisture contained in the solid ground:
(e) that, if drought set in, the mealies thus would have no source of moisture:
(f) that the hard solid ground below the mealie roots always contained more moisture than the broken ground on the surface; and, in case of drought, it often would suffice to prevent the mealies being scorched.

"From which he very logically concluded that his mealie seed required no more than a mere covering of soil."[1]

In one way it may be said that this discussion of native knowledge, which we have made in this chapter, is irrelevant in that this knowledge is not treated by the people themselves as an economic commodity. This is true, yet one of the features of change in Africa is that goods which formerly were free are now becoming scarce and desired. Land itself falls into this category. Firewood and a series of semi-wild products

[1] *Agricultural and Pastoral Prospects of South Africa.* Sir Owen Thomas. 1904.

of the forest are other examples. Knowledge may well follow this course. As we have seen, it is in no way foreign to Bantu culture to regard knowledge as an economic good. The time may well come, or indeed may be already here, when agricultural knowledge is something in which specialization may arise, in which one man will be better versed than his fellow and will be paid for his services. Yet quite apart from any such development, knowledge can no more be left out of an economic analysis of Bantu life than can land or labour. It gives or withholds value; pieces of land, products such as manure, are valued or not according to the people's knowledge. Further, it is in a way primary to the disposal of resources; a heavy piece of bush will have labour expended upon its clearing because it is known that the soil which produced it will produce food. Of the special type of knowledge which features so prominently in modern economic discussion, the knowledge of markets, the ability to forecast trends in the land, we are not able to speak. Uncertainty in Bantu economic life is discussed in another place. Here we have written only of that knowledge of Nature which is the basis of the African's application of his labour to his soil.

REFERENCES AND FURTHER READING

The Native Cattle of Southern Rhodesia (Art.). E. A. Nobbs. South African Journal of Science, 1927.
Report of the Chief Magistrate of the Transkeian Territories, 1913. Union of South Africa Blue Book.
Change and Exchange (Art.). W. H. S. Nada, 1934.
Wanderings in the Interior of South Africa. A. Steedman. 1835.
Zulu-English Dictionary. Bryant.
Kaffirs of Natal. J. Shooter. 1857.
An African People in the Twentieth Century. L. P. Mair. 1934.
Hunger and Work in a Savage Tribe. A. I. Richards. 1932.
The Life of a South African Tribe. H. A. Junod. 1927.
The Ila-Speaking Peoples of Northern Rhodesia. Smith and Dale. 1920.
The Bavenda. H. A. Stayt. 1931.
Ubena of the Rivers. A. T. and G. M. Culwick.
Modern Industry and the African. J. M. Davis (ed.). 1933.
Reaction to Conquest. M. Hunter. 1937.

TILLING THE SOIL

SECTION II

Land for Cultivation

The land chosen for the coming year may be either the garden land of the previous year, or newly cleared land. We may be sure that no clearing is done unless it is unavoidable. A previous garden will serve the purpose unless, at the last harvest, it showed unmistakable signs of exhaustion. But there is always virtue in new land, and it appears to be seldom that an existing garden is merely tilled once more; no Bantu garden is surveyed and fixed; the woman will let her pick or her hoe break up a little new land alongside of that which has already borne crops. Hunter tells us that fields are begun small, a little new land being added year by year. In all districts except those which have been thoroughly changed by European influence, and they are extremely few, some new land is taken from the bush each year and some old land allowed to revert. The clearing of bush, which may be merely thick undergrowth or which, on the other hand, may really be forest, is of economic significance in that, according to traditional Bantu agriculture, it is the men's contribution to the year's work. An immense amount of evidence goes to show that until quite recent years it was extremely heavy work, and even today it is by no means light in many parts of Bantu Africa. The men clear the fields for their wives. Each field is to be the asset and responsibility of a wife. There are important restrictions to this; among numbers of people, the man will have his fields, while among all peoples the children, especially the girls, also have their smaller fields. Children's fields, however, are entirely under the supervision of their mothers, while even a man's fields must be weeded by his wives.

It is very possible that in earlier times the work of clearing was a deciding factor in determining the area to be cultivated. It was, indeed, the cost of the land. Even today there is ample evidence of its playing such a role. The amount of land from which people may choose for purposes of cultivation is large, as a general rule, throughout our area. This in itself by no means entitles us to think of land as a free good. Local investigation is necessary before any such statement is justified. Even should the labour of clearing not be a limiting factor, the amount of really first-class land for particular purposes may well be limited so that people who do not succeed in getting such land for their gardens are obliged to take the next best. Further, women are well aware of the waste of their time and energy not only in travelling to their gardens, but also, and much more, in carrying back to their homes the heavy burdens of field produce. Even when, to all appearances, fertile land is unlimited, there will still be preferences by certain people for certain lands, and difficulties in satisfying these desires. It is quite unnecessary for these preferences to give rise to any visible or tangible payment. Such a payment would be most unusual in a Bantu community. The lucky people can easily make recompense by extra hospitality to headman or chief, and even this will not be formulated; or they may make no recompense, simply enjoying the extra proceeds of their skill or good fortune. The cost of suitable garden land will thus be represented, to the people, in the amount of work which the men have put into clearing them and in the extra labour required to work difficult ground. They will be well aware of the alternatives which they have foregone in order to perform this work.

The extent of land to be cultivated will thus depend upon the amount which can be secured, and the amount which it is expected that the people will be able to cultivate. These considerations, in turn, are quite consciously balanced with the desire to grow a certain amount of foodstuffs. If some stores are still left over from the previous year, the people may look forward to an easier time. If famine has been experienced, the women will press on with early gardens even before the main crops, and as soon as rains permit.

It is at this stage that the capital equipment of the household begins to play a part. By far the most important element in this equipment is the labour power of the people themselves. Apart from this and the resources necessary to pay the rain-maker, there is indeed little capital. But the labour power may be well or ill conserved. Much will depend upon how the food supplies have lasted from the previous season. Food is invariably carefully stored and its use regulated through the mechanism of the household. Accumulated food is capital in various ways; some of it will be used to reward work parties; much of it will have to support, by nutrition, the working power of the family; in each case it must be classed as capital, consciously conserved through all the opportunities of expending it upon hospitality and other immediate consumption soon after harvest time. The part which cattle play in the essential supply of food in the old days is illustrated by Steedman's report that at the time when the women were about to begin cultivation, the man of the household would kill an ox to improve their diet so as to support them in their arduous work. This necessity for special diet to cope with hard work is illustrated today, when a boy going to Johannesburg to work in the mines has to be fed up for a time before he has the necessary strength. The killing of the ox appears to have fitted into a seasonal scheme. By the end of winter, milk was very scarce. All other food was no more plentiful. It appears that it was customary to resort to flesh at that time. It was the time when, incidentally, the women expected their new cloaks, made from the skins of the beasts. The men's careful herding of their cattle would thus conserve an essential form of capital which, at the time for agricultural work to be begun, would be converted into human energy.

Apart from these forms of capital, only seed corn and the primitive picks or hoes were necessary. But, taking all the forms together, a given household might well be sufficiently or insufficiently supplied. A household which has lost its cattle would have to try to borrow from others. The work of clearing was, and is, done not so much by individuals working alone as by work parties. The household that could invest in work parties would have advantages over that which could not. The work party requires meat and beer. Beer, at this time of the year, would be much more expensive than earlier, for the grain would now have to be carefully conserved so as to make it last until the coming harvest. Also, the labour of making beer would be more expensive, since the women have much other work to do. It is very possible that in the old days meat was the real inducement to join a work party at this time of the year, for it appears that beer has come to play a much bigger part in these people's economy than was formerly the case. Or, on the other hand, it is very possible that beers of high nutritive value were the vogue until recent times.

After the clearing come the hoeing and the scattering of the seed. Before the introduction of ploughs, these were one and the same operation, as they still are in so many parts of Bantu Africa. They are almost entirely the work of women. The work party would be comparatively little resorted to for this hoeing. It occupies practically the entire day of those engaged in it, and the planting will go on, field after field, until the field first sown is ready for weeding. Weeding is the next item in the cycle. It involves many work parties and keeps the female population extremely busy until the next great event, the first appearance of the plant. Fructification, so far from being the stage at which the people are free to rejoice in coming plenty, marks a new intensification in the labour of men, women and children. Pests have to be scared, and this, in Africa, even today when big game is much less plentiful than formerly, involves the heaviest and most unremitting labour of the whole year.

The pests range from small birds to elephants. Over very large areas the people have been freed from the necessity of dealing with elephants, hippopotami, and lions, which have now been exterminated in South Africa but are still to be reckoned with in many other parts. Many records show that in South Africa the work of protecting the crops from the marauders was a major part of the men's work. In almost every territory of which we have any knowledge it is still the custom to erect fairly substantial platforms in the fields, often building a small hut on these platforms. These erections involve considerable labour and are a definite task for which the men must organize themselves. Often the whole family will live in the fields during the months of growth. The women will be busy all day scaring birds; the men busy at night, often cold and wet, frightening away the animals. Wherever agricultural lands are situated at a distance from the homesteads, as in Bechuanaland, the homesteads will be deserted during these months. This is work from which no Bantu people are free. At its lightest, it occupies the whole homestead for some months; at its heaviest, it involves very long hours of labour throughout night and day. It goes on until harvest, the next stage in the agricultural cycle. Harvest thus finds the people at the culminating stage of months of labour. It is itself a process which may even intensify that labour, and rest is not yet to come, for the work of carrying the produce to the homestead may, in certain circumstances, be the hardest in the whole year.

REFERENCES AND FURTHER READING

Communal Land Tenure (Art.). C. L. Carbutt. Nada. 1927.
Zulu-Land. Rev. L. Grout. 1864.
Wanderings in the Interior of South Africa. A. Steedman. 1835.
A Journey to the Zoolu Country. A. F. Gardiner. 1836.
The Akamba. C. W. Hobley. 1910.
The Ama-Xosa. J. H. Soga. 1931.
The Social System of the Zulus. E. J. Krige. 1936.
The Baganda. Rev. J. Roscoe. 1911.
An African People in the Twentieth Century. L. P. Mair. 1934.
The Life of a South African Tribe. H. A. Junod. 1927.
The Ila-Speaking Peoples of Northern Rhodesia. Smith and Dale. 1920.
The Bavenda. H. A. Stayt. 1931.
Ubena of the Rivers. A. T. and G. M. Culwick.
Modern Industry and the African. J. M. Davis (ed.). 1933.
Anthropology in Action. Brown and Hutt. 1935.
With a Prehistoric People. W. S. and K. Routledge. 1910.
Reaction to Conquest. M. Hunter. 1937.

SECTION III

The Economics of Agricultural Organization

This description has necessarily been summary. It has been necessary in order to provide us with a working basis for the analysis upon which we are now to embark. In what ways are economic decisions made? How are factors of production valued in their application to the growth of food? What evaluations are placed upon the labour units of men, women, and children respectively? How is the application of capital to the soil determined? How do the economics of the chief and tribe intertwine with those of the smaller units?

It will be seen that one of the largest investments of capital at the beginning of the agricultural year may be the payment of rain specialists. This payment is made by or through the chief, and, for an irrational service though it may be, it is a definite investment for guidance in which the people depend upon the chief. Our study will thus bring us to see how the irrational element is used in the Bantu agriculture to establish a link between the household and the ruling authority, linking the local economic units into larger territorial ones in doing so, and thus securing greater choice in the application of resources.

In the annual round of Bantu agriculture there is no doubt that the responsible parties, the adult men, the married women of the homestead, must make the really effective decisions as to the starting of the hard and necessary work. In some tribes, the chief plays an important role at some of the vital stages; but there is no evidence, from any part, of his inducing the people to begin the tedious and unspectacular work of clearing. There appears to be not even a vestige of supernatural stimulus to this work. We must definitely conclude that the people begin it in a very utilitarian way, knowing that they must, if they are to eat. We do not suggest that each person sits down grimly and makes up his or her mind that work must be begun. This would give a very misleading picture of the scene. The situation is rather that everybody is aware that the season for clearing is again upon them, and the work begins almost so as to appear automatically. Strong social compulsions, we are well aware, underlie this apparent automaticity, but it is not part of our work to delve into them.

It is at the time of the sowing and hoeing, which operations, we must remember, are simultaneous, that magic or religion, and, very possibly, the chief, come into play. As Willoughby sums up the matter: " All are free to fell trees and burn undergrowth in any garden-plot that they are entitled to reclaim from the forest, but actual cultivation must wait till orthodox tribal rites have been performed—rites marked by great diversity of practice, everywhere strangely magical, but always designed to secure fertility for the seed." This passage refers to the practice of the Bantu people in general, and not to that of any particular tribe. As Willoughby indicates, practices vary in detail to an immense degree; it is for us to single out the relations which have real economic significance. Three such relations, by no means found among every Bantu people, appear to be important. The chief engages the expert who gives advice about rain, the man who is so often designated the rain-maker. He also may supply medicated seed, a little of which, mixed with that of each homestead, magically ensures fertility. He also may call upon the people to cultivate, not his own homestead garden, but certain special gardens which are cultivated for him by his people, and which thus may set the pace for the rest of the cultivation. It is these gardens, incidentally, which agricultural demonstrators nowadays use, if they can, as demonstration plots to show the advantages of new methods. The chief appears to be unlikely to play any very special part in his people's agriculture until the time of harvest, when first-fruits ceremonies may be a great national event, with considerable economic significance in regulating the consumption of the various crops and possibly in conveying parts of the crops, as a kind of tax, to the chief.

Rain concerns, not any single homestead, but invariably a whole community. Therefore it is of no use to appeal merely to family ancestors. These play their part in the fertility of their descendants' soil, but not in the all-important matter, especially important in the semi-arid regions of Southern Africa and also in many other parts of Bantu Africa, of rain supply. Of all the single factors which control Bantu agriculture, rain is the most compelling. Note that it does not control the work of clearing; this must be done while the land is still dry. Since rain concerns the whole tribe, appeal for it must be made to a line of ancestors which is vitally connected with the whole people. Such are the ancestors of their chief. Again we shall accept Willoughby's judgment: ". . . a line that has occupied a demesne and buried generation after generation of its patriarchs in it, is the only one whose ancestor-spirits are thought to be concerned with the fertility of its soil and the weather which subserves fertility." Krige puts the matter plainly when she says, "The Zulu king is responsible for the growth of vegetation, and it is his duty to procure rain by asking his ancestors 'to pray for rain to the Lord of Heaven'. He thus cannot approach the 'Lord of Heaven' directly, but has to do so through his ancestors." Again, we shall refrain from concerning ourselves with the finer points of Bantu theology. Whether the appeal is made to ancestors of the chief, or, through them, to a Higher Power, the fact remains that the appeal must be made by the chief. Several writers, notably Richards and Hunter, have pointed out that this power makes the people economically dependent upon the chief. While not disagreeing, we point out that, as usual, there is fairly complete reciprocity in the matter. It is inconceivable that a chief should refuse to do what he can to bring rain. Further, the chief's function is not himself to bring rain, but to appeal to specialists who, according to all accounts, have to be substantially paid. It appears that among the Zulus the chief himself appeals for rain and has resort to specialists only when further steps are necessary. Among other peoples, it appears that the chief at once calls in the experts.

The oxen necessary for sacrifice in the rain rites, and the beasts needed to pay the experts, constitute an expenditure of valuable resources which must be reckoned among the capital outlay of the tribe as a whole at the beginning of its agricultural year. The party immediately responsible for finding the sacrifice for payment might vary with circumstances, but would almost certainly be either the chief himself or a sub-chief or influential man from the district which specially needed the rain. A distinction must be made between oxen sacrificed, and beasts paid to rain-doctors. The latter are a very definite payment for services rendered, and support a kind of rudimentary profession. On the other hand, when cattle are sacrificed, no parts of them are wasted; in the case of the rain sacrifices, the beast would be eaten by the chief and the men at his Great Place, but some special, and valuable, parts of it would go to the rain-doctor as part of his remuneration. Willoughby very effectively describes the situation in which rain is anxiously awaited while "the sun screams". Time and again clouds gather, only to disappear. The essential work of food-producing will be impossible unless rain comes. It is not surprising that the people are willing to go to much trouble and to see valuable animals being disposed of in order to perform the necessary rites.

It is, of course, impossible to estimate the numbers of cattle invested in the bringing of rain. It is clear that nowadays fewer cattle may be involved, and a larger amount put in the collection plates of the new men who seek for rain, the missionaries. Steedman's description, quoted by Hunter, leaves no doubt as to the economic aspect. According to this, if the rain-maker is successful he receives gifts of cattle from the chief. Sometimes he may not be satisfied and will "stop" the rain, demanding more cattle. Sometimes payments will be made in advance both by the chief and by private persons particularly anxious for rain. That the transactions may involve really large payments is clearly illustrated by Hunter's example of a man who, in 1932, had in his anxiety paid fourteen head of cattle, fourteen sheep and goats, as well as baskets of grain, wood, and thatch grass.

The strongly rational part of the attitude to rain-making must never be forgotten. Peoples, such as those who exist in very favoured regions of East Africa, who do not need to seek rain, do not invest in the proceedings which we have described. Yet it is worth noting that even exceptionally favoured East African tribes have rain rites, for even they are not free from all anxiety. Peoples in arid regions attach especial importance to rain-seeking. The gatherings of people for this purpose among such tribes as those of Bechuanaland may be among the greatest of national gatherings, subserving many secondary needs as well as the main one which brings the people together. The common tendency of resort being made to rain specialists from outside, from more favoured areas, is in itself an indication of what is called sympathetic magic, but has the economic implication that these specialists, going to the trouble of working for foreigners, would presumably have to be very substantially paid, and that this would entail the moving of commodities from one district to another. The fact that the richer district would benefit at the expense of the poorer only shows how strongly felt is the need for rain-seeking; how real the satisfaction which it produces.

REFERENCES AND FURTHER READING

Agricultural Ceremonies and Practices of the Balobedu (Art.). E. Krige. Bantu Studies, 1931.
Some Agricultural Rites Practised by the Valenge and Vachopi (Art.). E. D. Earthy.
The Economic Position of the Native in Rhodesia (Art.). Hon. W. M. Leggate. South African Journal of Science, 1927.
The "Little Rain" Ceremony of the Bechuanaland Bakxatla (Art.). I. Schapera. Bantu Studies, 1930.
Rain-making in South Africa (Art.). Rev. S. S. Dornan. Bantu Studies, 1927-29.
Zulu-Land. Rev. L. Grout. 1864.
Story of My Mission in South-East Africa. W. Shaw. 1860.
The Soul of the Bantu. W. C. Willoughby. 1928.
Valenge Women. E. D. Earthy. 1933.
The Baganda. Rev. J. Roscoe. 1911.
An African People in the Twentieth Century. L. P. Mair. 1934.
The Life of a South African Tribe. H. A. Junod. 1927.
The Ila-Speaking Peoples of Northern Rhodesia. Smith and Dale, 1920.
The Bavenda. H. A. Stayt. 1931.
Ubena of the Rivers. A. T. and G. M. Culwick.
Modern Industry and the African. J. M. Davis (ed.). 1933.
With a Prehistoric People. W. S. and K. Routledge. 1910.
Reaction to Conquest. M. Hunter. 1937.

SECTION IV

The Gardens of the Chief

The cultivation of certain fields for the chief may have a double significance; it is a means of giving essential tribute to him, of filling the store-houses without which he would not be a chief. It is also a means whereby a kind of economic leadership is invested in the chief. Just what part the cultivation of the public gardens may formerly have played in the regulation of tribal agriculture, it is now quite impossible to say. We regard it as highly probable, however, that the significance is now a sentimental rather than a practical one. This does not in the least imply that it is less important; the word sentimental is used to designate that vast complex of cultural needs, the religious, the political, and the others, which are certainly not of less importance than the growing of food. The chief's gardens, therefore, may be taken as symbolizing the interest of the chief in his people's agriculture. They have the significance, wherever they exist, that each household throughout the community has to remember to cultivate for the chief as well as for itself. The dependence, on the other hand, of the chief upon the vital activities of his people is reinforced by his having subjects to visit him and work for him as well as for themselves. A distinct transfer of resources takes place. The people must do the chief's work just when their own fields require attention.

The function of the public gardens in "keeping the people up to scratch" need not be underestimated. It is evident that many other agencies do this; yet the chief's gardens play their part as a sanction. No people will wish to see their own agriculture much behind that of these gardens, while, though they give but little positive leadership in the work of clearing, they may more or less set the time by which people should have their land ready to be hoed.

Casalis tells us of gatherings of men among the Basuto to till the fields of the chief and his great wife; the result is a work-party not entirely unlike those organized by private households, except that the numbers are greater, hundreds of men in line wielding their oval hoes; the chief, naturally, supplies these men with meat and beer. This brings us to the main difference between this work-party and those of the common people. In the chief's party there is no specific remuneration beyond the meat and beer, while in those of commoners there is also the most important consideration of a return of the services in kind. According to Ellenberger, the chief's parties would involve three days' work for the visiting men in each year. Bavenda chiefs, we are told, have large cultivated areas worked by the "Compulsory unpaid labour of their subjects". The Zulu chief is reported as opening the hoeing season in that "no one plants or reaps before the king". It appears that this custom is weakening today. Krige gives us interesting information of a ceremony which was practised up to 1879, in which a kind of independent agricultural expert, with magical powers, is indicated as working for the chief. This man would tell the chief when the time for planting was due, and they would then take magical precautions against ill-fortune while the regiments of this great military people were brought to cultivate the chief's gardens. The people as a whole could then proceed with their own household cultivation. Junod throws light on the regulation of agricultural work among a people whose institution of chieftainship is extremely weak as compared with that of the Zulus. Among these people, the Thonga, there appears to be no cultivating of chief's gardens, but it is forbidden to anybody to sow certain kinds of seed before the elder members of the family. This quite simply asserts and supports that idea of hierarchy which is of such immense significance in the regulation of economic disposal in Bantu life, for there is no difference in principle between the head of a homestead and the chief of a tribe.

The cultivation of chiefs', or public gardens, is by no means a universal practice among the Bantu. It exists, and apparently is still important, among those peoples whom we have mentioned, and a few others. It is described here simply as a practice playing its part in tribal economy under some conditions. Where the tribe is highly organized, with a powerful chieftainship and the rudiments of an army, it would appear that public gardens exist and are cultivated by this army, serving the important purpose of financing it. There is little or no evidence that they are ever worked by women. The army, being in existence, is capable of being put to this use, in which it also contributes to its own support. It costs the chief meat and grain in the form of beer; it gives him extra stores of grain. But we must remember that among all Bantu tribes there is the possibility of this practice arising. Invariably the chief expresses some vital interest in all stages of agriculture. Whether or not he has the control of tribal gardens would appear to be determined by historical circumstance.

REFERENCES AND FURTHER READING

Chieftainship in Modern Africa (Art.). L. P. Mair. Africa, 1936.
Social Aspects of First Fruits Ceremonies among the South-Eastern Bantu (Art.). M. Gluckmann. Africa, 1938.
The Sacred Fire of the Bapedi of the Transvaal (Art.). W. Eiselen. South African Journal of Science, 1929.
The Bavenda in the Bantu Tribes of South Africa. Vol. 1. A. M. D. Cronnin. 1928.
History of the Basuto. Ellenberger and MacGregor. 1912.
Bantu Beliefs and Magic. C. W. Hobley. 1922.
Kaffirs of Natal. J. Shooter. 1857.
Western Civilisation and the Natives of South Africa. I. Schapera. 1934.
The Bomvana. P. A. W. Cook.
The Social System of the Zulus. E. J. Krige. 1936.
Hunger and Work in a Savage Tribe. A. I. Richards. 1932.
The Life of a South African Tribe. H. A. Junod. 1927.
The Ila-Speaking Peoples of Northern Rhodesia. Smith and Dale. 1920.
The Bavenda. H. A. Stayt. 1931.
Ubena of the Rivers. A. T. and G. M. Culwick.
Reaction to Conquest. M. Hunter. 1937.

SECTION V

The Greater Economic Units

We thus see that although, in a peculiar sense, the unit concerned with Bantu agriculture is the homestead, it is by no means left to each homestead to make for itself all the vital decisions. In writing of social units we traced the many ways in which each homestead is vitally connected with others, notably with those of other members of the same family, of those with whom it is connected by intermarriage, and, simply, with those in the same neighbourhood. We have now seen how a larger regulation can be achieved, how the control of the chief over rain-making and public gardens may set the pace for agricultural work throughout a larger district. Since the chief must draw a considerable part of his revenues, directly or indirectly, from the agriculture of his people, and since the services which he will be able to render will depend upon this revenue, it is easy to see the significance of the relationship between the chief, the agriculture of the tribe, and the economic life of the people as a whole.

Owing to the circumstance that, among any Bantu people of whom we have a record, cultivable land was until very recently in considerable supply, there is exceedingly little evidence that the chief has ever controlled the area of land allotted to each homestead. In the event of land becoming scarce, it would presumably be the duty of chiefs to share it out among their people. We can say this with confidence, because, except in areas with a strongly developed system of councils of elders, no other authority exists to carry out this function. Our need is to continue to protect ourselves against the fallacy that cultivable land has commonly been a free good to most or all Bantu peoples.

Within historic times, the great majority of Bantu peoples have been migrant. Many are the statements that in the old days it was a duty of a chief "to lead his people to good land". What was meant by good land must usually have been pasture. There is no indication in this evidence that tribes ever moved in order to find new agricultural land. But there was clearly always a possibility that people would settle in some one place in such density as to give at least the rudiments of economic value to land for both agricultural and pastoral uses. This actually happened in the case of Kikuyu land. The instance is important as showing that Bantu culture is very capable of adapting itself to circumstances in which land takes on considerable economic value. Cultivable land, among the Kikuyu, came to be very actively owned by large families, perhaps better known as clans. If one clan found itself in need of more land, its elders had to obtain more, either by going to the trouble of clearing new forests, possibly in a distant place, or by purchasing from another clan which had been better supplied in the first place or whose numbers were declining. If more land could not be obtained, individuals had to erect their homesteads on the land of other clans, always after obtaining clear permission and almost certainly making some form of payment. On the other hand, by far the most usual state of affairs, even today, among Bantu peoples, is that there is no obvious scarcity of land suitable for cultivation. Yet other limiting factors have been seen to operate. The heavy work of clearing has already been mentioned. This exists with greater or less significance over nearly all of Bantu Africa. It represents part of the real cost of cultivated land, in the other activities which the people must needs forego in order to secure this land. Thus land as a general resource may be unlimited and only potentially an economic good, yet garden land, to each homestead, is undoubtedly a limited agent, more of which cannot be obtained except at further cost. Fully consonant with this is the intense feeling of private property, strongly implemented by legal and supernatural sanctions, in garden land.

Yet even uncleared fertile land is far from being, on closer examination, only potentially an economic resource. Almost everywhere we find that the people, far from being able to choose garden lands at random, have to choose carefully and have many preferences. A fair indication is given by Brown and Hutt in their book on the Hehe. They tell us that when the people select a plot for cultivation, two considerations operate. "They must belong to a community, and preferably a community in which they have kinsmen. The second consideration is agricultural; the land must be fertile, or, at worst, it must not fall below some minimum level of fertility. The social desires can be satisfied by any one of a large variety of conditions of residence; and the need for fertile land still leaves a wide range of choice. Other factors are also taken into account; for example, water must be near and firewood available." We quote this because it appears to apply almost exactly to so many other Bantu peoples, as well as to the Hehe, of whom it was written. There is "plenty of land", that is to say, there is a fair range of potentially fertile soil. But then practical considerations limit the choice.

That which is too far from the homestead not only denies a social life to the people; it also imposes upon them the very heavy work of carrying produce a long distance, thus giving a higher value to land which is nearer and more convenient. Among every tribe of whom we write, this consideration must carry weight. It never means, so far as we know, that garden sites become saleable. But there are many other ways in which differential values can be expressed. The best sites may be secured by luck, skill, or influence. Of their additional value to their holders, there can be no doubt. Precisely the same is to be said of land which is above the "minimum level of fertility". It has been necessary to make this digression into the economic value of agricultural land, because we cannot afford to fall into the common mistake of supposing that the Bantu people carry out their agricultural operations on land which is of no value to them.

REFERENCES AND FURTHER READING

The Economic Aspects of the Native Problem (Art.). E. Brookes. South African Journal of Science, 1924.
The Political Organisation of the Bechwana (Art.). G. P. Lestrade. South African Journal of Science, 1928.
The Natives and Agriculture (Art.). W. H. Tooke. South African Journal of Science, 1921-22.
The Transkei Trader (Art.). E. S. Haines. South African Journal of Economics.
The Bapedi by Eiselen in the Bantu Tribes of South Africa. Photographs and Descriptions by A. M. D. Cronnin. Vol. 2, Section 2. 1931.
The Bechuana in the Bantu Tribes of South Africa. Photographs and Descriptions by A. M. D. Cronnin. Vol. 2, Section 1. 1928.
Zulu-Land. Rev. L. Grout, 1864.
A Journey to the Zoolu Country. A. F. Gardiner. 1836.
Bantu Beliefs and Magic. C. W. Hobley. 1922.
Kaffirs of Natal, 1857. J. Shooter.
Seven Years in South Africa. Dr. E. Holub. 1881.
The Life of a South African Tribe. H. A. Junod. 1927.
The Ila-Speaking Peoples of Northern Rhodesia. Smith and Dale. 1920.

TILLING THE SOIL

The Bavenda. H. A. Stayt. 1931.
Ubena of the Rivers. A. T. and G. M. Culwick.
Reaction to Conquest. M. Hunter. 1937.
Native Land Tenure in Kikuyu Province. 1929.

Section VI

The Economics of Agriculture

It is now necessary, as briefly as may be, to follow the agricultural round among some of the more representative peoples, or those of whom we have best information. In this we shall select our examples in no definite order, leaving the reader to follow our progress by references to the map.

The Hehe grow a series of crops very common among the Bantu. Maize is the staple crop; they have also eleusine, sweet potatoes, marrow, and beans and ground-nuts. In the last few years cassava has been introduced owing to its resistance to locusts. Brown and Hutt give an estimate as to the proportions of each in the total produce, as follows:

Maize	.	.	75 per cent.
Potatoes	.	.	17 ,,
Cassava	.	.	5 ,,
Eleusine	.	.	3 ,,

These proportions hold for a hypothetical garden area of 5½ acres; on smaller or larger areas it is possible that the proportions may vary. It is pointed out that, as we know, but are inclined to forget, all the people are not equally industrious or equally keen on agriculture. A few people "run short of food regularly every year". It is estimated that, in average soil, a man with one wife and three children should cultivate 3½ acres to have food, seed, and some surplus for sale. Three instances are given. One is of a man with two wives and three children, cultivating 5½ acres; 4.2 acres would furnish their minimum requirements. Three-quarters of an acre was cultivated by the man himself, three acres by one wife, and 1⅝ acres by the other wife. In another instance a man with one wife and five children cultivated six acres. Another man with two wives and eight children cultivated just under six acres. This falls below their lowest needs, and they live short of food for two or three months each year.

The economics of the polygamous household are illustrated in that a man will generally, if he has one wife, cultivate one-third of her gardens, but if he has two wives his share will be less, and if he has four or five wives he will not cultivate at all. He will, of course, give much attention to managing both the economic affairs of his own circle and the public life of the neighbourhood. That fertile land is not a free good is shown by the fact that the family plantation is divided into strips, those of each person being scattered so as "to ensure a fair division of the more fertile land, an important factor in a polygynous household". These strips vary from four to ten yards wide and fifty to two hundred yards in length.

The hardest agricultural task is the clearing of land. When new land is being broken in, its clearing may be spread over two years. Then the family will move to live beside it. There is also annual clearing of some land, taking the place of other soil which is left fallow, to be covered by brush in its turn. Clearing is entirely men's work. Hoeing and planting are shared, the basis having already been indicated. All cultivation is done with the hoe. It is regulated entirely by rains. A well-defined form of rotation appears to be followed, differentiating the Hehe from most other Bantu peoples. Newly broken ground grows eleusine or potatoes. In the second year it grows maize and beans. In later years, maize only. It generally lasts six or eight years. As ground is worked out the man goes further afield to find new fertile lands. Another example of land having its economic value, although Brown and Hutt make it clear that the system would have to be modified if land were not so plentiful.

People in some areas can cultivate dry-weather gardens on the banks of small rivers, carrying out irrigation by means of furrows. But not all people are so lucky. In some areas the suitable land is limited; in others, there are no streams.

The work of cultivation is carried out sometimes by people working alone and sometimes by parties, the Bantu work party being an institution which secures co-operation outside of the individual homestead. Hehe children have their own strips to cultivate from the age of about twelve. We are not told of work involved in protecting the growing crops from pests, but the people cannot be so lucky as to escape this. This account serves to show some of the main routine, giving valuable information about the sharing of work, about the distribution of land, and about the variations in the amounts cultivated by different families.

Coming to the Bavenda of the Northern Transvaal, we find many interesting facts set out by Stayt. We are told first that "arable land is plentiful and every man can obtain the usufruct of as much land as he requires for himself, his wives, and other dependants". However, people living in the hills make use of every patch of ground, where no European farmer would think of working. The work of protecting the crops is such that temporary houses are built in the fields and whole families live in them during the planting and reaping seasons. When one family has gardens away from those of other people, the land may be hedged with bushes, but this type of fencing entails very little work. The people have no idea of the rotation of crops, but do know that soil must be left fallow from time to time. Private property in gardens and everything on them is rigidly respected. The clearing is done by the men, who cut, burn, and prepare the ground for tilling. The tilling is mainly women's work, but if a man has a plough he,. of course, ploughs for his wives. Both man and wife have their own gardens. The women weed their husband's garden, but a man does some of his own garden work, assisted by his male relations.

SECTION VII

The Economic Application of Resources

To move to the most northerly of the Bantu peoples, Mair has given us a most important study of the Baganda. The chief crop among these people is the banana, which is not a seasonal but a permanent crop. With all crops, however, clearing is the first process. A new banana grove may be started with a new household, being planted over two or three rainy seasons and then being extended from time to time. "The bananas require a good deal of attention. The grove is scrupulously weeded, and the more careful housewives heap up the weeds round the roots to serve as manure. Old trees are also used in this way." Mair makes it clear that there is no co-ordination of the activities of a district under one leader, so that it is impossible to speak of a fixed routine. Yet activities do characterize the different seasons, cotton having recently become the main crop. The preparation of the ground begins during the dry season. The seasonal crops are planted as soon as the ground has been softened by rain. The next six weeks are the busiest in the cycle, it being better to plant while the rain is heavy.

A more technical description of agriculture is given in *Modern Industry and the African*, relating to peoples in Northern Rhodesia. These include a wide variety of tribes, but a general pattern can be found in the agriculture of all of them. The homesteads vary in size, some having twenty huts and some a hundred. The paramount chief of one tribe has a homestead which is in effect a village of more than 2000 huts. In some cases gardens extend for twenty miles around a village, so that huts have to be built there for living during the busy season. Homestead sites are chosen with a view to the usual factors: fertility, water supply, and the distance to be moved. The method of preparing a garden is first "to select a likely patch of ground", then to chop the trees four feet from the ground, or only their branches if the trees are large, within a radius of twenty to thirty yards. This is when millet is to be grown. Some twenty of these gardens may be needed for a single family. Fences may be built. The cut timber is burned, and after rain has fallen the grain is planted in the ash. The method is economical of labour, little hoeing and weeding being necessary. The site is abandoned after three or four harvests, and then a new homestead established in another place, where the process is begun again. Variations of the method are used for sorghum and cassava. With sorghum, the village must be moved every four years. With cassava more permanence is possible, five to ten years in one place being the rule. Cassava is a relatively new native crop and shows the adaptability of an African culture when no deep social adjustments are demanded. With it there has grown up a system whereby each family cultivates three fields, of varying ages, simultaneously, with a system of fallowing. Cassava also is economical of labour, as it is not depredated by animals, so that no fences are needed except in one territory which is infested by elephants. Other types of agriculture are found, but the main characteristics remain the same. The usual immense amount of labour is expended, giving in return only enough to enable the family to journey through the year with the aid of wild products in the lean season.

It is in this district that the closest examination of the indigenous technique has been made, with the result that the Europeans have found that it is no easy matter to discover better methods. "Experiments are now being made to discover the peculiar advantages of this (the native system) in the local conditions and to devise alternative methods of securing equal results." Yet this is the system in which twelve acres of trees, and at least two and a half acres, must be cut down to provide timber to burn on one acre of land. The trees take some twenty years to recover, so that one family needs between two and three hundred acres of woodland to meet its needs. However, "It is almost impossible to discover another method equally safe and equally efficient". The work is carried on in a series of spurts; first there is tree-lopping, then fencing, then harvest. Between these there is rest.

This report states in the most emphatic terms two conclusions, both running counter to many preconceptions, and both of first-rate importance. The first is that, so far from the Bantu being typical "lazy savages", they in fact put an enormous amount of work into their agriculture for an exceedingly small return. One of our difficulties is that it is impossible to make any definite estimate of this amount of work. There are no such things as regular hours. In busy seasons the people appear never to be away from their fields.

In slack seasons both men and women go visiting, and this is one of the most valued occupations of their lives; yet there is something to do in the fields at almost all seasons, and enough people will be left at home to do what is necessary. Incidentally, it is shown in this report how the people's whole balance of work and income is accepted as inevitable or natural. This, of course, is one of the fundamental factors in the whole of our study. The Bantu wishes to increase his food supply only within the limits known to his culture. Anything beyond that does not mean anything to him. When examining the theoretical basis of needs in a culture, it is not surprising to find that Bantu men and women should be unimpressed by suggestions which would considerably increase the yield of their gardens. In this particular area in Northern Rhodesia, however, this point does not arise, for the agricultural experts found that absurdly wasteful as local methods seemed to be, European knowledge could not yet find ways of improving upon them.

The second point brought home by this report is that when it is really advantageous or necessary to do so, the people could make considerable adjustment. In some areas, owing to the exhaustion of forest, the staple food had to be changed from millet to cassava. In other cases ways were found of cultivating millet in open country, without timber-burning. The adjustments, apparently, were made successfully. The whole point is that such adjustments called for no major readaption of the social system. The work could still be carried on with the homestead as the main economic unit, without a drastic reapportionment of tasks among its members, without any revolutionary change in the placing of responsibility or in the basis of economic power.

The very realistic account of Ba-Ila's methods of agriculture given by Smith and Dale drives home many of the cardinal points. The closeness of the African to his soil is emphasized; the impossibility of any deficiency in foodstuffs being made good from other sources. "Hunger is speedily and actually felt." In these circumstances it is not surprising that the rain-maker plays an important role, and that his remuneration should be one of the primary ways in which the people's stored-up wealth is invested. Of the principles which we regard as most germane to agriculture, the Ba-Ila know nothing. Fallowing, rotation, manuring, seed selection are unknown to them; on the other hand, they have their own simple methods and apply them industriously. When Smith and Dale wrote, efforts had been made to induce the people to change these methods, but so far without result. There was a growing tendency to observe and enquire, but it is evident that the usual crux was yet to be encountered; supposing that the new methods themselves were well within the practical grasp of the people, could they be carried out without necessitating social and religious changes which might not be achieved even in the course of generations?

The indigenous methods, it is made clear, are "extremely wasteful, both of labour and land". No such thing as "land rent" is known. The necessities of the seasons effectively impose the routine of work. The people themselves, however, must find the stimulus to prepare for coming seasons. The cutting of timber must be done long before the rains are due. The ash must be on the ground before the wet season. Smith and Dale now give us an interesting example of how, in estimating the extent of the African's knowledge, we are only too likely to reveal deficiencies in our own. "While the native is aware of the fertilizing power of the ash, it must be admitted that he utilizes fire as the readiest method of getting rid of the timber." Research showed, more than a dozen years later, that the value of ash is not in its fertilizing properties, but in its providing a good seed-bed.

It is left to the wife to decide when, according to natural signs, it is time for her to apply the hoe to the gardens prepared by her husband. She sets to work, her husband meanwhile hoeing his own small patch. As is universally the case, hoeing and sowing go on together. Then comes rain, and the face of Nature is transformed. In the view of the people, rain comes or is brought through their approaches to the Supreme Being, just when they want it. It is not that they have been preparing for rain, which would come in any case. Work is now pressed on, and then comes the tiresome routine of watching. There are ten days of continuous guarding until the grain is firmly established. Any neglect at this time means that the ground has to be sown again and again. Then comparatively little in the way of hoeing serves to keep the plants free from weeds; but constant watch by night and day is needed to give protection from animals.

A newly cleared piece of soil is known to be not yet weathered and sweetened. It gives a fairly small crop. The second crop is better, and the third gives warning that the land must soon return to bush and another piece of bush must be cleared. The gardens of a homestead cover about three acres, producing 600 to 1000 pounds of crops per acre. The range of crops is the usual: maize, millet, tubers and beans.

In the course of our discussion we have already made considerable use of Hunter's invaluable information about the Pondo. This is the most detailed account of a Bantu system of agriculture. It is valuable not only in itself, but also in suggesting the discoveries yet to be made among other peoples. The Pondo round of work is typical of what may well be called the Bantu system. It is unnecessary for us to repeat the many features which we have found to be possessed in common by practically all of the peoples of whom we have knowledge. The main principles in the clearing of land, the size of gardens, the seeking for rain, the sharing of work between the members of the homestead, the weeding and guarding of the crops, all of these have already been indicated, not, indeed, as they are found in detail among the Pondo, but as they function among those and so many other peoples. Certain of Hunter's conclusions, however, must be specially noted.

The place of field magic is well indicated. In the mentality of the people it takes its place along with the technical processes as being essential to the production of food. The form of magic most common is that of burning a medicine to windward of the field. Much individual choice is possible both in the composition of the medicine and in the time at which it is burned. The knowledge of the medicines and of the methods is public property; specialists do not have to be paid. On the other hand, one wild plant is much sought after and in some cases may even be bought from neighbours. That the traditional element is not predominant in magic is shown by the fact that some people use a little coal, brought from the mines in Natal. Hunter probed to find out whether this burning could ever have been used to regulate work in a number of fields. It cannot be performed purely individually, for if one man or woman treats his or her field without first warning the neighbours, the result is that the neighbours' fields suffer. The people who failed to give warning are thus suspected of witchcraft, although there is no legal case against them. Thus when one person wishes to treat some fields, neighbours must be warned so that all may do so at the same time. Yet Hunter was assured that this arranging was never done by headmen or chiefs; it is simply that when one person wishes to apply the magic he or she notifies the neighbours. Thus although the magic does imply a clear social responsibility, if a negative one, it is apparently never used as a co-ordinating economic force. Other ceremonies are performed, and undoubtedly unite a district in their observations, expressing an interest in the growing crops which is undoubtedly shared by a whole district, and which does indicate that all of the people in the district are approximately at the same stage in their work. But, as we have seen, there are other forces to bring about this uniformity. It does not appear that the work depends upon the ceremonies.

Hunter shows how very difficult it is to estimate the amount of actual work put into fields. The people love to work spasmodically, taking days off to attend beer-drinks and other festivals during the busy times, and, of course, attending the work-parties of friends. The only possible kind of reckoning is that of which Hunter gives an example; a medium-sized field will be ploughed in two or three days, a big field in a week. People may work alone in weeding their fields for a fortnight, then call in a party to finish the job in one day. The work is done; it is not done with the monotonous regularity of peasants' labour. The main supports to the people's work are the festivals, the social events which are obviously desired as keenly as is the crop itself.

Many references have already been made to the work-parties which play so vital a part in all Bantu agriculture. We are not lacking in information about these, but Hunter gives a particularly full and clear account of how she found them to work. They are of especial importance to the study of Bantu economics. Conforming to no text-book type of labour organization, satisfying needs in no very direct way, wasteful of labour and materials in a utilitarian sense, they yet are the principal means whereby numbers of people outside the boundaries of individual homesteads co-operate for the performing of difficult work; they are the principal medium in which capital is invested for agricultural purposes, and they are one of the main groupings through which consumption is carried out.

Work-parties are used by practically all the Bantu peoples at all stages of agriculture, from the clearing to the harvest. The principle is simple. Individual toil is tedious, and it looks as if the man or woman will never get through the field. Nothing could be more natural than to invite the neighbours to help, and to make a social occasion. But resources are necessary. Beer must be provided, and possibly even meat. The woman who wants help may have enough grain to provide beer for her party. If so, her husband agrees, and word is sent round that there will be beer at So-and-So's place on such-and-such a day. The party does not turn up in any automatic way. At least, it does not automatically appear in the right numbers or composed of appropriately industrious people. Much depends upon the reputation of the woman who is giving it. Also, upon her circumspection in choosing a day when other people will be in the district and not too busy with their own fields. But most depends upon the amount of beer which is expected.

This depends upon two factors, first upon the amount of grain which the woman has succeeded in producing and in conserving throughout the winter months, despite all the temptations to consume it then. Secondly, it depends upon the amount of work which she, with probably her daughters and her co-wives, will put into making the beer. This is very heavy work. There is no doubt that in many cases it is heavier than that of cultivating the fields, and that if the woman followed rigidly direct rules of conduct she would effect a nett saving of labour simply by tilling her fields instead of preparing for the party.

But it is here that the complex nature of wants evinces itself. The woman definitely desires a change from the monotony of field labour. To obtain this she is quite willing to perform another, even more intense labour, but of a sort which breaks monotony and which brings other direct satisfactions. It brings contact with neighbours; the pleasure both of feasting and of working in groups. Not least among its satisfactions is that of seeing the fields being successfully cleared, tilled, weeded or reaped. The economics of the work-party have nothing abstruse about them; they are simply not directly utilitarian, and show, incidentally, that production is no more "direct" among these very backward people than it is in Western Europe or North America. The "roundabout" process by which capital is stored, its employment planned, and calculations made as to its present as apposed to its future use, is just as clearly evinced in Bantu Africa as anywhere else. Thus another text-book generalization as to the differences between "primitive" and "advanced" economics must go the way of all such pronouncements.

These facts have to be reckoned with in a very direct way when efforts are made to introduce more Western, more individualistic methods of work. To ask an individual to cultivate his or her gardens in a way which precludes the use of the work-parties is to ask him or her to give up one of the main satisfactions associated with the work of cultivation. It entails the loss, from one aspect, of an important social satisfaction and, from another aspect, of one of the most interesting uses to which grain can be put after it has been grown. Thus the motives for work, and for change to a much more monotonous kind of work, are removed by the removal of one of the main satisfactions.

If the woman has not enough grain in her own stores, or if a big party is suggested, which will do the fields of more than one wife as well as those of the man himself, the man must play a leading part in deciding just how the expense is to be shared among the various stores, and here the principles of the economics of the household come into play. Further principles of the work-party will emerge in our examination of its working in several areas.

That there is some direct correspondence between the value of the beef or beer given to the helpers, and the amount of help obtained, is shown by such facts as that a chief or very rich man might even kill a beast for a work-party, as against the pig or goat of an ordinary man, but that the people would be expected to give two or three days' work instead of the normal single day. Further, a work-party with beer always draws more people than one with meat, "for by summer the beer is scarce and people will do anything to get it". Even Hunter could collect no adequate data as to the quantities of beer involved. It is, however, known throughout the neighbourhood how many barrels have been prepared, and this plays a big part in determining the numbers of people who will attend. The attendance is greatly influenced by the scarcity and value of beer at any time. Sometimes it is plentiful, low in the communal scale of values, and thus a lesser attraction. Thus the successful head of a homestead is the one who, through his ultimate control over consumption, is able to make the grain last through the months of scarcity so that at a time when it is almost unavailable to the rest of the people he and his wives will be able to summon and reward substantial parties through its medium. The stored-up grain is thus true capital, stored resources capable of being used for further production.

It is only the man with a large household who can hope to achieve this surplus. The additional number of wives and dependants is necessary in the first place for growing the surplus grain, and in the second place for undertaking the labour of making the beer. The large household has a surplus of labour power denied to the smaller one. Usually this surplus labour is occupied to a considerable degree in providing more varied cooking; the division of labour among a number of wives means that the basic work of the household, the cooking of essential food, is got through more easily; there is more labour and time left over to make beer for a party.

The Culwicks show that in all agricultural work assistance

can be obtained by people who can give beer. This is especially prized at the right time, that is, when there is most field labour to be done at the beginning of the agricultural cycle. It is then that beer is scarce; so many people have, possibly for months, been husbanding their store with the utmost care. By the time of harvest among the Bena, and this is equally true everywhere else, beer is much more easily obtained and a weaker incentive. A well-to-do Bena man will organize a beer drink on a large scale perhaps two or three times a year.

The cheapness of beer at harvest time is reflected in the comparative absence of work-parties at that stage of the cycle. Hunter heard only of one party for reaping, and that given by a rich man. The Culwicks tell us that the work of reaping falls very largely to the women, because the men are able to get beer at that time without working for it.

The shading off of ordinary work-parties of commoners into the parties for cultivating the fields of chiefs and headmen is indicated among the Kondo, where it is shown that work-parties are used as among other tribes, and that, when a headman's garden is being done beer is provided, while the chief, rewarding his parties in an exclusive way, kills an ox. We have already shown how the cultivation of the chief's gardens among the Basuto was really done by an extension of the work-party principle. The main difference is that when a man of high rank requires several days' labour from his neighbours or subjects, instead of the normal single day, he rewards them not alone by beer and its attendant festivities, but also by the highly valued flesh food. Even this may not make a full payment for the services. The significant point is that he and his family will give perhaps insignificant service in return, so that a clear element of taxation may be distinguishable.

Attendance at work-parties of neighbours is almost entirely a neighbourly act. There can be no compulsion, but it is rather unfriendly not to go if one can and if one is likely to be needed. How much of the reward is through highly-valued beer and meat at a certain time of the year, these being, we should note, at that time invaluable as additions to diet; how much from the social intercourse, and how much from the reciprocity by which the giver of the party attends other parties in turn, it is quite impossible to say. The beer and meat are valuable, and by all evidence are real payment. The fact that they are distributed in the form of entertainment as a social function must not be allowed to blind us to this fact. Reciprocal work also is essential. Underlying both of these, the clear working of economic principles is to be discerned.

By the institution of the work-party, a considerable number of people are able to put their grain stores and their labour power into the market. Those with the available grain are able to receive labour in exchange for it, on terms which are dictated, directly, by the willingness of other people to give up work in their own gardens, or leisure, in return for the beer and meat; indirectly, by the other satisfaction derived by both sides to the transaction. People without the capital resources of grain and meat will give up working time to secure some of them, in the form, of course, of consumable goods. It is when work is becoming monotonous, and other activities rise in the scale of values, that people will think of going to a work-party, or organizing one. In all, the parties are a med um wherein people make economic choice and exchange; these result in an effective but far from direct means of applying labour to the soil and sharing the results.

REFERENCES AND FURTHER READING

Bantu Industries (Art.). D. A. Hunter. South African Journal of Science, 1921-22.
Cattle Magic and Medicines of the Bechuanaland Bakxatla (Art.). I. Schapera. South African Journal of Science, 1930.
Some Ethnographical Texts in Sekgatla (Art.). I. Schapera. Bantu Studies, 1930.
Story of My Mission in South-East Africa. W. Shaw. 1860.
Zulu-English Dictionary. Bryant.
Seven Years in South Africa. Dr. E. Holub. 1881.
The Life of a South African Tribe. H. A. Junod. 1927.
The Ila-Speaking Peoples of Northern Rhodesia. Smith and Dale. 1920.
The Bavenda. H. A. Stayt. 1931.
Ubena of the Rivers. A. T. and G. M. Culwick.
Reaction to Conquest. M. Hunter. 1937.

TILLING THE SOIL

Section VIII

Economic Conclusions

What are we to say, in conclusion, of the basic economic aspect of Bantu agriculture? It is a round of activities as simple in one way, as complex as others, as any other chain of human actions. Agencies are combined to produce a given set of results. The problem of imputing shares in the results to the various agencies is present, although but little formulated, and concealed from the superficial view by the fact that all proceeds go to the family. There is no question, for example, of the men having to prepare land and then receiving a proportion of the crop as their share. The crop belongs to the household in much the same way as, in Europe or America, a man's income belongs to his family. But the control over the Bantu food supply is shared in the ways which we have tried to describe. It will now be seen that this system does implement the imputation of results and the sharing of rewards. This is seen particularly in the case of a wife who, doing part of the work in her own garden, is able to claim an individual share for herself and her children on account of any specially successful management which she may have performed. There is plenty of room, in practice, for her to express the view that the specially good yield on her lands, better than that on the lands of her co-wives, must be due to her own skill and not to her husband's part in the work, which was given equally to all the wives. The ease with which a Bantu wife can return to her parents for a short time, or for good, makes this an effective piece of bargaining.

The man also is able to claim, in a very definite way, the results of his management. Should he succeed in clearing more or better land, in providing for better work-parties, or merely in making better implements, he is likely to be able to show the results of his skill. These results will only in small ways go to him and not to his whole household. Yet the formulation of his own share will not be absent. It will be known that through him food surpluses are obtained, cattle and other stock carefully husbanded, and every now and again a new

247

wife obtained with her working and her reproductive power. His personal reward will be the credit and prestige which result. By far the greater part of this imputation and distribution is within the homestead or kinship unit. This is correlated with the basic fact that this unit is also the unit of production. We thus have a substantial difference between the Western and the Bantu economic systems, yet even this makes it only more significant that in the Bantu system value is attached to the services of individuals, even though the product thus distributed may be consumed by all, all sharing in the advantages, for example, of a skilful economic leader as head of the kinship group.

The combining of agencies is carried out in a way very little different from that in Europe or North America. The people are fully aware of what they are doing when they put extra labour into clearing, or planting, or guarding. They are well aware that the relative value of pieces of land may change from time to time and from place to place. A scarcity of suitable land will leave no doubt that they have either to work it more carefully or to travel further to find better soil. A relative shortage of grain left over from the previous year, or of cattle, leaves no doubt that the people begin the season less well equipped, and that each unit of the supply is more valuable. If work-parties cannot be summoned, the drudgery of toil becomes apparent. If there is neither milk nor meat, the heavy work of clearing is felt to be more heavy through the lack of these resources which would have been converted into human capital.

The basic choice, that between putting labour into agriculture and devoting attention to the many other calls on a Bantu's time and attention, is often only too acutely present. If a man has but one wife and cannot leave his fields, then he has no chance of taking part in the councils of his tribe, nor may he be able to go and recover a debt of a cow from a son-in-law or someone else a distance away. The women have an even greater variety of calls upon them. Household work and the looking after of children will often bring a woman back from her fields. If she is a sole wife this means that she must cultivate less in order to cook, or cook less in order to cultivate.

If she is one of a number of women in a household her position will be more fortunate, for one will be able to come home and prepare the food for the whole household while the others carry on with the fields; this gives a very clear instance of the advantages of division of labour in a Bantu household. The wife must also visit her parents. This is a duty and a pleasure not to be forgotten. Again, it will interfere much less with her husband's food supply if there are other wives whose work will make her absence less felt. Altogether, nothing could be further from the truth than to suppose that the Bantu do a fixed amount of work because custom so dictates. Custom, as we shall see, does dictate the broad limit among the Bantu as among ourselves. Within these limits the choice is wide and very consciously made by individuals.

Superficial though it is, we must note the striking absence of those material aids to production which have become a main feature of Western industry. Bantu material resources are not stored up in great quantities and then converted into some piece of machinery which will transform their methods of work. To note this absence of what is known as the "roundabout" method of production is, however, to note a surface fact only. It is obvious that the Bantu lack capital equipment on a Western scale. Our task is to observe the whole social set of which this is but one facet. The Bantu are well aware of the advantages of providing themselves with such capital equipment as they know of. A good supply of food at the time of clearing is, as we have shown in some detail, the better part of this equipment. Their knowledge is an equally vital part of their capital equipment, and is, in a sense, a determinant. We have seen how it is knowledge or the lack of it which gives or withholds value. That land is valuable which is *known* to be good for crops. Manure, not known to be useful, does not become an economic commodity.

Needless to say, refinements in method requiring elaborate machinery are just as far outside their ken as is the machinery itself. This being so, we do not expect to find products being stored up for conversion into capital aids. Storing is limited by the means of storing. Grain pits are adequate only for year to year supplies. Herds are clumsy, uncertain, and not easily convertible into anything else. But storing or saving is yet more fundamentally limited by the limits to the demand for the stored resources. The people are very well aware that they may consume more or less of their grain or their cattle, and that what they do not consume is available for future use. The balance between immediate and future satisfactions is always appreciated, despite any loose talk about the improvidence of the savage.[1] A man stores grain because he knows that its power of giving satisfaction in the future will be greater than its present power. But all of this can mean only one thing, that the demand for savings is determined by the people's choice within the limits of their culture. The demand for savings is determined by the satisfactions which they may be expected to give in the uses to which it is possible to put them. Once again, demand exercises the controlling power, and demand is conditioned by the knowledge, the technical processes, the working organization of the people. To single out the absence of instrumental capital is to stress most unduly one superficial point. Notwithstanding all this, Bantu production is, as we have shown, just as "roundabout" as is our own.

The controlling power of demand shows itself in ways, if possible, even more fundamental yet. Within any given culture, the present writer suggests, people desire to increase their resources only in terms of that culture. Thus, if an Englishman is asked whether he would like to be richer, he may well reply that he would, but will have in mind only the things which are around him, which constitute the substance of his desires. Similarly, if we ask a Bantu whether he would like to be richer his answer will be Yes, or more probably a smile. He wants a better supply of food; to have enough even in the winter months, and meat and beer in plenty. In contact with

---

[1] The extent to which certain traits have become associated in our minds with the concept of "the savage" is well illustrated by the fact that even Knight, than whom no thinker has done more to clear away such misconceptions, says: "The improvidence of savages is proverbial." The statement is absolutely immaterial to Knight's argument. He simply feels, as does almost everyone, that it is perfectly safe to treat "the savage" as a sound concept, then to use it to illustrate the apotheosis of some thoroughly uneconomic tendency.

Western civilization, his horizon widens. For example, he may want enough food to be able to pay his tax without having to neglect his fields in order to work for wages. But always there is the cultural limit, and to teach people how to grow extra crops, for which they visualize no effective use, is pointless. Nor is the indigenous demand for food merely an undifferentiated desire to have enough to eat all the year round. Throughout this book we have shown that demand is itself formed by organized activities. At certain periods people must have enough to provide marriage feasts; on other occasions very large supplies of food are needed for funerals; at other times again the occasion of birth puts new strains upon the resources of the household, while we saw how the initiation of young people was further an activity shaping demand. Thus the individual, in disposing of his resources so as to produce "enough," must think of all of these components in his future demands. It is to meet these, as well as merely to have plenty to eat, that resources must be brought into existence. The resources will produce satisfaction in so far as they are brought into contact with these needs.

We begin to see how the economic aspect of Bantu life threads its way through the round of activities; how values are created and satisfactions produced in the process. As the man or woman toils in the field he or she thinks of the variety of ways in which the produce will finally be expended, and this awareness gives a unity to the whole cycle of production and consumption.

It would be unnecessary to labour the point of all these correlations, between the social organization of the people, their knowledge and technical equipment, and their organized activities controlling consumption, were it not so generally believed that one of these factors alone may be changed under outside influence. It is believed, for example, that people may be taught new methods of agriculture, and amazement is expressed that even when the advantages of these methods are demonstrated, only a few people, and those often out of touch with their fellows, will adopt the new methods. The reasons are not far to seek, and practical men are partially aware of them.

251

In the first place, the people adopting the new technique will very often find that it conflicts, not with their prejudices, but with their practical knowledge. This is a matter of which we know far too little, but the example of Northern Rhodesia alone indicates the difficulty. In the second place, social obligations have to be maintained as between the people themselves; thus a fact already mentioned, and which is of great importance, is that among all cattle-owning Bantu the gardens, after harvest, must be turned over to public grazing. This supplies the cattle with a very valuable food, and if any one man wishes to cultivate crops all the year round as the demonstrators teach him to do, he must refuse to give this customary grazing to his neighbour's cattle. Not only does he put himself on bad terms with his neighbours; he also forfeits his claim to graze his cattle on the stubble in his neighbour's fields.

Further, a married woman is to-day a most influential and respected member of Bantu society, but this is based upon the solid fact of her importance in agriculture. Since the essence of new methods very often is that the man takes charge and works larger fields in new ways, it will be seen that the woman finds herself in danger of losing all that she values most. The list could be continued indefinitely. Enough has been written to show how technique, knowledge, social organization, not to forget religion, all combine to make of Bantu agriculture a system of activities coincident at every point with the important elements of the people's lives. Agriculture satisfies not merely the primary need for food, but also the complex needs which are so intertwined with Bantu social organization. Agriculture is in itself a complete system of activities, having many aspects, which coincide with needs. Its social aspect is strong and gives direct satisfactions. Its religious aspect helps to control the outlay of resources. Its political aspect makes possible the government of units big and small, from the group of homesteads up to the great tribe. Its economic aspect, intertwined in practice with all of the others, is one of the dominant ways in which the Bantu share tasks, expend resources, share rewards and get the best results within the limits set by their own culture for effort made.

PART III

CHAPTER XIII

THE SIGNIFICANCE OF THE ECONOMIC UNITS

THE argument of this is that the customary division between Public Economics and economic theory may now be replaced by the concept that, in an important sense, all economics are public economics, and that we cannot presuppose two spheres of economic choice, in one of which the active unit is the individual, while in the other some kind of government is the object of study.

Economic discussion has, so far, proceeded quite justifiably on the assumption of economic decisions being made by individuals. Our contention is that this is a simplifying assumption, necessary for the progress of the science, but far removed from reality, and that the time is ripe to replace it by a more useful set of concepts.

Equilibrium economic theory could, obviously, never have been developed without the assumed existence of a clear and concrete economic unit. The "individual" has filled this role, in all discussions of economic theory, but always with one or two reservations. It has always been recognized that certain economic decisions were, in fact, not made by individuals. The activities of municipal and national governments, in their economic aspect, have thus been relegated to a different field of study, that of so-called Public Economics.

The effects of this splitting up are apparent now in discussions centering around the questions: Who? Whom? Who makes economic decisions? To whom are economic resources and obligations to be allocated?

When we have seen that for all practical purposes economic decisions are invariably made by some kind of group executive and never by an individual acting on his own behalf, we shall see how unnecessary it is to split, as de Marco would definitely

255

have us do, "general economics" off from "public finance or economics". Our conclusion will be that there can be but one body of economic theory, that of the evaluations arising from and guiding the disposal of economic resources; and that the decisions considered in this theory may be made by great groups or small, national governments or parish councils, the households of feudal chiefs or of manual labourers, but that, whoever or whatever makes the decisions, *these decisions are the data of economic theory*, it being impossible without serious error to set apart the activities, in an arbitrary way, of certain groups and to treat them under the heading of Public Economics while assuming that all other decisions are made by individuals.

De Marco, in his section on *The Methodological Nature of Public Finance*, speaks of "the two fields of theoretical investigation". There are two fields, but not in the way in which de Marco thinks. De Marco goes on to explain that "Public Finance is a concrete science—that is, it must be brought down finally to real phenomena. Economics, on the other hand, is an abstract science . . . ". He elaborates this a little later by saying "The statement that Public Finance seeks, in its investigations, to approach as near as possible to reality, and therefore makes an effort to study real phenomena, taking into account all the factual elements of which the latter are composed, is to be taken simply as meaning that it is a concrete science, as opposed to other sciences that are more abstract"; and from this he draws his "important methodological corollary: viz., that Public Finance cannot use logical abstraction to the same extent as does general economics". Our comment upon this is that economic theory deals with the decisions made by human groups (and possibly, in very exceptional cases, even by individuals). It deals with only the economic aspect of these decisions. The other matter is the way in which the decisions are arrived at. This cannot be split off into a study of the activities of governing bodies alone. It must try to analyse the sociological processes behind the formation of all decisions. In doing this, it may, for all we can now know, develop instruments of logical abstraction just as useful as those now in the hands of the economic theorist.

It does not yet have, we shall probably agree, such well-developed instruments. But it must be granted a field no less than, in fact strictly coinciding with, that of theoretical economics. Economic theory deals with the *results* of economic decisions; sociological theory will, in time, deal with the *formation* of such decisions. Further discussion may succeed in showing the inadequacy of any treatment which depends upon the isolation of a subject known as Public Economics, and its treatment as if it were a kind of appendage of general economics.

De Marco's reasoning appears to depend upon two main assumptions: first, the division of wants into two kinds, collective and individual; second, the existence of two distinct economic subjects, the state and the individual. It appears to us that these two main assumptions are not only unnecessary but misleading. We shall argue that *all wants are of one kind*, all being socially conditioned and having their ends in individuals. We shall argue further that *there is but one type of economic subject*, the human group through which decisions are almost invariably made.

All wants are collective or social. Let us examine the difference "which exists between individual wants, on the one hand, and collective wants, on the other." De Marco tells us that collective wants presuppose the existence of a community. But can we ever, without being nonsensical, presuppose anything else? "So long as man lives in isolation, one can conceive of the existence only of individual wants"; it is, apparently, when man passes into a state of society that a new type of want, the collective, is added to the original individual type of want. We must hold that anything which depends upon reasoning of this type ought to be suspect. Nothing is known of any time when man was not a social being. We can speak of man only as we know him. But de Marco presses home his point. "Individual needs, on the other hand, are those which arise and remain within the life of a man who is isolated or who believes himself to be isolated." This indicates, if anything, nothing better than a form of lunacy. Any such supposed needs can have no relevance for us.

R   257

De Marco, in his section on *Classification of Collective Wants*, reverts to classification according to age or antiquity. The oldest collective wants are given as the need for defence against enemies. Since this is made to include internal enemies, it covers causes of friction and conflict of interests between individuals. These, however, are usually covered by legal arrangements, nearly always paid for by the individuals who go to law. It provides a clear example of the fact that, whatever kind of want de Marco can indicate, it has both its collective and its individual aspects; in fact, that it is social.

De Marco comes next to a second category of collective wants which, according to him, were originally individual but which have been modified by the fact that people live in society. Once again, we have the inadmissible term "originally", as if we had knowledge of some state of mankind other than that of which the whole of history tells us. Abandoning, however, de Marco's fruitless evolutionism, we have to ask whether his second group of wants can in fact be classed as either "individual" or "collective". This group covers the need for personal and domestic hygiene. These, we are told, are individual needs "that even isolated man feels". But, apparently, they take on a new social value when man comes to live in society because of the dangers of contagion. We are told that it is because of these dangers that rules of hygiene are imposed by society. Even a slight acquaintance with primitive peoples, and a slight examination of our own habits, should be enough to show that rules of hygiene are by no means explicable through the fear of contagion. Savages who have no knowledge of contagious diseases, as such, will yet have elaborate rules of personal cleanliness. We ourselves would be very hard put to it if we had to account for our washing habits, our preference for clean finger-nails, through fear of contagion. We should often be much nearer the mark if we said that we are clean because we like it and because we know that other people like it, that cleanliness is a social value, doubtless a symbol of other things; that it may have no more to do with health than table manners have to do with nutrition. When a man decides to devote time and money to achieving cleanliness of himself and his belongings, this is a decision taken by himself, but on account not only of his own preferences for cleanliness but also because he knows that his acquaintances also will value the result, partly judging him by it. The satisfactions end not merely with the man himself but with his social group, with the people who get additional satisfaction from using his clean house, and so on. These needs are exactly like all others in that they centre in individuals but have a strong social aspect.

De Marco's third group of collective needs appears to be taken on an entirely different basis. The example is that of water, which is taken to satisfy a collective want when it is collectively supplied. The source of supply is taken as the criterion. In this way, any want which according to other tokens might be individual, may become collective, and any distinction between individual and collective needs would depend merely upon the choice of the people as to how they were to be satisfied. In fact, any functional distinction would disappear. If we are to classify the collective wants at all, we must have a consistent rule. We may note in passing that the only example given of this third group is that of water which "unquestionably, satisfies an individual need". And which becomes a collective commodity only when supplied by a monopolistic group. Our comment is that water, if anything, satisfies collective needs. A community needs it just as definitely as it may need an army. Cultivation and washing, especially washing of household utensils, involve the use of water by groups. A father of a family has to secure a supply of drinking water for the individual members, and this is an example of a smaller group at work, but operating on precisely the same lines as a government securing, say, protection against attack for its people.

Is it possible to classify wants, whether we call them collective or individual? De Marco's classification of collective wants "according to their degree of urgency for man in society" appears to have so little success that the attempt had better be abandoned. The defence of territory is given as the most urgent need, since without it no society can exist. But we are not entitled to argue from our Western communities to those of the whole world. It would be easy to supply examples of people who are in the happy position, or who have been so within historical time, of not having the defence of their territory as a major preoccupation. De Marco says that his list ends with the apparently least urgent collective want, that of the hygienic defence of the community. In many communities this is not a conscious want in any sense. It depends upon the state of the people's medical knowledge. In any case, it will vary enormously with the extent of the dangers from transmittable disease; in some parts of the world this presents a far more urgent danger than that of territorial invasion.

It becomes necessary to ask ourselves whether we are in the least clear about the nature of human wants. Nothing would be easier than for us to bemuse ourselves with endless speculation as to the nature of "collective", "individual", "aggregate" and other sorts of wants, and then to multiply our difficulties by attempting to put them in some perfectly unattainable order of priority or urgency. Since the distinguished Italian economist, whose work we are now trying to build upon, makes efforts to classify wants, and constructs theoretical conclusions upon the results, we must not merely criticize his work but must offer our own alternative.

Malinowski has classified human wants into those which are primary and those which are secondary, or derived from the others. Common sense will soon give us a sufficient list of primary needs; nutrition, supply of air for breathing, a degree of warmth to maintain bodily temperature, sufficient room to move in, are examples. At once they reveal one characteristic; they cannot be placed in order of urgency. All must be satisfied, or people cannot live. This, indeed, gives us the very definition of primary needs. The extent to which they are translated into wants, or consciously felt needs, is another matter and will not be dealt with here. Then come the derived needs. Man requires not merely food, but a food-producing organization. He requires this organization to function efficiently, and this presupposes the existence of effective legal sanctions and many other arrangements. The need for warmth also can be satisfied only by social arrangements. Even if only the fire in the hut of a savage is in question, it is clear that a number of people will co-operate to produce it and to satisfy their wants from it. We shall not now discuss in detail any full list either of primary or of derived needs or wants. It is enough to see that primary needs cannot be classed in order of urgency and that derived needs are for means of satisfying these primary requirements.

It now becomes clear that any division of human needs into individual and collective is likely to be a spurious one. All needs are ultimately the needs of individuals. The need for territorial defence is just as individual as that for food. It may well be satisfied through each person making a contribution according to his desire for the protection. Again, no need, when translated into a want, has a purely individual action. It is here that we come to our fundamental objection to de Marco's division of wants into two kinds. It appears to us that even the most apparently individual expression of a want is really social. When a man buys a newspaper, there is a strong probability that it will satisfy, and that he knows it will satisfy, the wants of other people besides himself. If he is a member of a family, as very nearly every man is, the newspaper will be read by other members of the family. It may be read by other people at the man's place of work. It may be exchanged. The particular newspaper bought may well be chosen, not according to the man's own preferences, but according to those of his wife or other secondary readers. Another point is that the man may well buy, not that newspaper which he himself, or even he and the secondary readers would prefer. He may buy a newspaper with a presumed higher social standard, so that various people upon whom he wishes to make a good impression may get satisfaction from seeing him reading it. Some of the satisfaction will come back to him, and his family, but he may certainly give satisfaction to other people.

If even the purchase of a newspaper can be shown to satisfy the wants of a collection of people, it is clear that almost every other purchase will be of the same nature. A piece of furniture will obviously give what de Marco would call a collective satisfaction, though he would certainly, according to his own reasoning, class it as satisfying an individual want. A suit of clothes or a tie may be thought of as giving a very individual type of satisfaction—until we realize that not merely the wearer but his wife must be satisfied. The tie or a hat worn by a man may even be chosen by his wife and may certainly give more satisfaction to her than to him. We have deliberately selected examples of the most personal and apparently individual kinds of wants and satisfactions. We see that in every case the want is not merely individual; more than one person has to be satisfied. Cases could be multiplied indefinitely; expenditure on food is another clear example. A mother, possibly assisted by other members of the household, has to provide food in precisely that way in which, according to de Marco, a government has to provide the things which it does provide. The only difference is the size of the group involved.

If our reasoning is correct, it follows that de Marco's distinction between the aggregate of individual wants as an arithmetical sum, and the aggregate of collective wants as an algebraic sum, is pointless.

The question as to whether a man should buy a newspaper is, even if we take for granted the expenditure of the penny on *something*, quite sure to have positive and negative aspects. Some people, other than himself, are almost sure to want him either to buy the Daily Howl or to buy, not the Daily Howl, but the Daily Wail. If a mother gives castor-oil to her children, we can scarcely suppose that each child, left to itself, would decide to purchase the same dose for its own consumption. The executive of the group, in this case the mother, makes the only relevant decision, and makes it on the basis of her estimates of the needs of the children. A shifting of power within the group might materially affect the disposal of its economic resources. The writer well remembers hearing from a well-known man that he bought precisely the newspapers which he liked—but that the porters on the Underground to whom he gave them after reading them often asked him to get different newspapers, and that he sometimes bought more popular ones in order to satisfy them. These illustrations show negative satisfactions at work, giving a kind of algebraic sum even in the case of the most individual expenditure.

In the case of the newspapers and the porters there was no question of the porters paying any of the costs. But in the vast majority of cases this consideration does arise and enormously strengthens our argument. A working man in particular, spending carefully and maintaining a family, will know that even though the money spent upon an ounce of tobacco will be *primarily* for his own satisfaction, the money might be spent in some way giving more satisfaction to other members of his family. The expenditure upon tobacco may well involve a negative satisfaction for other members of the household, and this may be quite in evidence even though the man has a strongly established customary right to that expenditure. With any reduction in income or rise in the cost of living, he may reduce on that item so that his dependants will need to make less sacrifices in other directions. It cannot possibly be maintained that the demand for ounces of tobacco in a given community is merely the arithmetical sum of individual demands, in the sense in which de Marco uses these terms. Again we come to the point that all wants are collective in his sense; they all involve positive and negative quantities. This is because they are all satisfied through the activities of group executives. De Marco's example, illustrating his point, is that of the supply of hats, which, earlier in this book, we showed to miss its point. Whether this demand is expressed by an army department, or a school or cricket team buying hats for its pupils or players, or a father buying hats for his children and perhaps for himself because his *wife* feels a want for him to have a new hat, makes no difference to the hatter.

De Marco's example, illustrating his point, is that of the supply of hats. "Thus the hatter produces exactly as many hats as there are individuals requiring them; but he does not take into account those who do not wear hats. The State, however, if it furnishes headgear to its soldiers, must produce as many hats as there are soldiers, including those who do not ask for them." Our comment would be that the hatter

263

produces the number for which there is a total demand. (Whether this demand is expressed by an army department, or a school or cricket team buying hats for its pupils or players, or a father buying hats for his children and perhaps for himself because his *wife* feels a want for him to have a new hat, makes no difference to the hatter.) "Including those soldiers who do not ask for hats." But are there any soldiers who do not, or who do? It makes no difference whether they ask for them or not. They get them; the mere fact of their being soldiers means that they "want" all parts of the soldier's equipment. If any individual soldier would rather not have a hat, that fact cannot interest us because it cannot be expressed in economic demand. Throughout any taxation system there may be people paying for services which they do not really want. But, as economists we have no means of knowing this. We can but assume that people want the things for which, in fact, they pay. We must go on the assumption again, simply as economists, that all soldiers do want their hats. As sociologists, we should be able to do something in the direction of investigating what we may here call. as a rough beginning, the real as distinct from the economic want or demand.

The same writer, in his section on *The Active Subject*, refers to the State as the active subject or unit in general economics. He is careful to point out that the State is not a physical person "as is the *homo economicus* of general economics". Without discussing the physical existence of economic man, we may repeat that economic discussion has so far gone on the assumption of decisions being arrived at by two kinds of subject, by some governing body on the one hand, and by "the individual" on the other. "The individual" has served as a piece of shorthand. Economists were concerned with economic decisions; they did not go into the question, Who made them? until they came to deal with decisions which most obviously were not made by individuals. These came to be treated separately because economists were aware, at least when dealing with the obvious and well-marked economic powers of modern governments, that the nature of the bodies making decisions is likely deeply to affect the decisions made.

SIGNIFICANCE OF THE ECONOMIC UNITS

If a government takes over the duty of supplying water to the people, each household may spend either more or less upon its water supply than it may have done if it had its own well, *but it is extremely unlikely to spend exactly the same amount.* The really important point is that the total decisions arrived at are affected by the nature of the active subject. It is for this reason, that it is most important to carry out every possible investigation into the nature of the groups whose executives make economic decisions. It becomes all the more important if, as we believe, virtually all decisions in the economic world are made by group executives.

"The motives and the wants that induce the State to produce public goods are a resultant of the motives and the needs of individuals and groups who have *actually* contributed toward the formation of the State's calculation of financial advantage and disadvantage. For this reason, theoretical enquiry must, as far as possible, break down the State's calculation into the economic calculations of the individuals or the groups which represent the constituent elements of the State's calculation.

"This is a fundamental principle. In order to do this, however, it is necessary, first of all, to take account of the political constitution that is in force in a given country at a given time, in order to know which wants and which individual and group interests help to form the State's calculation of advantage and disadvantage, and which wants may happen to be excluded from this calculation."

In this statement, de Marco arrives at an important truth which is, however, limited by his inability to see beyond the conception of economics as being divided between the individual on the one hand and the State on the other.

We have already seen some of the reasons for believing that the individual will have to be dropped altogether. It also becomes clear that the State is merely one of a vast number of economically significant organizations. The family is always, so far at least as human experience has been able to go, responsible for the disposal of more economic resources than is the State. De Marco indicates the necessary line of advance when he says that theoretical enquiry must break down the

265

State's calculation into the economic calculations of its component parts. It is very true that in order to do this we must take account of the political constitution of the State. But what kind of theoretical enquiry will this be? It will not be economic. Economic theory cannot perform the work of analysing the pulls and pressures behind the formation of an economic decision. This, in the case of the State, would require political research, but then something more. It would require full sociological analysis. The study of the political constitution would be but the beginning, and economists are not theoretically equipped even for this. The analysis of individual and group interests, which de Marco rightly sees to be essential, must take into account the whole range of activities of all persons and groups; of, to mention only one or two, their religious interests, the state of their knowledge and tastes in general, the economic evaluation which they place upon health or education.

All this becomes even more significant when we see, as we should see clearly, that each group within the community has to be studied with precisely the same technique as that applicable to the State itself. This indicates that nothing less than a full sociological analysis of the community. We should, for example, make the minimum of progress if we were to begin with de Marco's surface division of States into two types, the absolute and the democratic.

"Public goods" are not, as de Marco would indicate, goods produced by the State. They are goods produced through the agency of any group managing the affairs of its members. Goods produced by the State may, if we wish, be designated "State goods". We shall see that the vast number of groups into which almost any human society is organized all produce or obtain goods which have the full characteristics, for each group, of public goods. That is to say, they are produced or obtained by drawing upon the resources of the group members and are then in some way placed at the disposal of these members. The principles according to which members contribute their share, and consume their share, are as yet formulated only in the studies of some primitive peoples.

SIGNIFICANCE OF THE ECONOMIC UNITS

It will probably be found that all goods, in any community, not only have some of the characteristics of public goods, but that they satisfy our full definition of public goods. This results from a simple but as yet imperfectly realized fact; that an individual practically never operates, or comes to an economic decision, simply as an individual. He is invariably a member of a group, or rather of a series of groups. Presumably the nearest approach ever existing to an individual who expends his resources without taking account of the requirements of other people is the individual living in lodgings, the product of modern Western civilization. Yet even he is not likely to be permanently without a family. He is very possibly saving up to get married, in which case his present economic decisions are influenced by the future, instead of the present, pulls and pressures of family members. His group is in the future. Or he may well have other family obligations, as to support elder people. Yet if we grant that there do exist some people who are without family or substitute groups, we but emphasize the rarity of such people in human culture.

The family is responsible for a much greater total expenditure than the State in any known country. How is it, then, that the State has been studied almost exclusively as the subject of public economics? The answer doubtless lies in the State being obvious and in the fact that it has always been right and proper to discuss State expenditure, but not family expenditure. The accounts of the State are open for all to see. The accounts of the family are intensely private. This imposes a great difficulty upon a most important line of research, but it does not diminish the value of that research.

Once it is stated it becomes fairly obvious that a piece of furniture is a public good for a family in precisely the same sense as that in which a gasworks is a public good for a city. The family is the primary organization through which economic resources must pass. When a pay envelope is brought home, its contents are at once brought under the consideration of at least two persons, the man and his wife. In a great many cases there is more than one pay envelope, since the husband is not always the sole earner. What is of even more importance, the wife contributes her work in the home, even if not a monetary source of income. The total family income is sure to be composite; several contribute, whether monetarily or otherwise. At once we see the first problem of "public finance": how is the total income of the group to be made up, in what proportions are the members to contribute? It appears just as clearly in the family as in the State. The second problem follows: to whom are the resources to be given? What utilities is each individual to get out of the common pool? In the first place, even if we could suppose, though it is an impossible supposition, that each person got a certain amount of money to spend just as he or she wished, upon his or her wants, the question of how much money would remain.

But it cannot be like this. Rather, we come back to our argument in the first part of this paper, that all significant expenditure is in respect of the wants of the group. Food supply, furniture, house rent, are obviously in respect of the public wants of the group. More personal expenditures, we have argued, are scarcely less so. In each case, underlying the economic decisions which are the data of economic theory, there is the process of the formation of these decisions, of the registering of the pulls and pressures of the individuals, of the sorting out of the forces which each individual is able to register. These can be dealt with only by sociological theory. Since the different ways in which these pulls can be organized, whether through the State, the family, or any other group, deeply affects the decisions arrived at, we see that, for the purpose of analysing and predicting human behaviour, a thoroughgoing consultation and continuous comparing of notes between economists and sociologists is a necessity. Even if economics goes upon its present assumption of regarding the active economic subjects as consisting of the State on the one hand and the individual on the other, other experts, as de Marco insists, must be called in to analyse the ways in which the State's economic decisions are arrived at, and, presumably, yet others to discover how the "individuals" form their

268

decisions. But since, as we have seen, this division of the subject is a thoroughly misleading and inadequate one, the need for co-operation is infinitely more pressing. At present there is a strong tendency for economists to say that the study of State taxation and expenditure is "economics" and that the study of the ways in which the family manages its resources is "sociology". This paper is a protest against any such assumption.

It remains only to note that the present writer has confined himself to putting the family on the map. The mere fact of doing this involves an important theoretical recasting. He does not in this paper indicate the lines along which, he believes, sociological theory will proceed in its co-operation with economic theory. That must remain for another study. Nor must it be supposed that the important decision-forming groups are fully enumerated when we add the family to the State. The family has been taken merely as an important example. The essence of any society is that it has a whole network of functioning groups, all producing their public goods, and that, as soon as we have enumerated these goods, we shall find nothing left to correspond to the term "private goods", just as the list of active economic groups will leave no room for "the individual" in the theoretical picture.

CHAPTER XIV

IF a sociological observer reports that among a primitive people there is a set of customs whereby resources are taken from people thought to have "too much" and given to other people thought to have "too little", and that thereby greater satisfactions appear to be given to the society as a whole, how is the economist to react to this report and judgment?

His present reaction is likely to be a curt "How does the sociologist *know* that satisfactions to the society as a whole are increased? he cannot compare the satisfactions of different people".

There has, of late, been a very strong tendency to rule interpersonal comparisons out of the considerations of economic theory. The object of this paper is to combat any such tendency. It appears to the writer that economic resources are disposed of according to *two sets of principles*, of equal importance and equally necessary if economics is to guide us in the study of human affairs. First is the principle of the economic application of resources according to the subjective evaluations of the functioning unit or subject. This is the subject-matter of the great majority of present-day economic studies. Second is the principle that, the economic unit seldom or never being an individual, resources are disposed of not only in the market, but within every group which formulates economic decisions, and that this involves some practical comparison of the needs of the individuals making up each group.

The importance of interpersonal comparisons has until now been somewhat limited owing to their being discussed mainly, or only, in connection with progressive taxation. Reference to another chapter will show that the question is in no sense limited to State taxation. It is shown that the State is merely one of a very large series of groups which registers economic decisions. It is shown that within each family, and, *a fortiori*, within many other functioning groups, precisely the same problems have to be solved before a purchase can be made or a supply of purchased goods distributed among the individual members. It was further shown that it is extremely difficult to regard any economic decision whatever as being made simply by an individual. If these conclusions have any degree of validity, they will show that, far from it being possible to outlaw interpersonal comparisons, it is rather the case that every single disposal of economic resources is made on the basis of a set of these comparisons, as well as upon the subjective evaluation of resources, and that, indeed, the two principles run *pari passu* and are inseparable.

The reconsideration of the nature of the economic unit is thus destined to bring interpersonal comparisons into the forefront of economic considerations. Before any father or mother spends any part of the family income, he or she is practically certain to consider the needs of the other members of the family. It will be considered that A had enough of something last week, and can afford to do with less this week; that B requires a certain supply of a given commodity because of certain circumstances; that C has too much of something and that consequently some of it can be given to D, so that it will not be necessary to purchase a new supply. In exactly the same way a national or municipal government will decide that certain people can be taxed more; that others ought to be relieved of some taxation; that certain other people must get an additional supply of some commodity, and that certain other people have no need of such an additional supply. Both in government and in family considerations, the needs of individuals are in fact compared, and it is on the basis, or result, of these comparisons that the executive of the group, the Chancellor of the Exchequer or the father or mother of the family, decides to expend the resources at his disposal in one way rather than in another.

We can rule out interpersonal comparisons on one condition only: on the condition that we work entirely upon the supposition of economic decisions being made by individuals; of the individual being the only effective economic unit. As

PRINCIPLES OF ECONOMIC SOCIOLOGY

the present writer has elsewhere stated, such a supposition is entirely justified in a methodological sense, as simplifying the treatment of subject-matter and thus enabling equilibrium analysis to be pressed further than could otherwise be possible. It is an abstraction, and its value depends entirely upon its being recognized as such. The first necessity, in using an abstraction in scientific thought, is to widen its basis or to link it up with other principles which, in their turn, describe active elements in human conduct. It is thus necessary for us to recognize that economic decisions are not in actual life made by individuals, but rather by what, as a first approximation, we shall refer to as group executives, and that these group executives can be described as forming their decisions by feeling the pulls and pressures of individuals, as well as of smaller groups, within their units. Is it possible to put down in a few words any principle or axiom which may be taken to describe the behaviour of these group executives?

Sociology will, in all probability, be found ready to supply one or two useful principles. At present, however, we wish to discuss one only, that known roughly as the diminishing marginal utility of total resources for any given person, and we wish to show that this principle, whatever its logical standing, whether it can philosophically hold water or not, is in fact indispensable in the formulation of any sound economics.

The philosophic quality of any such principle must be determined by one test only: whether it gives results which describe reality. Even principles which can be taken apart and analysed into mere tautologies can still be of the greatest service in enabling us to analyse human conduct. No better example could be given than that of the economic disposal of resources, whereby each individual is regarded as expending those at his disposal in such a way as to obtain for himself the maximum total satisfaction.

It is sufficient to point out that whatever he does, no matter how unexpected or illogical his behaviour may appear, we are still in the position of having to say that that was how he achieved his maximum of satisfactions. We can say nothing else. A critic of economics can therefore say, quite truly, that the whole science is based upon a mere tautology. Our answer may take two forms; having admitted the completely circular nature of such an argument, we reply, first, that nevertheless the principle does appear to correspond to something in human behaviour, to some activity whereby we all feel that we would rather expend our resources in one set of ways than in another; second, that even a tautological principle may be very useful in organizing human thought. Though the principle of economic disposal of resources may in itself be little better than a meaningless statement, yet, for reasons which it is not here within our scope to discuss, it makes possible extremely useful advances in the investigation of economics.

Likewise, the principle that, on the whole, to take goods from a rich man and give them to a poor man is likely to increase the sum-total of both men's satisfactions, because of the diminishing marginal utility of the total resources of each, may or may not be philosophically valid or "provable". The extent to which it may be proved will be discussed. In the meantime it is suggested that it is, without more ado, well worthy of admission into our scientific equipment because, in the first place, it describes an extraordinarily prevalent factor in the behaviour of human beings; and, in the second place, because we shall use it scientifically only as an assumption, abandoning it at once if it leads to conflict with observable reality.

Whether interpersonal comparisons are possible or not is not for the economist, by himself, to say. Obviously, other people must be consulted. There is the clearest case for calling in the social anthropologist, for example, and the psychologist. It is enough to remark at this stage that several highly expert and consistent sociological investigations of primitive societies have been made, paying great attention to their economic aspects, and that the investigators appear to agree upon the fact that those societies all have elaborate means of taking from those who had plenty and giving to those who were starving; of arranging that districts suffering from shortage would be supplied by more fortunate districts; that even persons, individuals, who had no means of earning sufficient incomes by their own work came to be supported by others. Investigators such as Malinowski, Firth, Hunter and a number of others have, in investigating the means whereby primitive societies hold together and secure their survival, all put this aspect, based upon the making of interpersonal comparison, in the forefront. It is significant that these investigations are much more thorough than any that have yet been made of Western communities, and, at the same time, they show that the dividing line between so-called primitive societies and our own societies is infinitely less definite than we had previously supposed. The conclusion is inevitable that when we achieve a correspondingly full sociological account of our own community, we shall find activities based upon interpersonal comparisons to be of equally great importance. In fact, our common observations to date show that, even in England or the United States, the disposing of resources according to comparisons of the needs of individuals is a major principle.

Can we *prove* that total satisfactions are likely to be increased by redistributing economic resources as between people who are relatively well supplied and people who are not?

In the first place, let us take an extreme case. A is starving to death; B is suffering from overeating. By taking from B and giving to A, we may observe an actual physiological improvement in the persons of both. B is healthier through having less to eat; A is saved from a painful death. This simple example shows two things; first, it shows the utter impossibility of making interpersonal comparisons in any ultimate sense; second, it shows the absurdity of not making them in a practical sense. For all we know, B might have preferred to retain his indigestion, his high blood pressure, his fatty heart. He may actually resent being made healthier. To him, quite conceivably, his infirmities, resulting as they did from surplus, were a symbol of the whole success of his life. He probably enjoyed talking about them, nursing them, getting sympathy on account of them, and taking them to expensive specialists. A more sparse and healthy diet may, while transforming him into a healthy man, have diminished his total satisfactions. On the other hand, A may, for all we know, resent being kept alive. Yet, we can only say that anyone who would let such considerations weigh with him would be at once regarded as completely anti-social. Something in society demands that its component members should be kept reasonably fit and efficient. We shall not here ask what this is; it is enough to indicate that certain minimum conditions of social survival must be satisfied. Any executive would, in real life, make the redistribution so as to improve the condition of both A and B, and, as economists, we must take account of his behaviour.

In the same way, taking another extreme case, we cannot but agree with Wicksteed that it is of extreme importance to get *some* supply of economic resources. Without this, life is literally impossible. So that, considering a person's total resources as a series of units of supply, we see that as a plain physical fact, the first unit makes the difference between life and death, whereas a later supply may make little or no observable difference. To refine upon this extreme antithesis, we shall see that whereas the first unit means life itself, the second may be absolutely necessary for freedom from disease; the third may be necessary for the maintenance of essential energy, and so on. Later supplies will make very little difference to these essential states. Thus the diminishing marginal utility of total resources becomes something correlated with physical fact. Again, we cannot in the least measure the various satisfactions of the man under consideration when he is in possession of one unit of supply, or of two or more units. For all we know, he may value the twentieth unit of supply, giving him so little practical satisfaction that he may scarcely trouble to spend it, more highly than the second or third units, without which he could never have had the twentieth. There is no accounting for tastes. Again we are brought to the position that in making interpersonal comparisons we are not dealing with what we may call the mere satisfactions of the individual; we are dealing with some deeper kind of needs. The whole indication is that, whereas equilibrium economics deals with wants, another type of economics, which we may here term social economics, deals with needs. It is in this connection that the relationship of wants to needs may have to be further explored.

Next, in discussing the diminishing marginal utility of total resources, we shall have to note how extremely firmly equilibrium economics is based upon the concept of the diminishing marginal utility of each commodity to each person, as further supplies of it come into his hands. The concept is held to with complete firmness, and very justifiably, even though it may be observable that a person may want more of a certain thing, the more of it he gets. Wicksteed goes so far as to suggest that with the development of his tastes, he becomes virtually a different person, thus accounting for his greater appetite for something already in his possession. We shall indeed step on to dangerous ground if we think in terms of individuals attaining new personalities. It is quite enough to say that, on the whole, second helpings are less wanted than first helpings, and that the diminishing marginal utility of supplies of a given commodity is an acceptable fact.

But is the number of commodities, available to any individual, infinite? The number of commodities in the world at large is certainly infinite. The number effectively at the command of almost any individual is just as certainly finite. Any of us could make a list of the economic commodities entering into our lives. We should find that, while, with increasing total resources, we should doubtless extend the range of our commodities to some degree, yet that we should to a much greater degree extend the supplies and qualities of those already on our list. It may be indicated that a millionaire in this country has extremely few actual kinds of commodities which are not in the possession or at the disposal of a person of ordinary means. House, furniture, clothes, travel, food, entertainments, objects of aesthetic satisfaction, means of religious observance, all of these are in the possession of any but the very poorest, and, it might be more accurate to say, are actually in the possession of even the poorest people. A poor man, as regards means of travel, may own only that part of a bus for the use of which he pays by means of his ticket, whereas a millionaire may have all kinds of private conveyances. Yet the commodities are the same; to each, they are means of travel. The number of commodities, in any basic sense, upon which any person can spend his income, is finite, and we are led inevitably to the conclusion that if each single commodity is subject to the condition of diminishing marginal utility, then all commodities together may well be subject likewise to this same condition. It may be an unwarrantable logical jump to pass from one commodity to the whole set in a person's possession. To the present writer it appears to be fully justified. If units of a single commodity can be taken as diminishing in value as the supply increases, it is extremely difficult to avoid the conclusion that units of all commodities together, or of total resources, will have the same tendency. Again, we find some ground, at least, for believing that the diminishing utility of total resources is a concept which we would do well to accept.

In a sense, the basic judgment which can be made about other people's satisfactions is that, of two supplies of economic resources, taken at their market valuations, any person will prefer the greater to the smaller. This judgment, or axiom, is quite as simple and fundamental as the axiom at the basis of subjective value and of equilibrium economics. It is also important to realize that the proposition that each person will dispose of his total resources so as to attain the maximum of satisfaction for himself, is by no means deserving of being considered a statement of purely subjective value. It is a proposition made about the subjective states of people's processes, but it is made objectively. In making it, economists are making an objective statement about other people. When it is made about more than one person, then it is *very difficult to see that it is not itself within the realm of interpersonal comparisons.* The objective and the subjective are only two ways of looking at the same thing. Subjectively, a person may or may not feel that he values one thing more than another, that his supply of one thing is becoming so large that he would rather begin to have units of something else; but, just as subjectively, he may feel that he would rather have more total resources than he now has, and that, equally, additional units of total resources will be less vital to him than the units which he already possesses.

Both of these are types of subjective judgment when looked

at from the point of view of the person making them. Equally, they are both objectively stated when formulated by one person about another or about others. It is by getting rid of a purely misleading antithesis between subjective and objective that we may hope to see that a proposition to the effect that a given person prefers more wealth to less, or that he values additional units of wealth less, the more he gets, is both subjective to the person feeling the satisfactions and objective to the scientist making statements about that person; and that precisely the same is true of the axiom of the economic disposal of resources.

This being so, it is unnecessary to appeal to the argument that, though we may find one individual who would not prefer more resources to less, yet we may be sure that in dealing with groups of people we shall not encounter such a perverse tendency. It is true that the appeal to large numbers may strengthen the argument that interpersonal comparisons can be made; yet it is no less true that we do not need to appeal to large numbers in the case of the preference of more to less, any more than we do in the case of the principle of the economic disposal of resources.

Two well-known writers have dealt with what we regard as the second necessary principle of economic administration, the weighing of the needs and preferences of individuals as against each other; an examination of the views of Wicksteed and de Marco may serve to reinforce our argument and to clear up doubtful points.

The key passage in Wicksteed's *The Common Sense of Political Economy* would appear to be on page 19: "Beginning our study of the administration of domestic resources, then, we note that in marketing, shopping, giving orders to tradesmen and so forth, the mother of a family is administering her pecuniary resources and trying to make the money go as far as possible; and when her purchases have been brought home she still has the kindred task, sometimes a delicate and difficult one, of so distributing them amongst the various claimants (whose wants they may be very far from completely satisfying) as to make them tell to the utmost. In marketing she is constantly compelled to buy less of this or that than she would like, because her whole resources are inadequate to the satisfaction of every desire, and the thoughtless indulgence of one would involve disproportionate neglect of others. At home she is compelled to give one child less than she would wish of something he wants, because the whole stock is inadequate to meet all the claims she would like to admit, and too liberal indulgence of one child's desires would involve disproportionate neglect of another's. Her doings in the market-place and her doings at home are therefore parts of one continuous process of administration of resources, guided by the same fundamental principle; and it is the home problem that dominates the market problem and gives it its ultimate meaning. The problem of the limitations which she must face at home in concrete detail is the same problem of which she is conscious, in a more collective form, in the market."

In this passage we have a perfect indication of several points of the utmost significance. The fundamental nature of the economic unit or subject is clearly indicated. It is a group, in this case a family, acting through an executive, here, the mother. The disposal of the economic resources of the group is made by the mother, who buys, not according to any self-contained set of evaluations in her own mind, but according to (a) the market prices of goods, and (b) her estimates of the needs and wants of the members of her group. It is indicated further that the wants to be satisfied are, while ultimately destined to culminate in the physiological processes of individuals, yet eminently social in their nature, from the very essence of the group through which they are satisfied.

It follows that the task, "of so distributing them (the purchases) amongst the various claimants . . ." is indeed part and parcel of the whole process of economic administration. The mother must make interpersonal comparisons; ". . . too liberal indulgence of one child's desires would involve disproportionate neglect of another's". We shall agree that the mother's doings in the market-place and at home are parts of one continuous process of administration of resources. We shall also agree that it is the home problem that dominates the market problem and gives it its ultimate meaning.

It is by thinking on such lines that we shall make progress in the understanding of the nature of the economic subject and of the correlated characteristics of social wants. Where we would suggest a rewording is in Wicksteed's statement that the mother's activities in the market-place and her doings at home are *guided by the same fundamental principle.* We suggest that it would be more useful to say that these two sets of activities are conducted according to *two major principles*; that the expending of resources in the market-place is carried out according to the principles of equilibrium economics; whereas the distribution at home corresponds to the principles of inter-personal comparisons. It is by disentangling what appear to us to be two different and equally important principles that we may make progress in the principles of social economics.

On page 87 of the same book Wicksteed returns to the topic. He asserts again that when the mother has *brought home* her provisions for the day or week, " she is still engaged on the same problem of adjusting marginal significances in accordance with the law of diminishing psychic returns". With the important difference, however, that the marginal significances are now as between the members of the household, and thus not of the same nature as those between goods in the market-place. The significance for the total administration of resources must, however, be seen to be equally great.

On page 89, Wicksteed further proves his essential under-standing of the dual nature of the problem. "The cost of giving more to one applicant is giving less to another. . . ." "But as well as balancing all the uses of milk, at the margin, one against the other, the housekeeper has to balance them all, collectively, against every other alternative expenditure of the money she paid for milk, and this opens up another source of possible mistake." The housewife must, first, balance all the uses of milk involved in its distribution among the members of her family; and second, decide how much of the family's total resources should be devoted to the purchase of milk. Wicksteed fails to differentiate theoretically between the two problems. As we know, the rest of his work is devoted to elucidating one only. But it is significant that when he thinks

THE TWO ECONOMIC PRINCIPLES

in terms of the family, both problems are so strongly present in his mind that he sees them practically as one. It is through the examination of basic economic units, primarily the family, that the equal significance emerges of the two economic principles.

It is only on page 146 that Wicksteed encounters philosophic doubts as to the possibility of comparing the sensations and experiences of two different minds. He is able, in the name of common sense, to cut through his doubts. Theoretic differences would hardly restrain us from saying that a halfpenny meant more to a poor man than to a millionaire. ". . . we habitually form estimates as to the relative urgency of wants experienced by different men. . . ." He points out that, measured by every conceivable test, such comparisons can be made. He sees that they are at the very basis of the ways in which men govern their lives. He goes on to say, however, that his philosophic doubts are resolved when he has recourse to large numbers. An individual may have unaccountable preferences; a hundred men will certainly prefer a gnat-bite to being put on the rack. It is in these ways that Wicksteed, virtually only in those parts of his work in which he thinks of the family and the individual, rather than of the processes of business, indicates clearly the equal significance of interpersonal comparisons and of the market disposal of resources.

De Viti de Marco in his *First Principles of Public Finance* writes on the problem of interpersonal comparisons, but, unfortunately, only from the point of view of the practicability and justice of progressive taxation. This is particularly regrettable in a work which does make a good contribution, if only by making mistakes more apparent, to the study of the economic unit or subject. Nowhere does de Marco appear to realize that the whole nature of the economic unit is that it is the group within which interpersonal comparisons are made.

In his study of progressive taxation, however, de Marco has much to say on the subject of interpersonal comparisons. Progressive taxation, he says: ". . . supposes that the 'rent' enjoyed by a consumer depends only on the size of his income;

that the readiness of the taxpayer to pay different prices increases uniformly with the increase of his income; and furthermore, that it increases equally for all taxpayers" (see page 173). He says that the validity of these assumptions must be demonstrated, and that the demonstration will consist in measuring the willingness of the taxpayers to pay increasing prices per unit for goods supplied by the State. He appears to link the higher prices paid for public goods with the less urgent wants which the richer person is able to satisfy from that part of his income which remains after taxation has been paid. Frankly, we do not see how the assumptions, as stated by de Marco, can be demonstrated. If the richer taxpayer gets a supply of State goods on about the same terms as a poorer man, we can only say that a very wide range of practice, in actual life (see, for example, *Coral Gardens*, by Professor B. Malinowski, *Primitive Economics of the New Zealand Maori*, by R. Firth, and *Middletown*, by R. S. and H. M. Lynd, reported by social anthropologists), does not allow him to do this. Again, we cannot speak of the readiness of the richer man to pay a higher tax, or price, for State goods. Only the sociological enquirer, probably after much work, will be able to discover whether such a readiness exists; but, whether it does or not, the executives are likely to base their practice on the assumption that whether the richer man is ready or not ready to pay more, does not matter very much, since he can be made to pay more with apparent all-round advantages. Here again we see a recourse in practice to some working concept of human needs and corresponding capacity to pay, rather than to the satisfactions felt by the individual. These satisfactions may be a fairly private matter; his needs are regarded as a very public matter.

Again, we should indeed get into difficulties if we tried to prove that the readiness to pay higher prices out of higher incomes "increases equally for all taxpayers". All that we can ever say is that in large economic units such as the State, wide assumptions of this nature have to be made in practice. In smaller, but not less important units, such as the family, it may be possible to make finer adjustments.

"'The rich man *is willing* to pay prices that *increase uniformly* with the increase in his income.' This is the fundamental concept underlying the doctrine; and it is clear that, if the taxpayer is willing to pay the higher price, the incentive to increase production, savings, and wealth, is not restrained," says de Marco, page 174. We would suggest that the concept of willingness is here shown to be of relatively small value. We can know nothing of an individual's willingness to pay taxes save by his continued industry while paying them. If his industry is apparently not less than it otherwise would have been, we can only say that this indicates his willingness to be taxed. Actually, his whole personal attitude may be one of bitter resentment. We are once more driven to seek something more objective than "wants" or "willingness" to pay.

Wants are something which may be very imperfectly felt even by the individual when he is, as he always is, one member of an economic unit. He has no way whatever of expressing his private wants, as they are compounded into the one economic decision which his group must make. If he is unable to express his purely private wants, it seems risky to say that we can ever know what these are. In any case, even if they are in some way formulated to the individual, they are most certainly overborne by the group executive which considers not only any wants or preferences of its individuals, but also, perhaps in a rough but certainly in a practical way, his needs. In just the same way, the willingness of a man to pay higher prices for public goods because he has a higher income is something that virtually cannot be known. What we do know is that if the group executive makes flagrantly wrong estimates of this willingness the man will cease to function as an efficient member of society. If this does not happen, we can but assume the willingness to exist, though in no sense do we need to say that it will increase uniformly with the increase in the man's income. All that we can say is that other members of his group will think in terms of his needs, and that, in a purely practical way, these will be regarded as diminishing more or less uniformly in intensity with the increase in his income.

De Marco encounters the fundamental difficulty—"namely, that the principle of subjective value does not allow comparisons of sensibility", page 175. Our comment is that obviously it does not, that it has nothing to do with the matter. It is here that we see that the principle of subjective value, like any other principle, is useful only in its proper sphere, and that we must realize that the total disposal of economic resources is governed by two distinct principles, that of subjective value, and that of the diminishing marginal utility of total income, with its corollary of the possibility of interpersonal comparisons; giving us, if we wish to use the expression, a "principle of objective value".

The next step in de Marco's argument is, if the present writer interprets it correctly, at variance with the sound principle enunciated by Wicksteed, that although an individual may have an eccentric set of evaluations, yet a sufficiently large group will cancel out these eccentricities and leave us fully justified in assuming that people prefer more to less, and that the vital significance of an income diminishes the further it goes from the first satisfying of primary needs. De Marco considers the decreasing importance attached by three imaginary taxpayers to successive portions of their incomes. He holds that the elementary principle upon which the structure of progressive taxation is built is, assuming it to be true, "true on condition that one confines oneself to the budget of each separate individual", page 175. But, he says, we must get out of the closed economy of an individual and make comparisons between different individuals. This is very true, so true indeed that it seems to be fruitless to try to draw up a scale for any one individual. The whole essence of the matter is that we are making comparisons between different individuals. Yet de Marco considers that "The progression seems to be an automatic result of the decreasing importance that each taxpayer attaches to the successive portions of income within his budget, without comparison with other individuals", page 177. He goes on to say that in the three examples which he has given it is supposed that the decreasing scale of sacrifice is equal for all three taxpayers, "whereas the theory of subjective value does not permit us to adopt such an hypothesis". It can neither permit us nor forbid us; it has nothing to do with the matter. As scientists we are permitted to adopt any hypothesis which we think may be useful.

Actually we have no wish to adopt the hypothesis mentioned here. It is not only probable, but wellnigh certain, that the scales of the three people are different from each other. It would be one chance in a million if any two of them coincided. Yet executives of economic units must come to decisions. Hence "two individuals receiving the same income owe the same amount in taxes". But this is not, as de Marco goes on to say, "obvious on the basis of the theory of objective value". Nor is it false according to the theory of subjective value which, as we have shown, has nothing to do with it. It appears to be from the theory of subjective value that de Marco concludes that even if incomes are equal, the pain or sacrifice of the two taxpayers may be and usually is different. It is indeed evident that no two taxpayers even with equal incomes are very likely to get equal satisfaction from them. In any case, we cannot too strongly insist that satisfactions may only be compared; they cannot be accurately measured, so that we can never say that those of two persons are equal. Nor can we see exactly what de Marco means by the "theory of objective value". If it is a summary, from human experience, to the effect that, the more people have, the less urgent the needs which they are able to satisfy, and that on this basis comparisons can be made between persons, then this principle is the second guiding rule to the disposal of economic resources. It in no way conflicts with the theory of subjective value; the two are complementary. To say that a certain proposition is "obvious on the basis of the theory of objective value; but . . . false on the basis of the theory of subjective value", page 177, is an impossible proposition.

De Marco does not deny that the progressive principle may be taken as demonstrated for each individual. He holds that its practical application is impossible only because of the theoretical impossibility of comparing the scales of different people, and also because of the technical impossibility of establishing different progressive taxes for each individual. As regards the first difficulty, it seems clear that the mere fact of our being able to construct scales for individuals is the surest guarantee that, having constructed a number of such scales, they will be comparable. Once we admit the possibility of making useful judgments about the total satisfactions of people, whether of ourselves or of other people, the pass is sold. De Marco's position virtually appears to be that we can make any number of valuations of the total satisfactions of different people, but that by some mystical "theoretical impossibility" we are precluded from formulating any observable uniformity arising from our observations. The whole essence of scientific method would rather appear to indicate that if we can make a number of isolated observations, it is not only possible, but our duty, to state any general tendency which appears to result from the individual operations.

In general it appears, then, that interpersonal comparisons are made as a universal practice among mankind. They are absolutely essential because of the fact that practically all economic decisions are made by group executives, each group, whether the family, the State, or any intermediate organization, being an effective economic unit or subject. The group executive, whether mother, or Chancellor, can arrive at the economic decisions of the group only upon the basis of a comparison of the needs and resources of the members. Thus, arising from the fact that interpersonal comparisons are at the very basis of wellnigh every economic decision, we cannot exclude these comparisons from economic theory. We must admit them on a basis equal with that of the theory of the economic disposal of resources according to subjective evaluations, and, this being so, it is necessary for us to enquire into their nature, their logical standing and the bases of their utility.

INDEX

INDEX

Rain specialists, 222
Reaction to Conquest, 185
Reciprocity, 9
Resources, economic, 40 ; economic disposal of, 10 ; management of, 57 ; universal limitation of, 44
Routledge, 117

Sacrifice, 190
Sacrifice, cost of, 103
Satisfactions, 11
Satisfaction, and production, 66
" Savage ", carefree nature of, 121
" Savage " and " Civilized ", 5
Saving, motives in, 70
Self-interest, 16
Sense data, 20 ; and specialization, 21
Services, valuation of, 9
Shepstone, 169
Smith and Dale, 102, 136, 239
Social evaluation and price, 51
Social fact, construction of, 18
Social facts, and their aspects, 33
Social organization and economic management, 59
Social law, 31
Social science, universality of, 4
Social world, knowledge of, 18
Sociology and economics, 272
Specialization, 6, 28
Stayt, 123, 235
Steedman, 168
Store houses, 62

Taxation, progressive, 270
Tembu, 169, 170

Thonga, 109, 111, 122, 197
Tobacco as payment, 121
Transkei, 168
Transkeian General Council, 178

Ubena, 107, 204
Uganda, 131

Valuation of units, 42
Value, 41
Values, a cultural product, 15
Village, structure of, 150

Wants, 257 ; indirect satisfaction of, 8
Wants, collective, 74 ; all collective, 255 ; economic, 40 ; formulation of, 59 ; groups of, 67 ; and needs, 18 ; pressure of, 60 ; and production, 73 ; organization of, 73
Wealth, exchange of, 127
Wicksteed, 6, 275-281
Wife, apprenticeship of, 185
Willoughby, 222
Witchcraft, 201
Wives, crops of, 207 ; and homestead, 183 ; property of, 161, 187 ; status of, 176
Women's work, economics of, 249 ; work of, 105
Work-parties, 63, 64, 155, 160, 206, 219, 242-246
Working power of the group, 63

Xosa, 169

Zulus, 108, 111, 193

For Product Safety Concerns and Information please contact our EU
representative GPSR@taylorandfrancis.com
Taylor & Francis Verlag GmbH, Kaufingerstraße 24, 80331 München, Germany